MEASUREMENT

Walker Maths Essentials: Measurement 4+
1st Edition
Charlotte Walker
Victoria Walker

Designer: Cheryl Smith, Macarn Design
Production controller: Michelle Gordon

Any URLs contained in this publication were checked for currency during the production process. Note, however, that the publisher cannot vouch for the ongoing currency of URLs.

Acknowledgements
Cover photo courtesy of Shutterstock.

We wish to thank the Boards of Trustees of Darfield and Riccarton High Schools for allowing us to use materials and ideas developed while teaching. Our thanks also go to all past and present colleagues, especially Kath Wilson, who have generously shared their experience and ideas.

For product information and technology assistance,
in Australia call **1300 790 853**;
in New Zealand call **0800 449 725**

For permission to use material from this text or product, please email
aust.permissions@cengage.com

National Library of New Zealand Cataloguing-in-Publication Data
A catalogue record for this book is available from the National Library of New Zealand.

978 0 17 044721 8

Cengage Learning Australia
Level 7, 80 Dorcas Street
South Melbourne, Victoria Australia 3205

For learning solutions, visit **cengage.co.nz**

Printed in China by 1010 Printing International Limited.
5 6 7 25

Throughout this book:

1. Assume that diagrams are not drawn to scale.
2. Where appropriate, round your answers to 2 dp.

CONTENTS

Glossary

Make your own glossary of key terms:

Term	Definition	Picture/Example
Units		
Perimeter		
Area		
Volume		
Capacity		
Polygon		
Compound shape		
Regular shape		
Dimensions		

ISBN: 9780170447218

Vertical		
Cube		
Cuboid		
Two-dimensional (2D)		
Three-dimensional (3D)		
Weight vs Mass		
Kilo		
Centi		
Milli		

ISBN: 9780170447218

The language of measurement

Volume and capacity

- **Volume** measures how much **space** is taken up by an object.
  Units: mm^3, cm^3, m^3.
- **Capacity** measures the **amount that an object can hold**.
  Units: mL, L.
- Sometimes these terms are used interchangeably.

Example: Consider a thermos flask.
Its volume is the amount of space taken up by the flask.
Its capacity is the amount of water that the flask can hold.

Match these words to measurement ideas below.

icy	gradient	light	age	heavy	reach
long	cold	fortnight	heat	steep	pitch
slant	century	long	space	distance	generation
slope	far	decade	wide	warm	room
bulk	incline	hot	period	load	flat

Length ______________________________

____

____

Angle ______________________________

____

____

Time ______________________________

____

____

Temperature ______________________________

____

____

Volume/Capacity ______________________________

____

____

Mass ______________________________

____

____

ISBN: 9780170447218

Useful expressions for periods of time

10 years	1000 years	100 years	About four weeks
About 25 years	Two weeks	366 days	365 days

Match the periods from the box above to the terms below.

Term	Period of time
Fortnight	
Month	
Leap year	
Generation	

Term	Period of time
Century	
Millennium	
Decade	
Year	

Measuring devices

Match these words to measurement ideas below.

ruler	pedometer	cup	timer
protractor	measuring cylinder	clinometer	tape measure
tablespoon	syringe	clock	scales
stopwatch	teaspoon	thermometer	odometer

Length ______________________________

____

____

Capacity ______________________________

____

____

Mass ______________________________

____

____

Angle ______________________________

____

____

Time ______________________________

____

____

Temperature ______________________________

____

____

ISBN: 9780170447218

Units

Abbreviations (shortened versions) for units

s	~~cm~~	m	tsp	c
kg	km	min	h	mg
ha	g	d	°C	mL
t	dsp	L	mm	tbsp

Write the shortened version of these terms from the box above and identify what they are used to measure.

Unit of measurement	Shortened version
Kilogram	
Centimetre	cm
Metre	
Minute	
Litre	
Hectare	
Milligram	
Teaspoon	
Dessertspoon	
Day	

Unit of measurement	Shortened version
Kilometre	
Millimetre	
Degree Celsius	
Second	
Tablespoon	
Tonne	
Millilitre	
Cup	
Gram	
Hour	

Add each of these abbreviations to the boxes below.

Length	Area
Capacity	**Mass**
Temperature	**Time**

 ISBN: 9780170447218

Time

- Time can be measured in **seconds**, **hours**, **days**, etc.

Use the following chart to help you convert time.

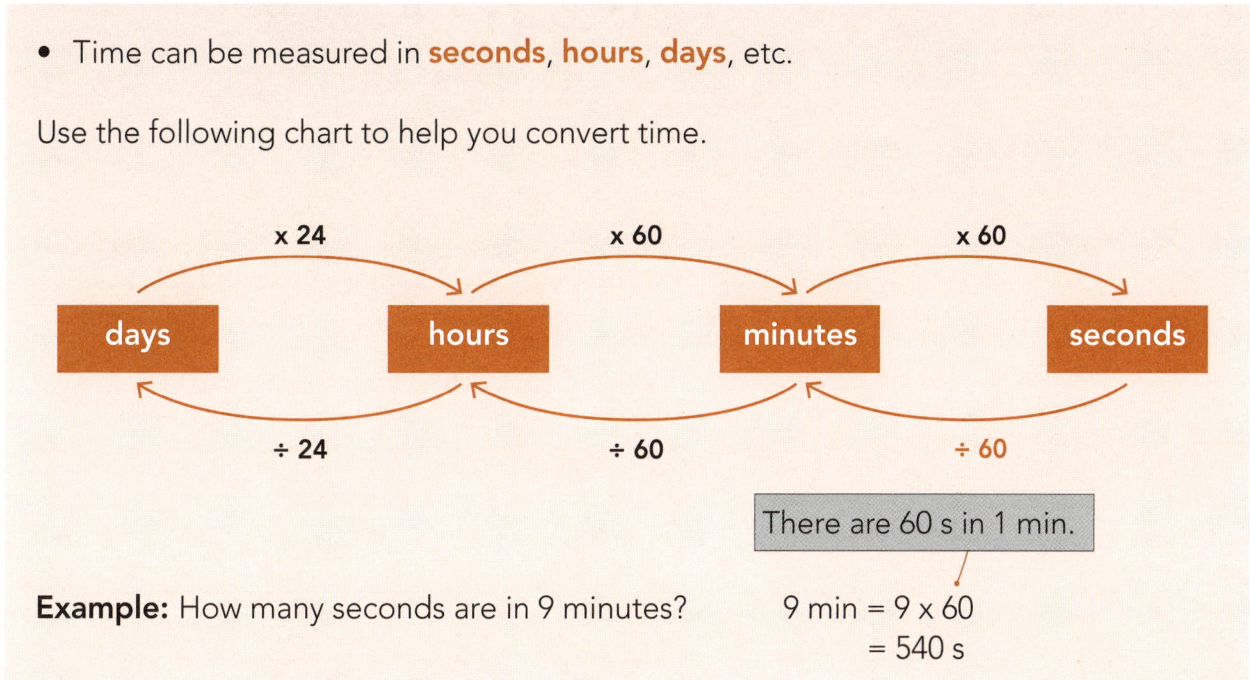

Example: How many seconds are in 9 minutes?

9 min = 9 x 60
= 540 s

Highlight the correct conversion for each of the following.

1	120 minutes	3 h	2 d
		2 h	720 s
3	72 hours	4300 min	1.2 d
		2 d	3 d
5	1.5 days	24 h	90 h
		2106 min	2160 min

2	90 seconds	2 min	1 h
		0.05 h	1.5 min
4	420 seconds	7 min	7 h
		0.1 h	17.5 min
6	0.6 days	51 840 min	14 h 24 min
		864 s	14 h 40 min

Convert the following.

7 480 s = ________________ min

8 1 d = ________________ h

9 180 min = ________________ h

10 3.5 h = ________________ min

11 60 min = ________________ s

12 120 h = ________________ d

ISBN: 9780170447218

Highlight the longer period of time.

13 3.5 h 200 s

14 2.5 d 3500 min

15 90 s 2 min

16 3 d 70 h

17 5 h 301 min

18 8.5 min 150 s

19 5000 min 3.5 d

20 1.5 d 4500 s

Put these times in order from shortest to longest. Hint: Rewrite them using the same units.

21

84 min	0.05 d	3960 s	1.3 h

Shortest Longest

22

2.1 d	180 000 s	50.5 h	3003 min

Shortest Longest

Circle or highlight the most appropriate unit of time for these intervals.

23 The time it takes to eat breakfast.

days hours minutes seconds

24 The time it takes to tie your shoelaces.

days hours minutes seconds

25 The time it takes for a posted letter to arrive.

days hours minutes seconds

26 The amount of time you slept last night.

days hours minutes seconds

27 The time it takes to boil an egg.

days hours minutes seconds

28 The time it takes to fly from New Zealand to Australia.

days hours minutes seconds

ISBN: 9780170447218

Length

- The basic unit for measuring length is the **metre**.
- All other units of length in the metric system are based on the metre.

Use the following chart to help you convert lengths.

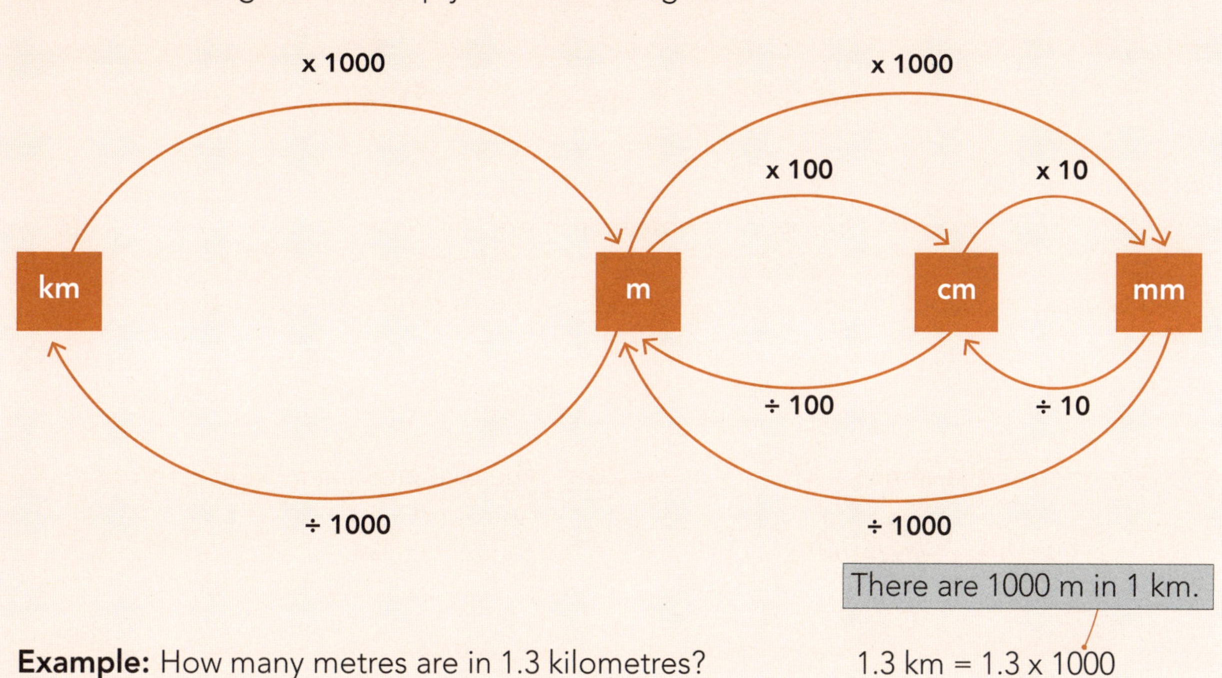

There are 1000 m in 1 km.

Example: How many metres are in 1.3 kilometres?

1.3 km = 1.3 x 1000
= 1300 m

Highlight the correct conversion for each of the following.

1	20 cm	200 m	0.2 m
		0.02 m	2 m
3	2.6 km	26 000 m	2600 m
		26 m	260 m

2	500 mm	50 m	0.05 m
		5 m	0.5 m
4	0.8 m	8000 cm	8 cm
		80 cm	800 cm

Convert the following.

5 9 cm = ________________ mm

6 20 m = ________________ cm

7 3000 m = ________________ km

8 2.5 km = ________________ m

9 1700 cm = ________________ m

10 9.5 cm = ________________ mm

ISBN: 9780170447218

Highlight the greater length.

11 12 cm 110 mm

12 35 m 315 cm

13 45 m 5.4 km

14 650 mm 56 cm

15 3.4 cm 0.3 m

16 9000 mm 0.9 m

Circle or highlight the most likely unit of measurement for these items.

17 The height of your chair.

km m cm mm

18 The thickness of your calculator.

km m cm mm

19 The length of a pencil.

km m cm mm

20 The distance from Wellington to Auckland.

km m cm mm

21 The length of your shoe.

km m cm mm

22 The thickness of a ruler.

km m cm mm

23 The length of a sprinting race.

km m cm mm

24 The width of this book.

km m cm mm

Estimating length

From the list on the right, select the most likely for the following.

25 The height of Mt Everest: ______________

26 The height of a Lego block: ______________

27 The width of a tennis court: ______________

28 The height of this book: ______________

29 The distance for a half marathon: ______________

30 The length of a cricket bat: ______________

31 The height of a mug: ______________

10.97 m
9.6 mm
21 km
961 mm
81 mm
8848 m
29.7 cm

ISBN: 9780170447218

Mass

- The basic unit for measuring mass is the **gram**.
- All other units of mass in the metric system are based on the gram.
- Mass is often mistakenly called weight.

Weight is a measure of the pull of gravity on an object and is measured in **newtons**.

Mass is the amount of matter an object contains and is measured in **grams**.

Use the following chart to help you convert mass.

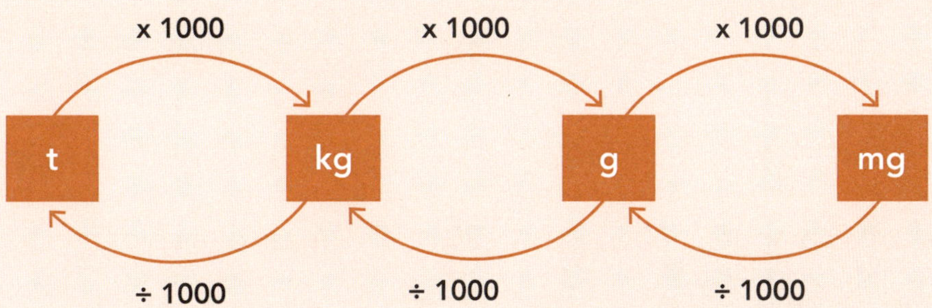

There are 1000 mg in 1 g.

Example: How many milligrams are in 1.2 grams?

1.2 g = 1.2 x 1000
= 1200 mg

Highlight the correct conversion for each of the following.

1	1500 g	0.15 kg	1.5 kg
		15 kg	5.1 kg
3	2 t	200 kg	20 000 kg
		2000 kg	20 kg

2	1.8 kg	180 g	180 000 g
		18 000 g	1800 g
4	2600 mg	0.26 g	2.6 g
		260 g	26 g

Convert the following.

5 16 kg = ____________ g

6 0.9 t = ____________ kg

7 630 mg = ____________ g

8 785 g = ____________ kg

9 94 g = ____________ mg

10 236 kg = ____________ t

ISBN: 9780170447218

Highlight the greater mass.

11 80 g 80 001 mg

12 4.5 kg 5400 g

13 1000 mg 10 g

14 0.3 t 3000 kg

15 52 kg 0.05 t

16 900 000 mg 1 kg

Circle or highlight the most likely unit of measurement for these items.

17 The mass of a cat.

t kg g mg

18 The mass of a brick.

t kg g mg

19 The mass of an orange.

t kg g mg

20 The mass of a spider.

t kg g mg

21 The mass of a truck.

t kg g mg

22 The mass of a $2 coin.

t kg g mg

23 The mass of a toddler.

t kg g mg

24 The mass of this book.

t kg g mg

Estimating mass

From the list on the right, select the most likely masses for the following.

25 The mass of this book: ____________

26 The mass of a teaspoon: ____________

27 The mass of a dog: ____________

28 The mass of an apple: ____________

29 The mass of the *Titanic*: ____________

30 The mass of a housefly: ____________

31 The mass of a paracetamol tablet: ____________

284 g
10 mg
136 g
500 mg
28.4 kg
52 310 t
22g

ISBN: 9780170447218

Capacity

- The basic unit for measuring capacity is the **litre**.
- All other units of capacity in the metric system are based on the litre.

Use the following chart to help you convert capacity.

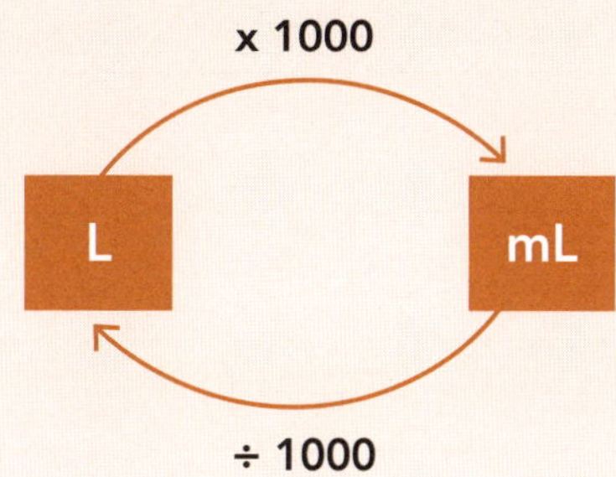

There are 1000 mL in 1 L.

Example: How many millilitres are in 2.6 litres?

2.6 L = 2.6 x 1000
= 2600 mL

Highlight the correct conversion for each of the following.

1	600 mL	60 L	6 L
		0.6 L	0.06 L
3	0.001 L	10 mL	100 mL
		1 mL	1000 mL

2	1.2 L	120 mL	1200 mL
		2100 mL	12 mL
4	15 000 mL	15 L	150 L
		0.15 L	1.5 L

Convert the following.

5 70 L = ______________ mL

6 450 mL = ______________ L

7 9800 mL = ______________ L

8 4 L = ______________ mL

9 15 L = ______________ mL

10 84 000 mL = ______________ L

11 10 mL = ______________ L

12 0.9 L = ______________ mL

ISBN: 9780170447218

Put these capacities in order from smallest to largest. Hint: Rewrite them using the same units.

13

1.2 L	2100 mL	1100 mL	2.0 L	1001 mL

Smallest Largest

14

1.9 L	9010 mL	0.91 L	9001 mL	9.1 L

Smallest Largest

Estimating capacity

From the list on the right, select the most likely capacities for the following.

15 The capacity of a watering can: ____________

16 The capacity of a car fuel tank: ____________

17 The capacity of a small saucepan: ____________

18 The capacity of an eye dropper: ____________

19 The capacity of a spa pool: ____________

20 The capacity of a tube of toothpaste: ____________

21 The capacity of a mug: ____________

22 The capacity of a tablespoon: ____________

100 mL
55 L
15 mL
350 mL
1000 L
1.5 L
12 L
1.5 mL

ISBN: 9780170447218

Appropriate units

- Length is measured in mm, cm, m or km.
- Mass is measured in mg, g, kg or t.
- Capacity is measured in mL or L.
- Time is measured in seconds, minutes, hours or days.

Example: The capacity of this bucket would be measured in which of the following units?

cm **kg** **t** **L**

The most appropriate answer is L (litres).

Circle or highlight the most appropriate unit of measurement for these items.

1 The length of a pencil.

kg mL g cm

2 The amount of a milk in a cup of tea.

t L mm mL

3 The mass of a mouse.

km kg cm g

4 The length of a shoelace.

mL L cm mg

5 The time it takes to get your hair cut.

min km t s

6 The amount of body wash in a bottle.

mL mg m g

7 The amount of drink in a can.

g m mg mL

8 The width of a TV screen.

km kg L cm

9 The mass of a newborn baby.

cm g mm t

10 The length of a movie.

min mL cm s

11 The amount of water in a bath.

mL t L kg

12 The mass of a dolphin.

t kg g L

13 The length of an eyelash.

km kg mm mg

14 The amount of butter in a biscuit recipe.

mL kg g cm

15 The length of a TV advert.

mL s g days

16 The mass of a truck.

cm km t g

ISBN: 9780170447218

Estimating quantities

Use the most appropriate quantities from the list on the right to complete the following sentences. You may need to do some research.

1 The mass of a hippo is most likely to be ____________.

2 The height of the Statue of Liberty is most likely to be ____________.

3 The mass of an average human brain is most likely to be ____________.

4 The mass of a cellphone is most likely to be ____________.

5 The length of your index finger is most likely to be ____________.

6 The capacity of a dessertspoon is most likely to be ____________.

7 The arm span of an orangutan is most likely to be ____________.

8 The length of a basketball court is most likely to be ____________.

9 The width of your school desk is most likely to be ____________.

10 The capacity of a shoebox is most likely to be ____________.

11 The mass of a basketball is most likely to be ____________.

12 The capacity of a matchbox is most likely to be ____________.

13 The length of your hand (including fingers) is most likely to be ____________.

14 The mass of a grape is most likely to be ____________.

15 The capacity of a bath is most likely to be ____________.

16 The capacity of a can of tomatoes is most likely to be ____________.

17 The length of a ladybird is most likely to be ____________.

18 The length of a newborn baby is most likely to be ____________.

19 The mass of a kiwi is most likely to be ____________.

Quantities
8.4 cm
0.5 kg
5 L
5 mm
93 m
400 mL
2.3 kg
1.5 t
2.1 m
28 mL
150 g
5 g
76 cm
50 cm
12 mL
17 cm
1300 g
80 L
28 m

  ISBN: 9780170447218

Word questions

1 Angus has one litre of milk. He needs 190 mL to make scones and 250 mL for his chocolate drink. How much milk will be left for breakfast?

---

2 Aroha's beehive contains 80 000 bees. Bees weigh, on average, 100 mg each. Calculate the mass of the bees in the hive. Write your answer in kilograms.

---

3 Bess needs 850 g of flour each day to make scones for the shearers. If shearing takes five days, how much flour will she have left over from a 5 kg bag?

---

4 An ant can run at 8.5 cm per second. How far would an ant run in a minute? Write your answer in metres.

---

5 As community service, the class is wrapping Christmas presents for a charity. Each present needs, on average, 95 mm of sticky tape. If there are 250 presents, how many metres of sticky tape will be needed?

---

6 Cleaning your teeth should take about 6 minutes per day. How long would you spend cleaning your teeth in a year (365 days)? Give you answer in hours.

---

7 **a** Eric has a rectangular run for his chickens. It measures 5.5 m by 4.3 m. Will his 20 m roll of netting be long enough to go around the pen? If so, how much netting will be left over?

---

b His hens need 800 g of feed each day. How long will a 10 kg bag of feed last him?

---

c The eggs weigh, on average, 55 g each. He collects 7 eggs per day for a week. Calculate the total mass of eggs collected during the week. Write your answer in kilograms.

---

d He needs 200 g of egg white to make a pavlova. Each egg contains 35 g of egg white. How many eggs will he need to break in order to get enough egg white? How much spare egg white will there be?

ISBN: 9780170447218

Time

There are two ways of writing times:

12-hour time can also be written with a full stop, e.g. 1.00 a.m.

24-hour time can also be written without the colon, e.g. 0000.

Midnight or 12:00 a.m.

a.m. tells you that a time is in the morning.

Midday or noon or 12:00 p.m.

p.m. tells you that a time is in the afternoon or evening.

24-hour time has **four digits**, so a **0** is added to the start of times earlier than 10 a.m.

Between 1 p.m. and 11:59 p.m: To convert 12-hour times into 24-hour time, you need to add 12 hours.

12-hour time	24-hour time
Midnight	00:00
1:00 **a.m.**	01:00
2:00 **a.m.**	02:00
3:00 **a.m.**	03:00
4:00 **a.m.**	04:00
5:00 **a.m.**	05:00
6:00 **a.m.**	06:00
7:00 **a.m.**	07:00
8:00 **a.m.**	08:00
9:00 **a.m.**	09:00
10:00 **a.m.**	10:00
11:00 **a.m.**	11:00
Midday or noon	12:00
1:00 **p.m.**	13:00
2:00 **p.m.**	14:00
3:00 **p.m.**	15:00
4:00 **p.m.**	16:00
5:00 **p.m.**	17:00
6:00 **p.m.**	18:00
7:00 **p.m.**	19:00
8:00 **p.m.**	20:00
9:00 **p.m.**	21:00
10:00 **p.m.**	22:00
11:00 **p.m.**	23:00

ISBN: 9780170447218

Examples:

		12-hour time	24-hour time
1	Five minutes past midnight.	12:05 a.m.	00:05
2	One minute before midday.	11:59 a.m.	11:59
3	Ten minutes past midday.	12:10 p.m.	12:10
4	Two minutes before midnight.	11:58 p.m.	23:58

Highlight the correct conversion for each of the following.

1	4.12 p.m.	04:12	16:12
		14:12	04:24
3	21:20	8.20 p.m.	9.20 a.m.
		9.20 p.m.	8.20 a.m.
5	15:51	3.51 a.m.	3.51 p.m.
		3.15 p.m.	1.51 p.m.

2	2.14 a.m.	14:14	14:12
		02:14	2:14
4	7.17 p.m.	17:19	19:29
		19:17	07:17
6	12.12 a.m.	12:12	00:12
		24:12	12:24

Convert the following.

7 16:01 = ______________

8 2.17 p.m. = ______________

9 20:42 = ______________

10 Midnight = ______________

11 
a.m. = ______________

12 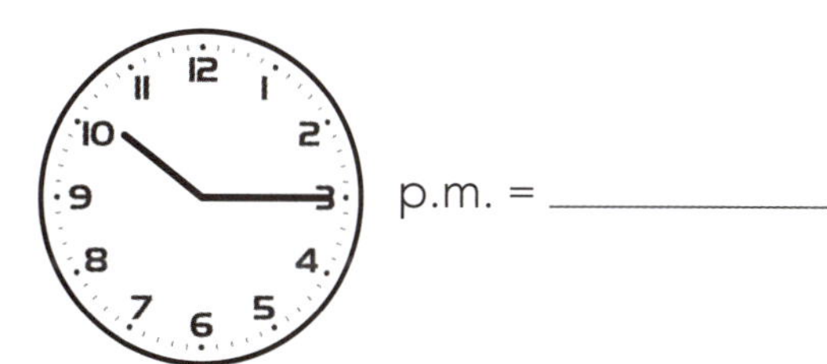
p.m. = ______________

13 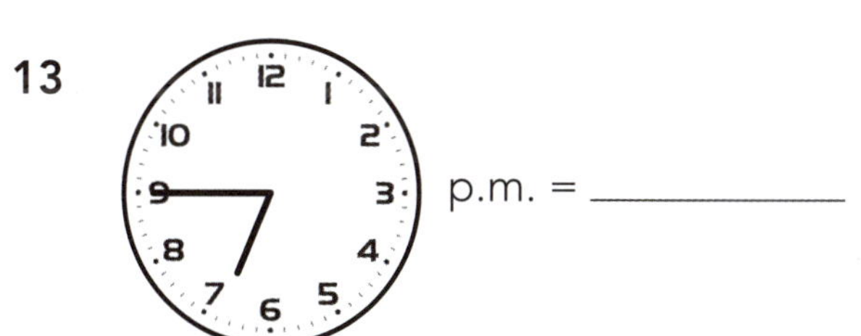
p.m. = ______________

14 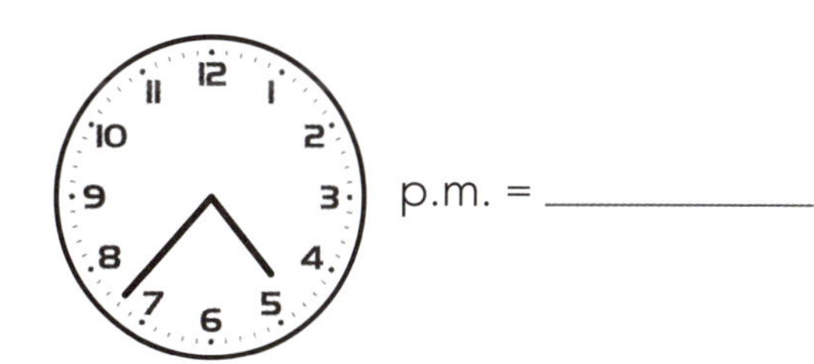
p.m. = ______________

Highlight the time that is later in the day.

15	3.20 a.m.	02:30	**16**	1.59 p.m.	14:00
17	4.16 p.m.	16:14	**18**	17:45	7.45 p.m.
19	10:01 a.m.	01:10	**20**	24:00	12:00 p.m.

Put these times in order from earliest to latest in the day. Hint: Rewrite them using the same time format.

21

15:03	3.15 p.m.	13:05	5.13 p.m.	10.53 p.m.

Earliest — Latest

22

12.21 p.m.	21:12	11.22 p.m.	22:11	12.12 p.m.

Earliest — Latest

Complete the table.

		12-hour time	24-hour time
23	Nine minutes past midday.		
24	Twelve minutes before midnight.		
25	Just before lunch at five minutes to twelve.		
26	Quarter to one in the morning.		
27	One forty five in the afternoon.		
28	Ten to nine in the evening.		
29	Quarter to six in the morning.		
30	Quarter past midnight.		

ISBN: 9780170447218

Reading tables

Answer the following questions.

Train timetable

Aranui	Kaiwera	Mānui	Ōkiwi	Te Horo	Wairere
09:13	09:19	09:32	09:41	09:48	10:02
10:04	10:10	10:23	10:32	10:39	10:53
10:55	11:01	11:14	11:23	11:30	11:44
11:32		11:49	11:58	12:05	12:19
12:09	12:15	12:28	12:37	12:44	12:58
13:46	13:52	14:05		14:18	14:32
15:17	15:23		15:43	15:51	16:04
16:22	16:28	16:41	16:50	16:57	17:11
17:01	17:07	17:20	17:29	17:36	17:50
18:36	18:42	18:55	19:04	19:11	19:25
19:11	19:17	19:30		19:43	19:57
20:03	20:09	20:22	20:31	20:38	20:52
21:16	21:22		21:42	21:49	22:03
22:28	22:34	22:47	22:56	23:03	23:17

1 If you took the 17:01 train from Aranui, what time would you arrive at Ōkiwi?

____

2 If you want to get from Kaiwera to Te Horo before midday, what is the latest train you can catch from Kaiwera station?

____

3 How long does the trip take from Aranui to Mānui on the 1.46 p.m. train?

____

4 Gus wants to meet his friend at Kaiwera station for lunch but he needs to arrive at Wairere before 4 p.m. He allows 35 minutes for lunch.

a Which train from Kaiwera will he need to catch?

____

b What is the latest time that he and his friend should meet?

____

Bus timetable

Harakeke Ave	06:15	07:23	07:51	08:03
Rimu Lane	06:19	07:27	07:54	08:07
Totara Rd	06:25	07:33	08:00	08:13
Manuka St	06:34	07:42	08:09	08:22
Horopito Pl	06:38	07:46	08:13	08:26
Karaka Rd	06:45	07:53	08:20	08:33

5 a What is the latest bus that Maia can catch from Rimu Lane if she must arrive at work at Karaka Rd by 8.30 a.m.?

____

b It takes her 5 minutes to walk from home to the Rimu Lane stop. What is the latest time she can leave home?

____

ISBN: 9780170447218

Scales

Reading scales

- Find **zero** on the scale to make sure that you read in the **correct direction**.
- If zero is not on the scale, make sure you read from **smaller values to larger values**.
- Include **units** in your answer.
- **Think** about your answer. Does it seem reasonable?

Example:

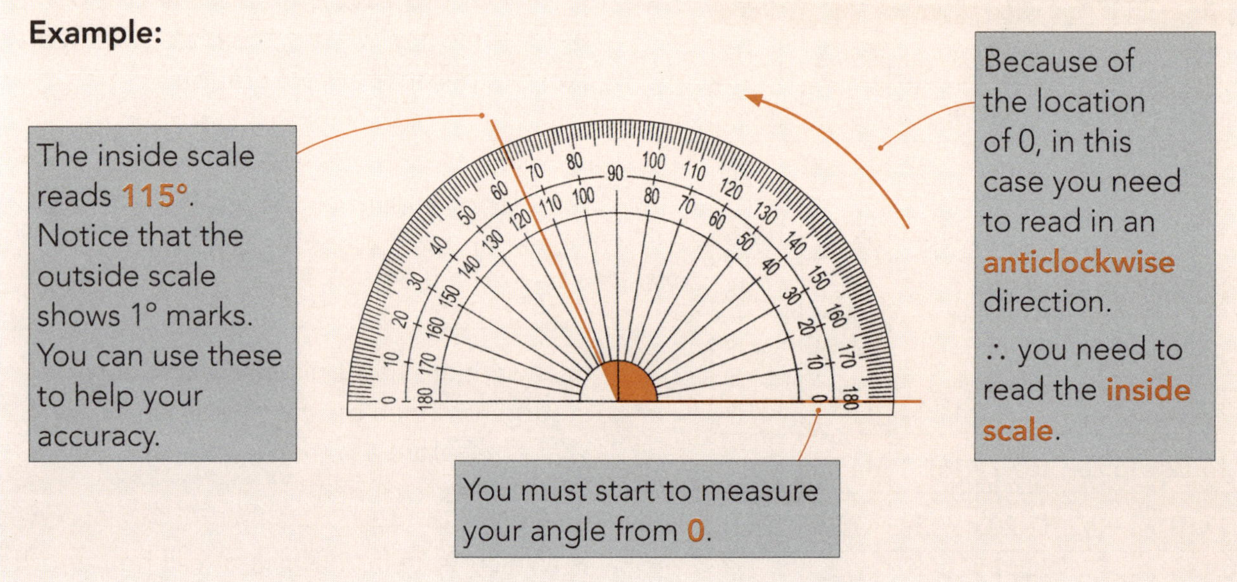

Write down the measurements shown on these scales.

1

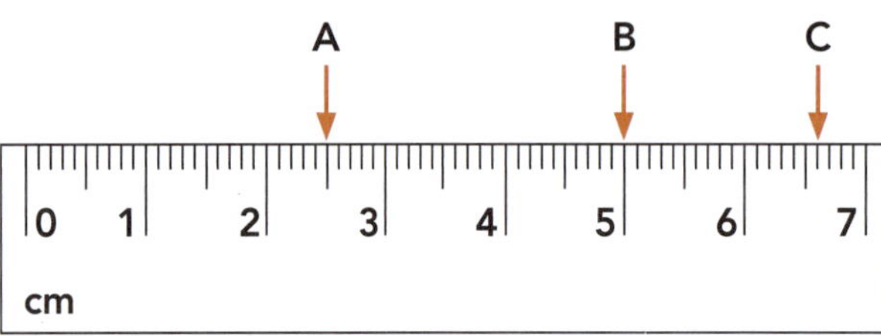

A = ____________

B = ____________

C = ____________

2

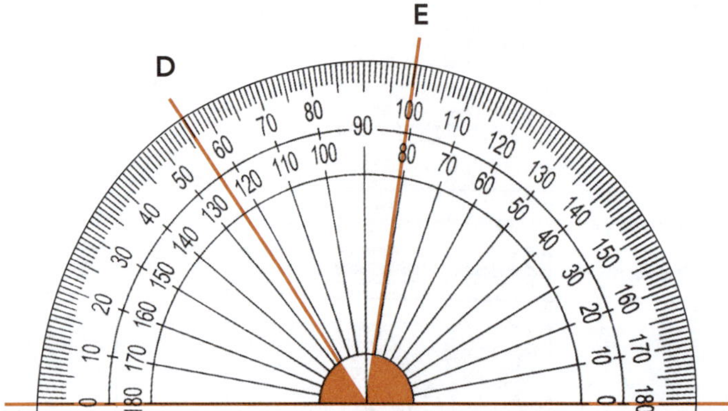

D = ____________

E = ____________

  ISBN: 9780170447218

3

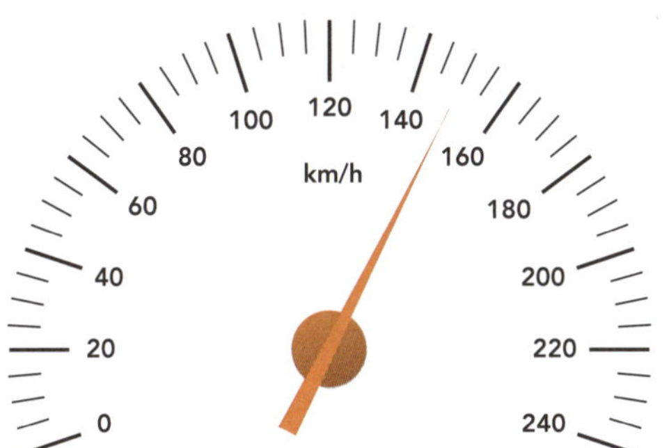

Speed = ______________

4

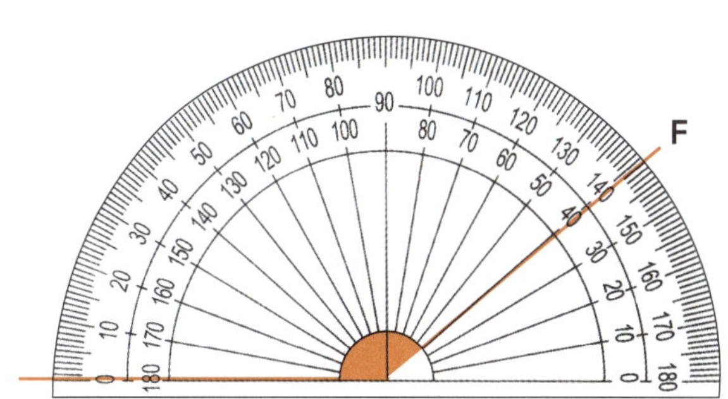

F = ______________

5

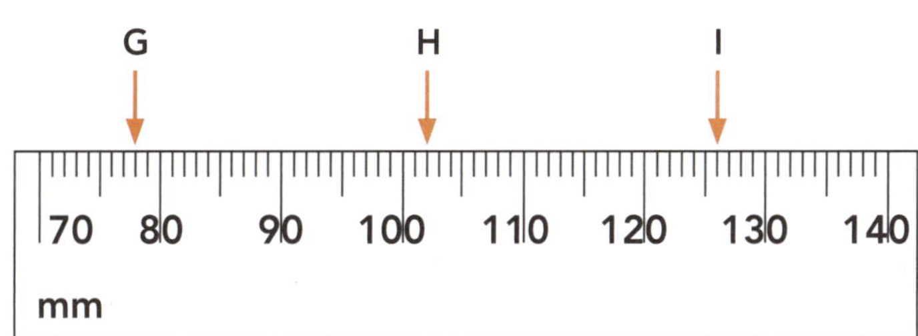

G = ______________

H = ______________

I = ______________

6

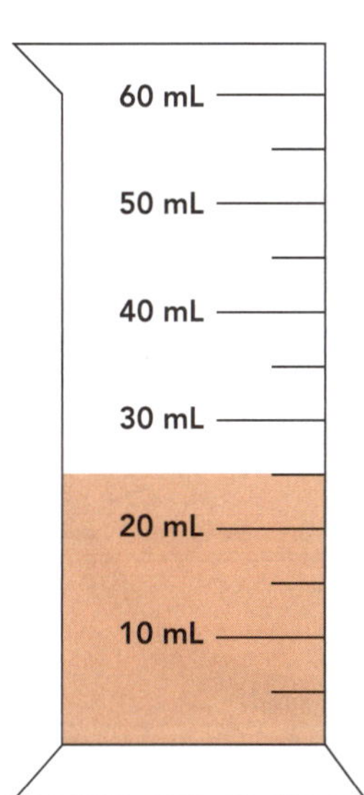

____

7

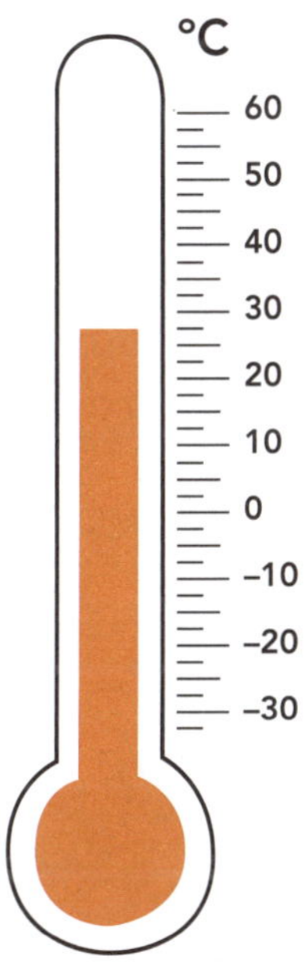

____

8

____

Showing values on scales

Colour the diagrams or add an arrow to show these measurements.

1 74°

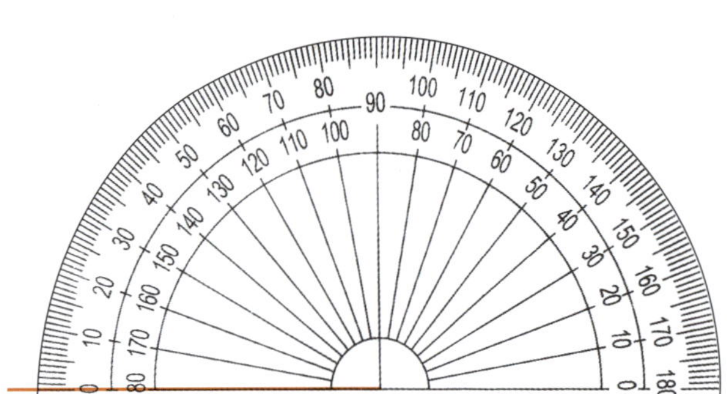

2 75 km/h

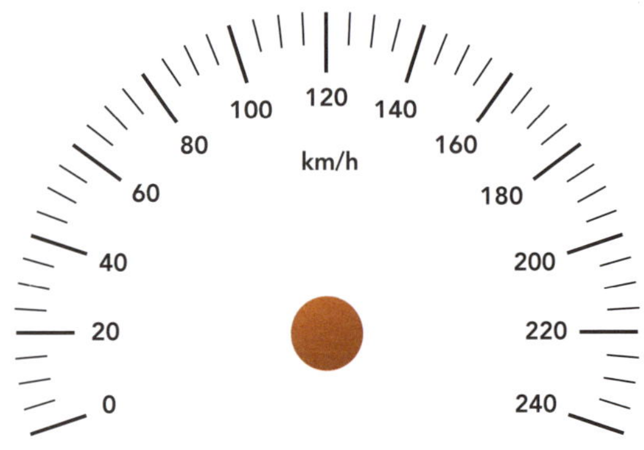

3

A = 2.6 cm

B = 4.1 cm

C = 0.7 cm

4 120 mL

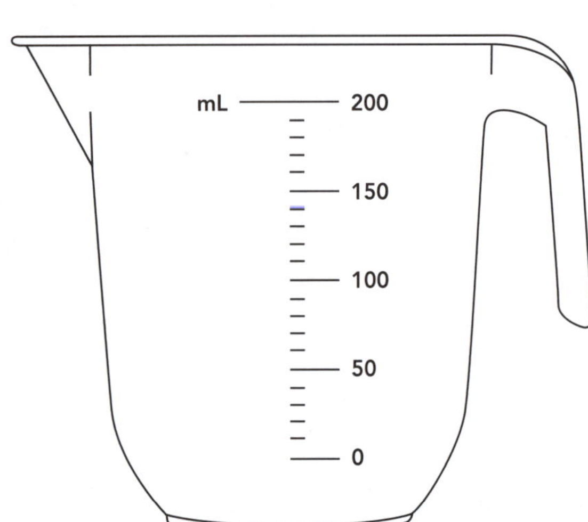

5 108°C

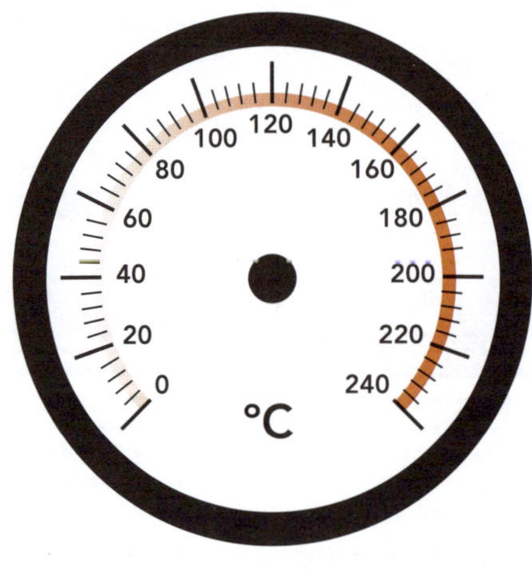

 ISBN: 9780170447218

6 45 mL

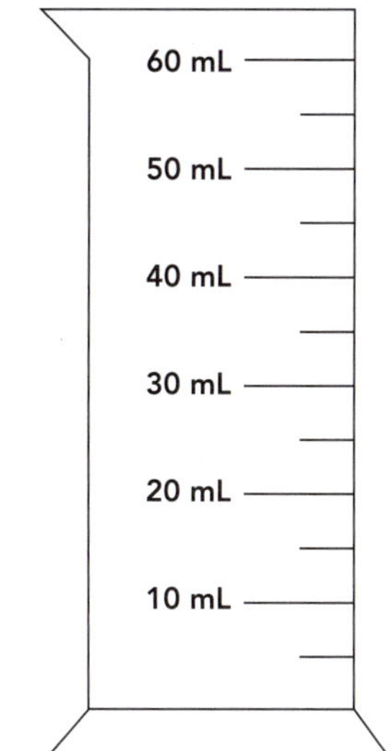

7 96°

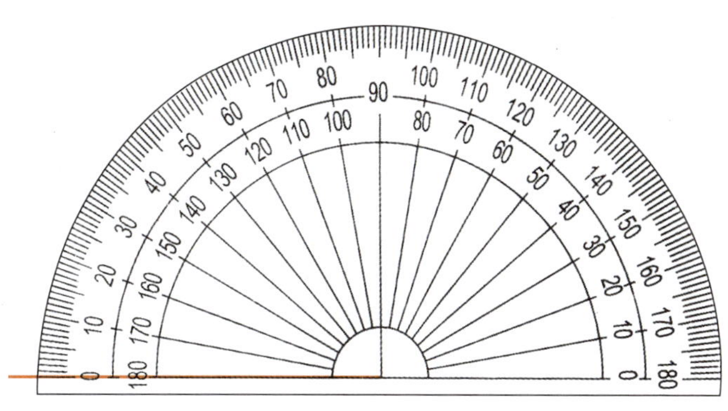

8

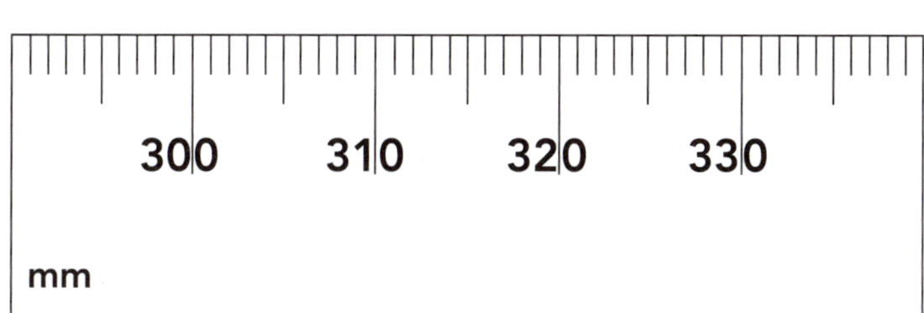

D = 304 mm

E = 331 mm

F = 316 mm

9 Write decimal values for each point along the ruler. Choose the most appropriate values from the list below. You will not need all the values on the list.

3.8	2.2	4.4	0.3	6.9	3.3
1.6	6.2	8.1	6.5	5.3	7.8
8.4	2.7	4.9	1.2	0.8	7.4

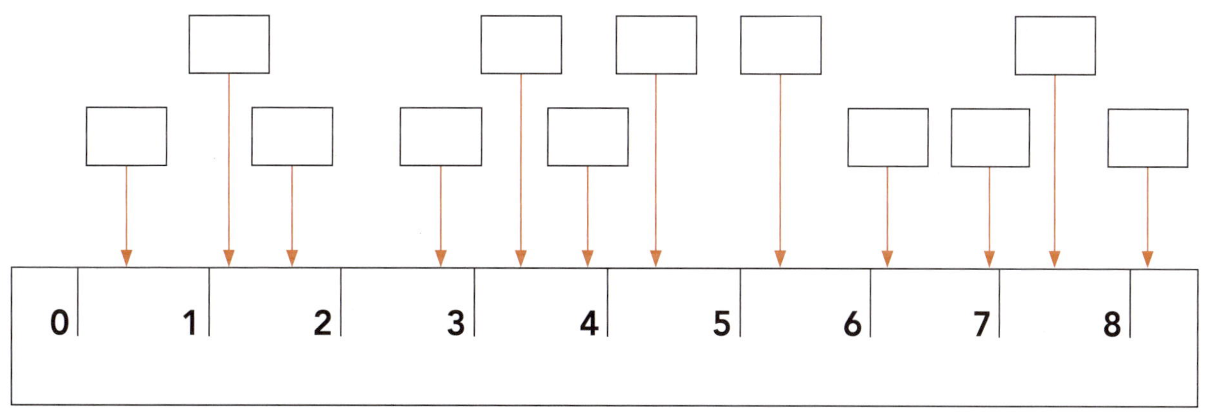

ISBN: 9780170447218

Perimeter

Shapes on a grid

- The perimeter is the **distance around the outside** of a two-dimensional (2D) shape.
- To find the perimeter, you need to **start at one corner** and **add** the distances around the outside of the shape.
- The shapes are drawn on a 1 cm by 1 cm grid.

Examples:

1 **2**

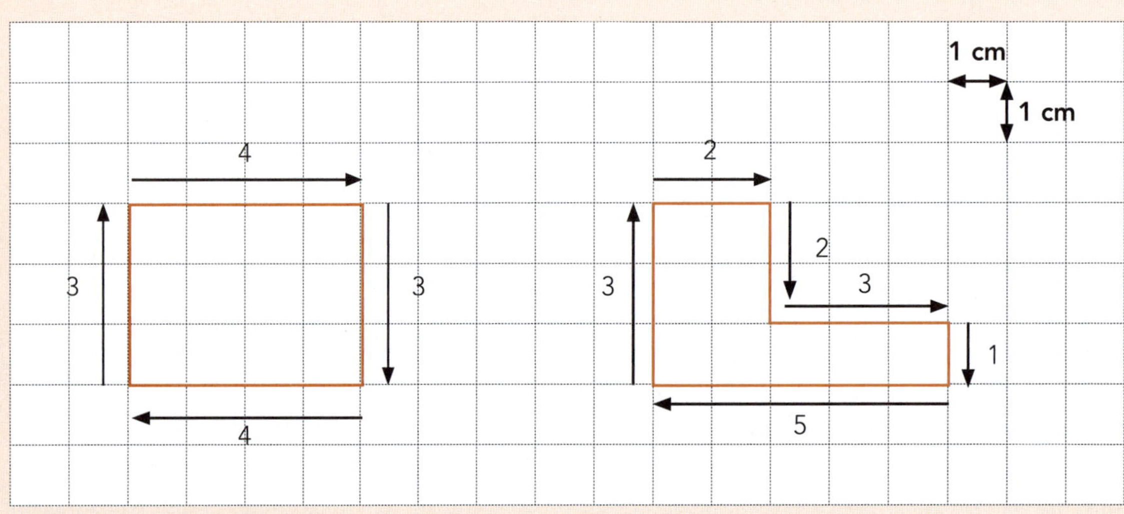

Perimeter = 4 + 3 + 4 + 3
= 14 cm

Perimeter = 2 + 2 + 3 + 1 + 5 + 3
= 16 cm

Calculate the perimeters of these shapes.

1

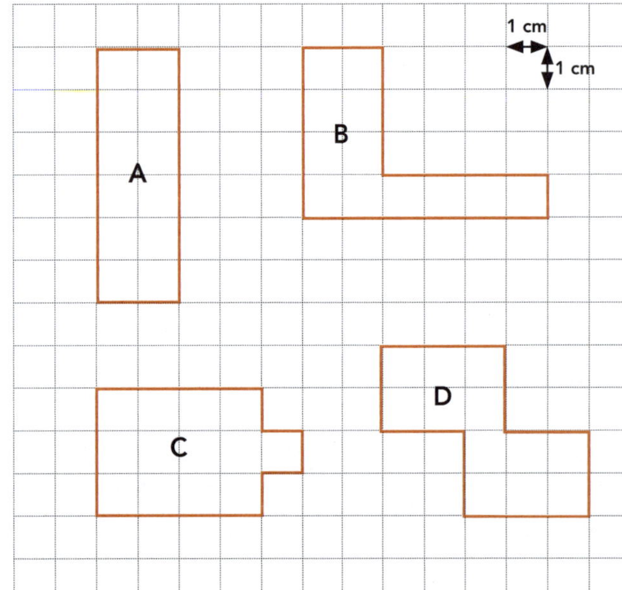

A = ______________________

____

B = ______________________

____

C = ______________________

____

D = ______________________

____

 ISBN: 9780170447218

2 Calculate the perimeters of these shapes.

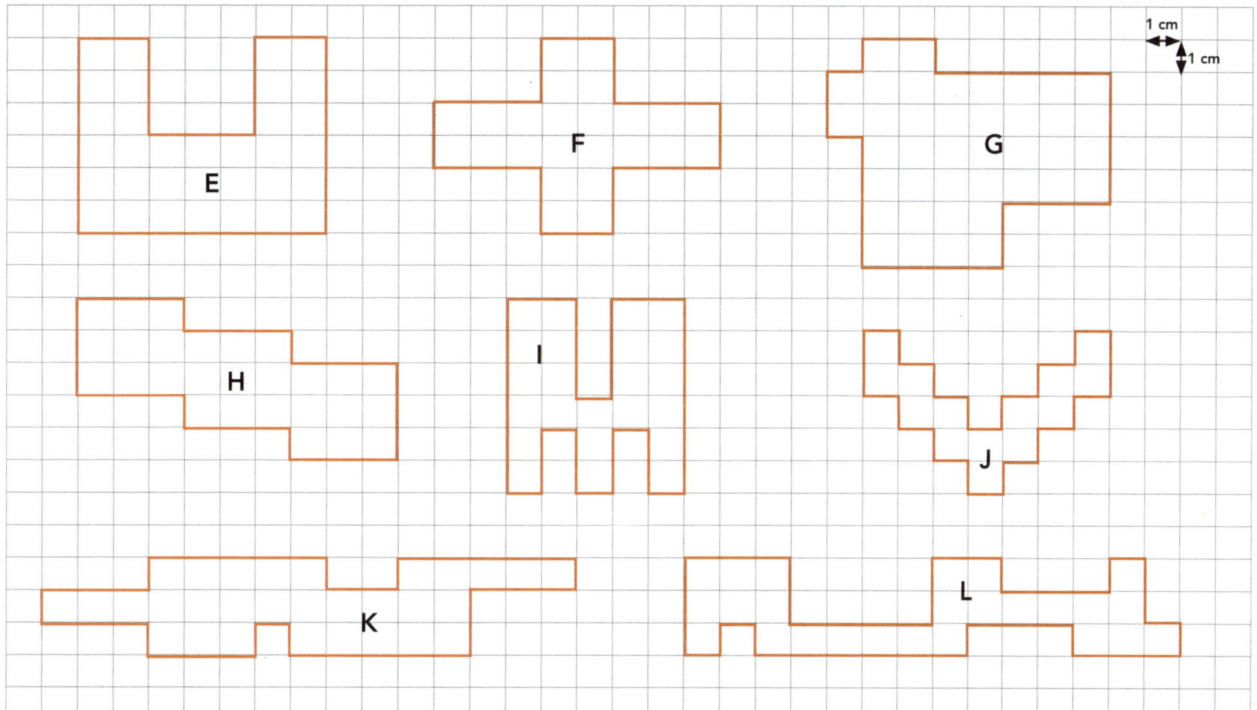

E = ____________________

I = ____________________

F = ____________________

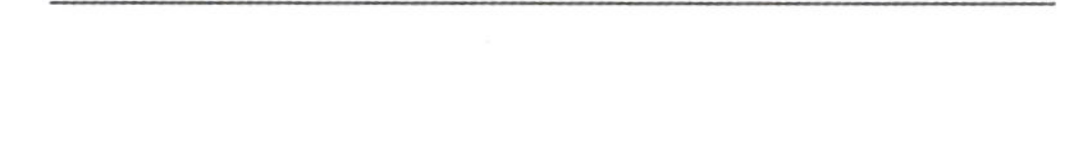

J = ____________________

G = ____________________

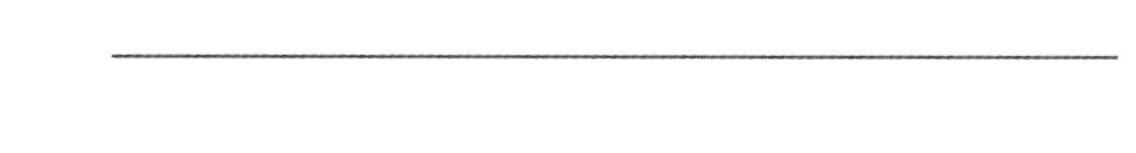

K = ____________________

H = ____________________

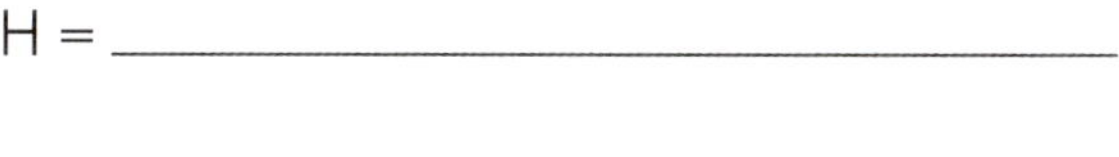

L = ____________________

Shapes with linear sides

- Remember, to find the perimeter you need to **start at one corner** and **add** the distances around the outside of the shape.

Examples:

1

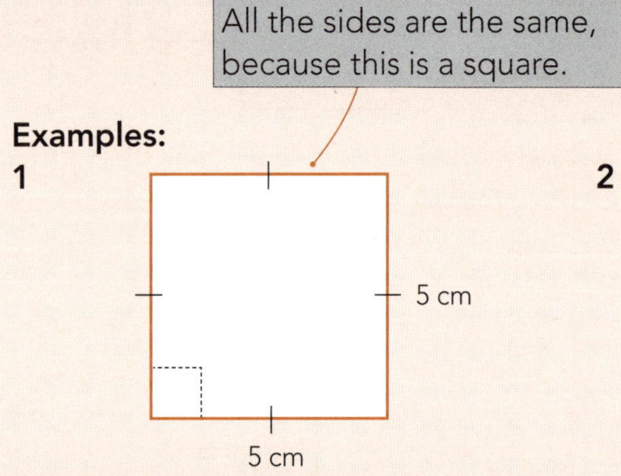

Perimeter = 5 + 5 + 5 + 5
= 20 cm

2

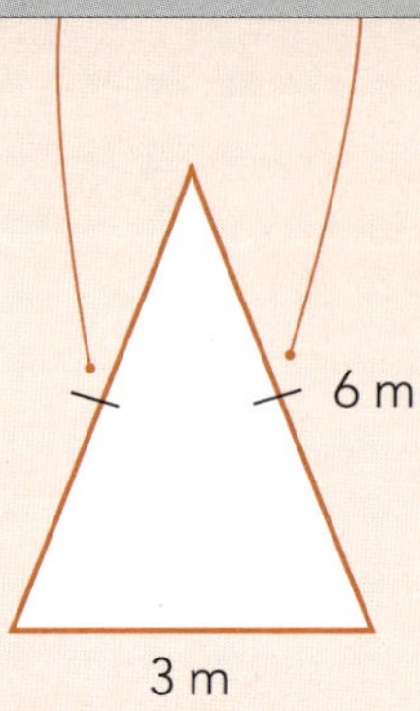

Perimeter = 3 + 6 + 6
= 15 cm

Calculate the perimeters of these shapes.

1

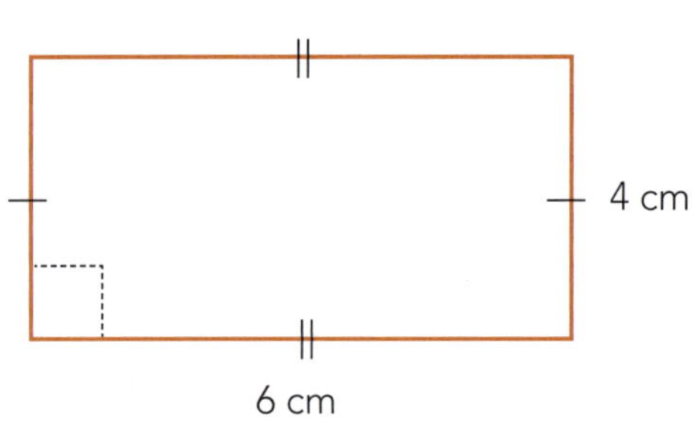

2

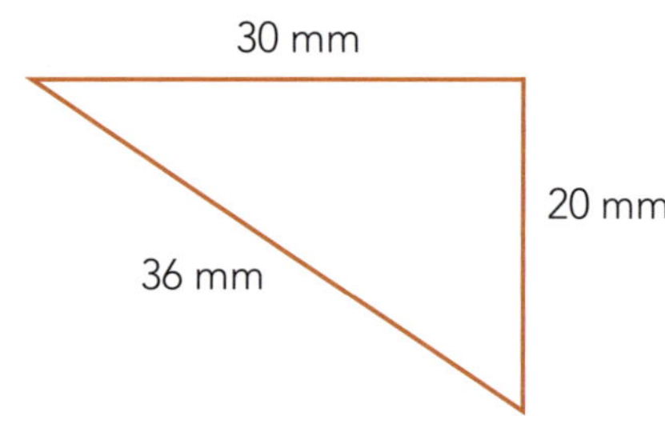

3

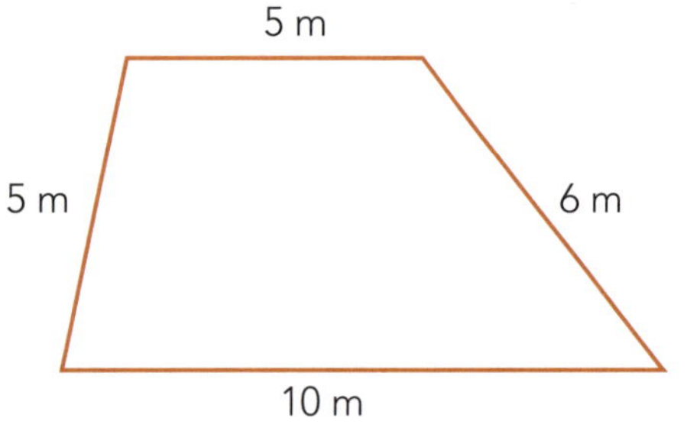

4

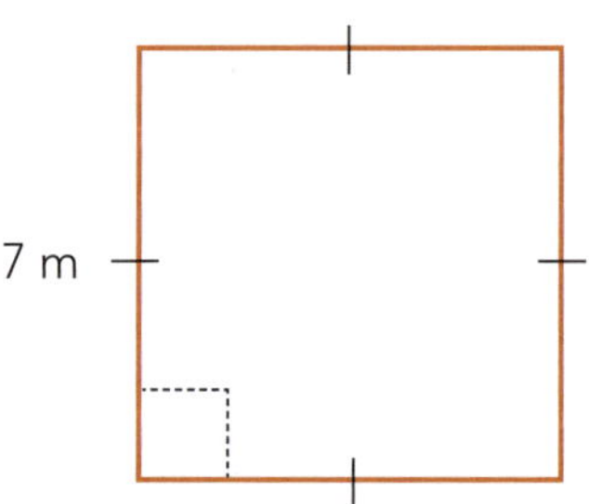

ISBN: 9780170447218

5

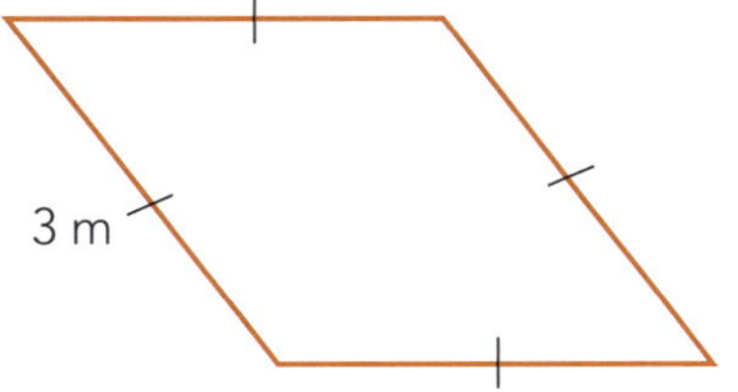

6

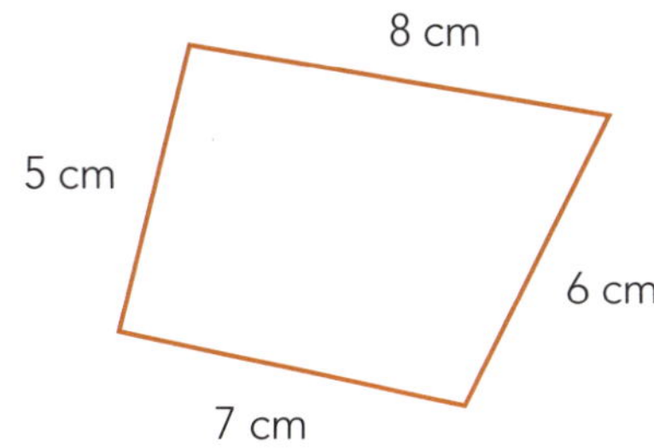

7

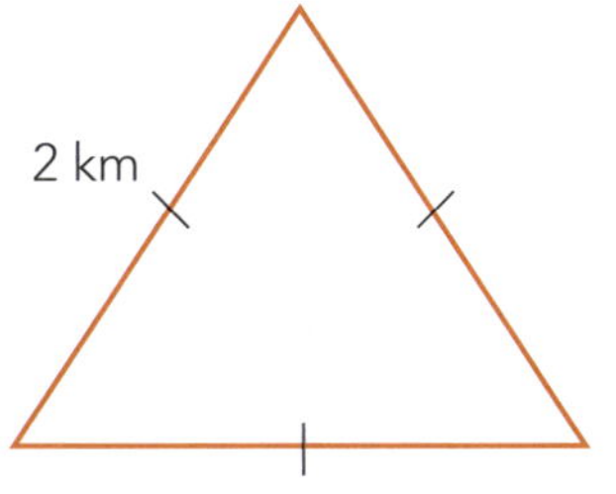

8

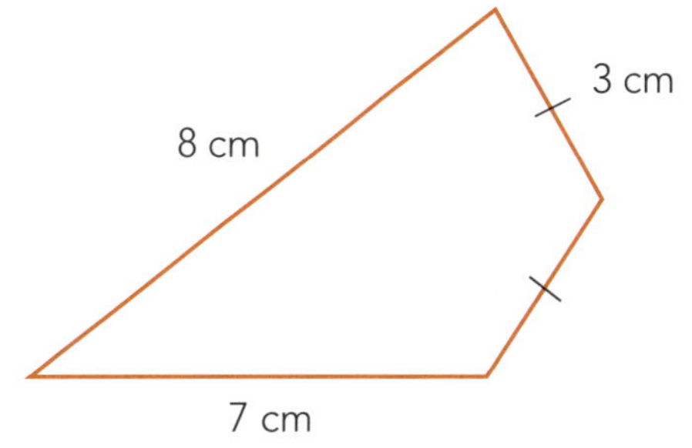

9

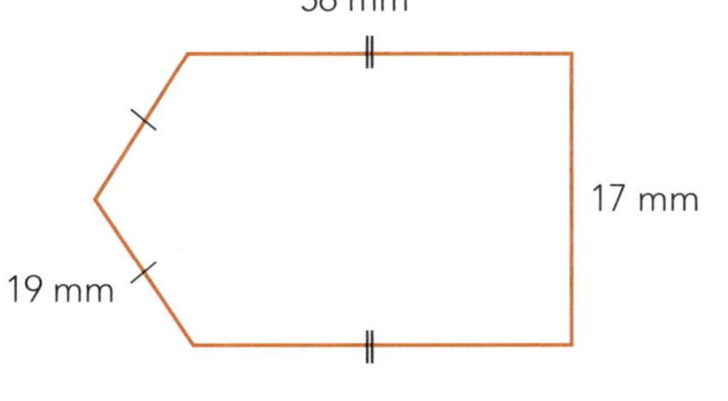

10

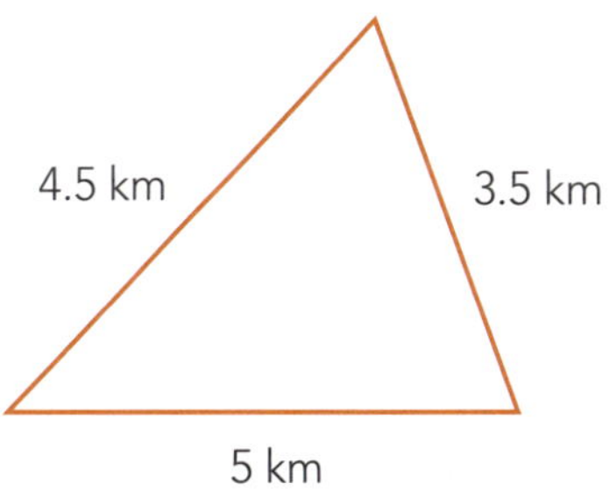

11

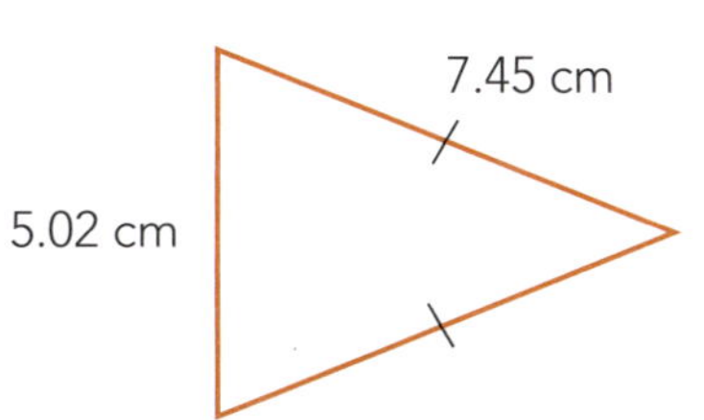

12

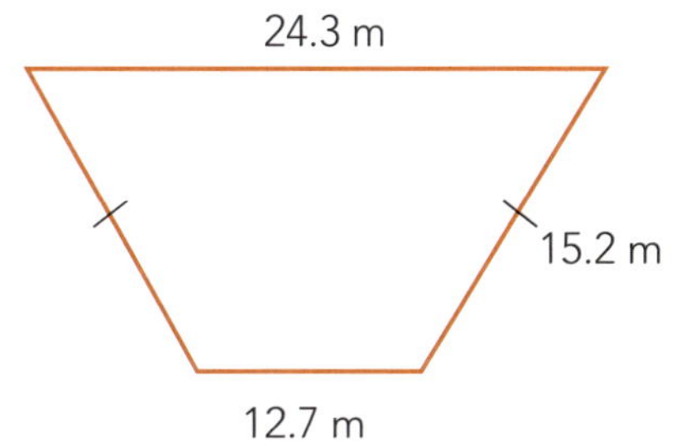

ISBN: 9780170447218

Things to look out for

Regular shapes

- 'Regular' means all the sides are the same length. In this case, each side is 12 mm long.

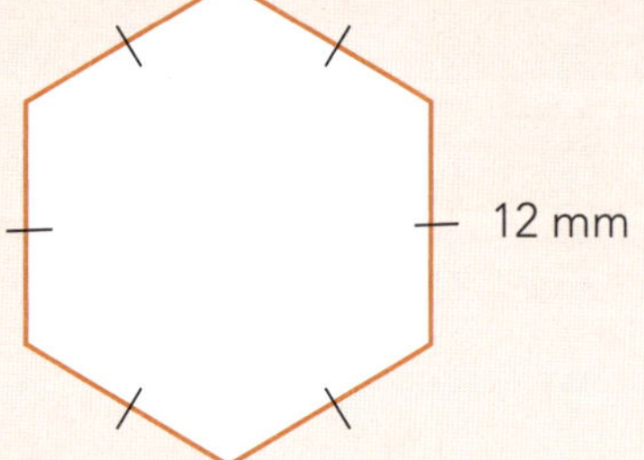

Perimeter = 12 + 12 + 12 + 12 + 12 + 12
= 6 x 12
= 72 mm

Extra measurements

- There may be measurements that are not needed for calculating the perimeter.

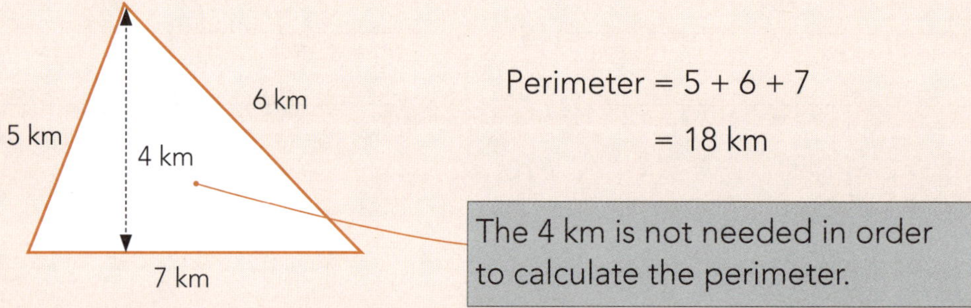

Different units

- Some shapes may have measurements with different units.
- You need to make sure that all the information you need is in the same units before calculating the perimeter.

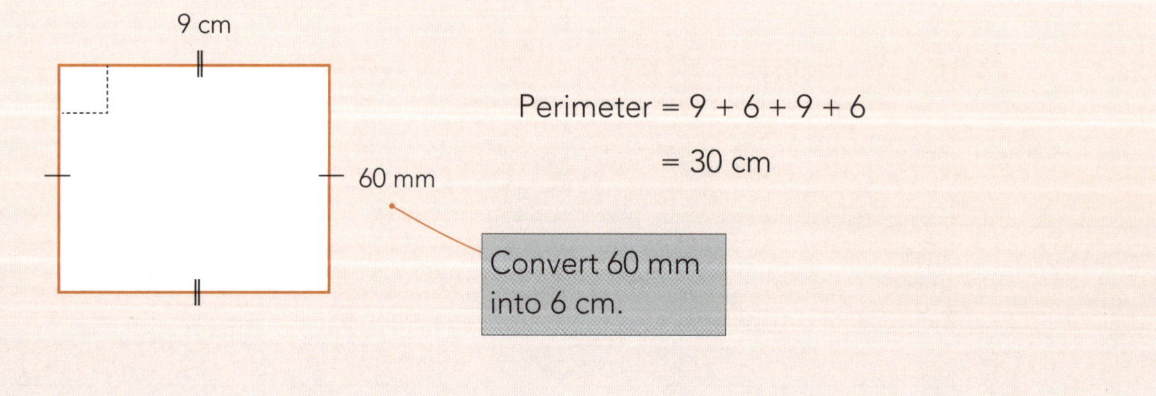

ISBN: 9780170447218

Calculate the perimeters of these shapes.

1 This is a regular pentagon.

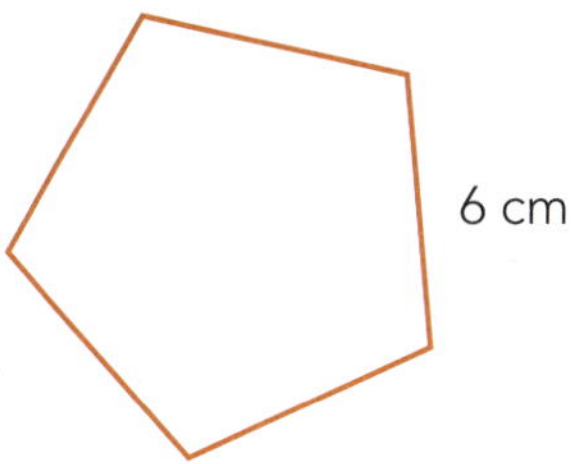

2 Write your answer in kilometres (km).

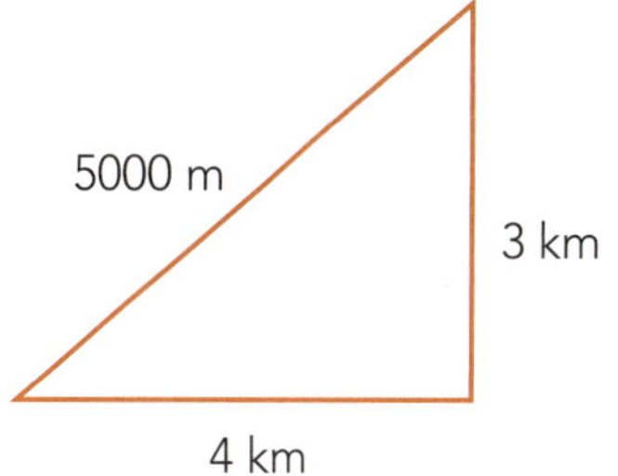

3

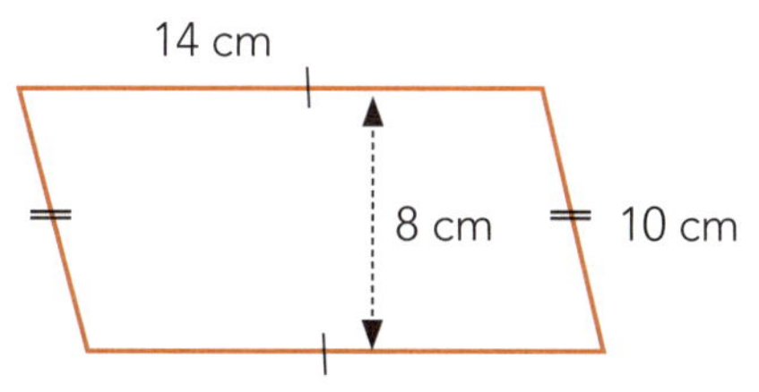

4 This is a regular decagon.

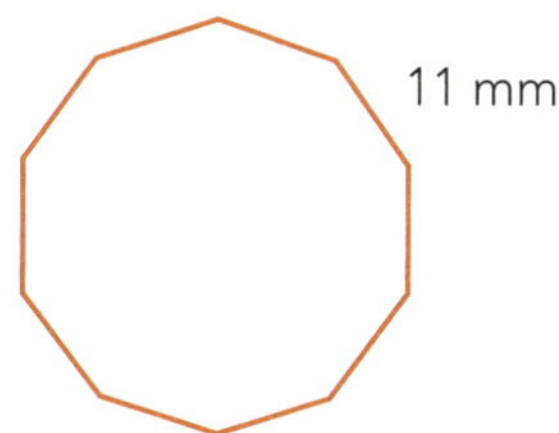

5

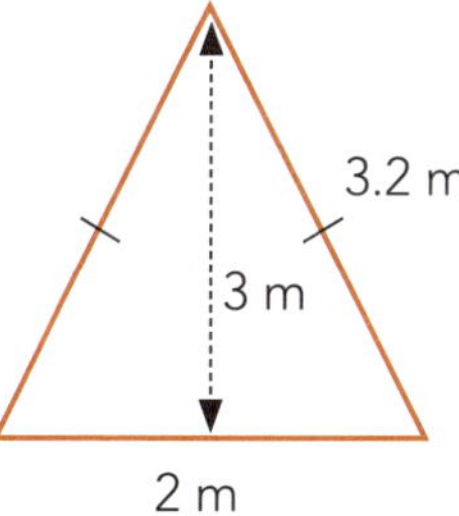

6 Write your answer in metres (m).

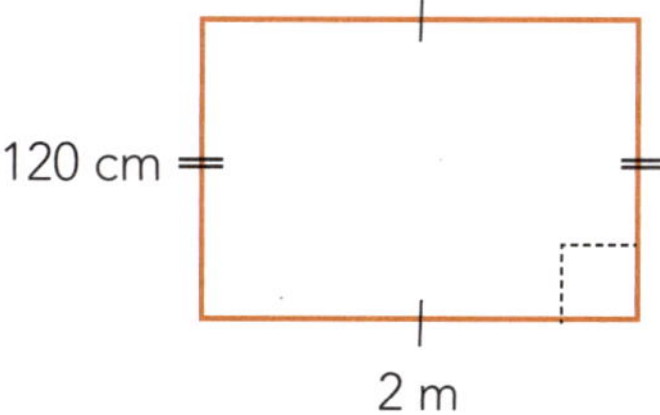

7 This is a regular heptagon.

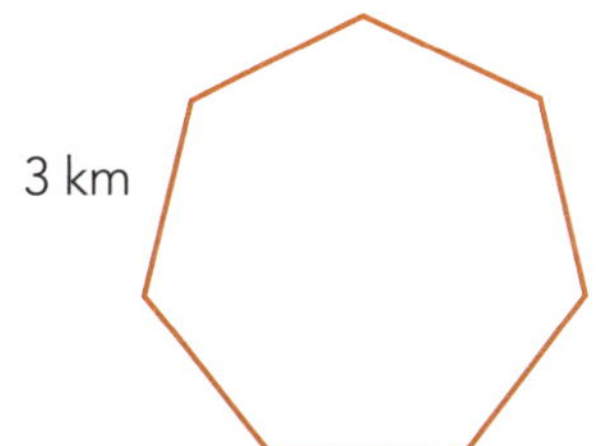

8

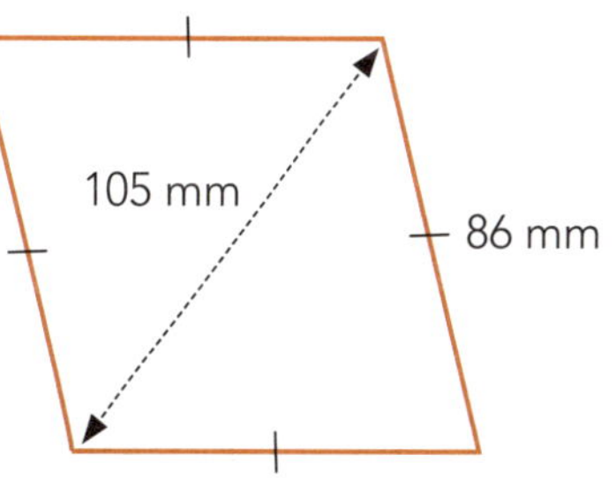

ISBN: 9780170447218

9 Write your answer in kilometres (km).

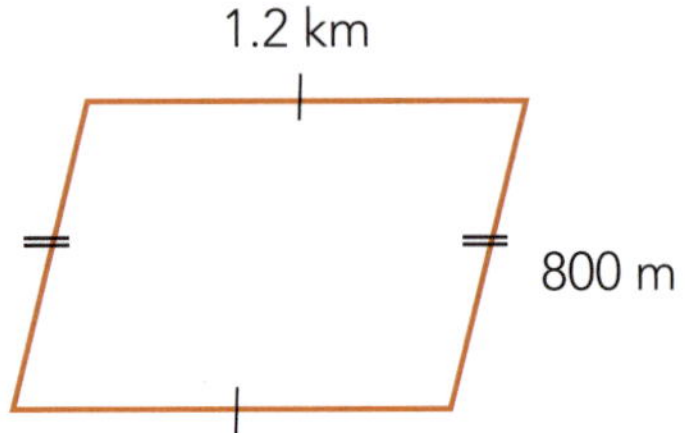

10

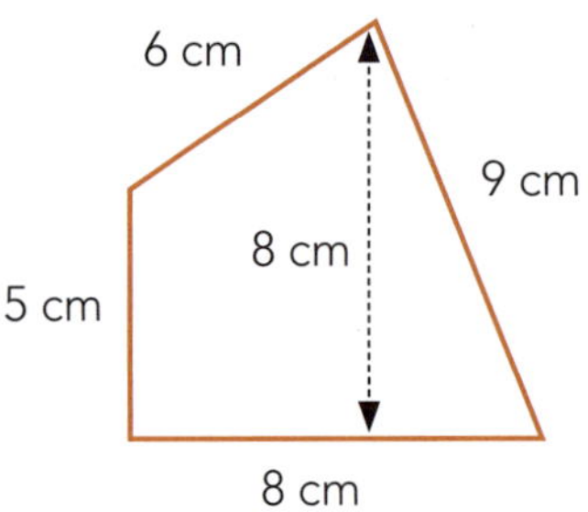

11

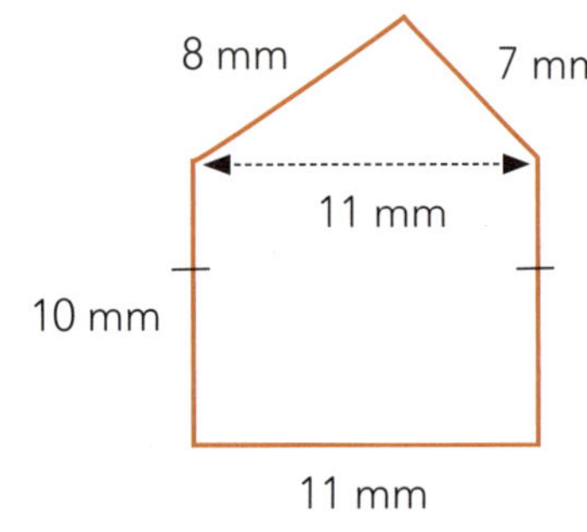

12

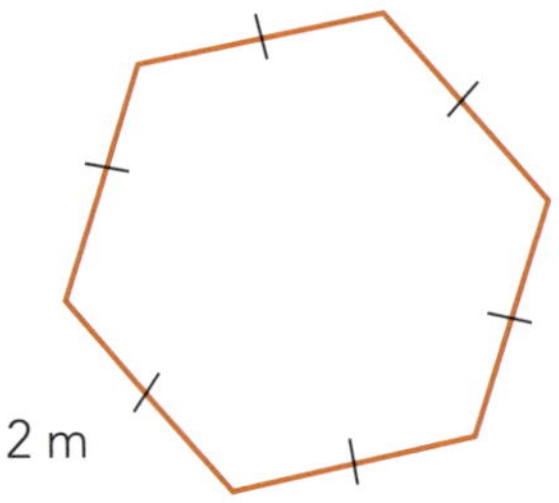

13

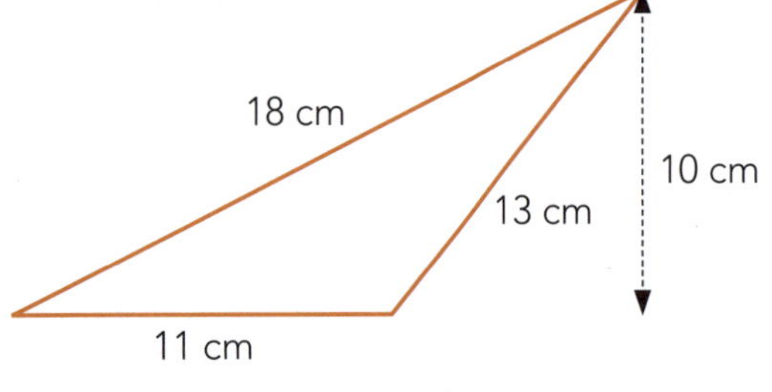

14 Write your answer in metres (m).

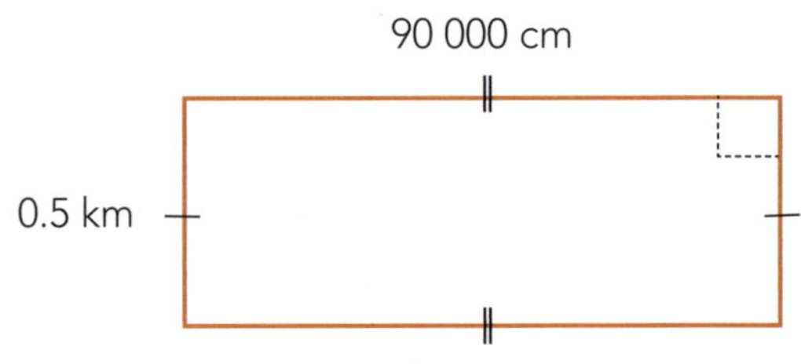

15 Write your answer in metres (m).

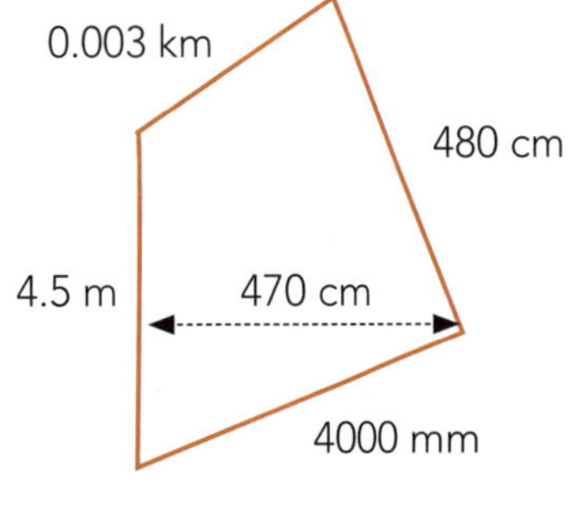

16 Write your answer in metres (m).

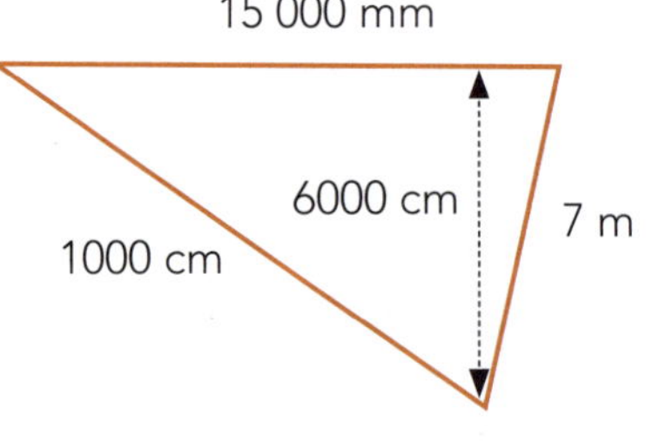

ISBN: 9780170447218

Challenge 1

1 The perimeter of this rectangle is 38 cm. Calculate the length of side h.

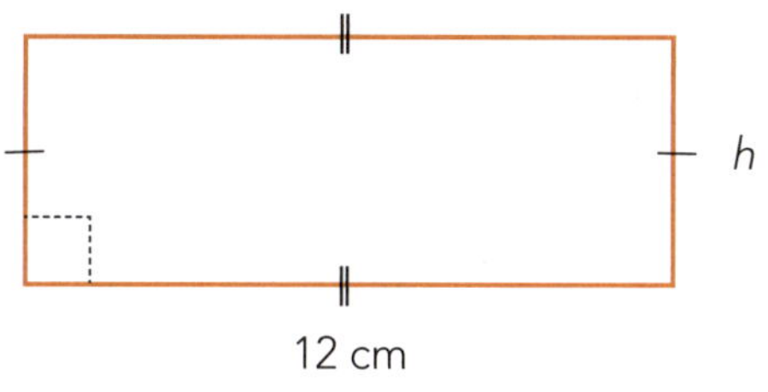

2 The perimeter of this equilateral triangle is 9.6 km. How long is each side?

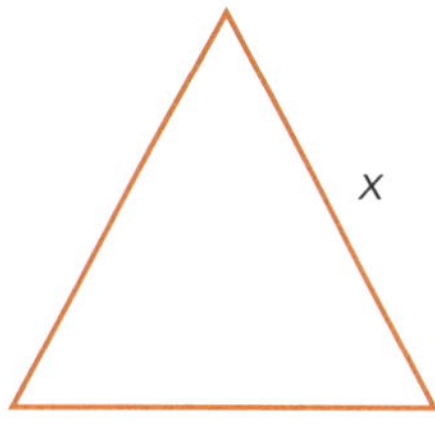

3 The perimeter of this square is 24 m. Calculate the length of the sides.

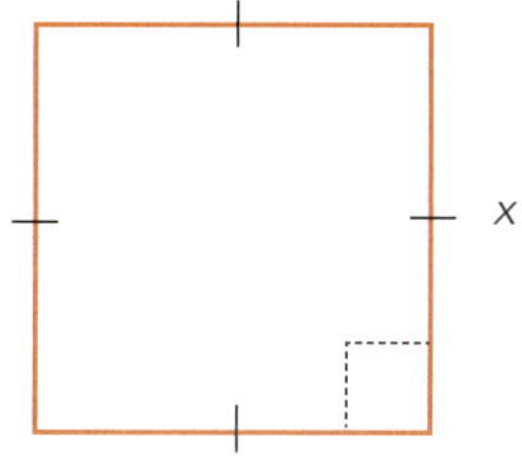

4 The perimeter of this isosceles triangle is 205 mm. Calculate the length of the missing sides.

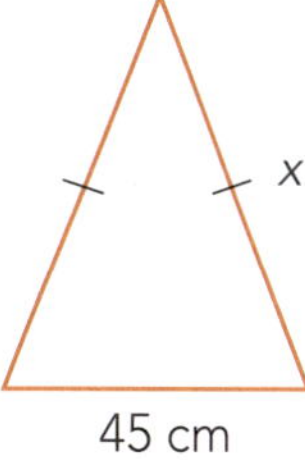

5 The perimeter of this shape is 0.19 m. Find the length of the missing sides.

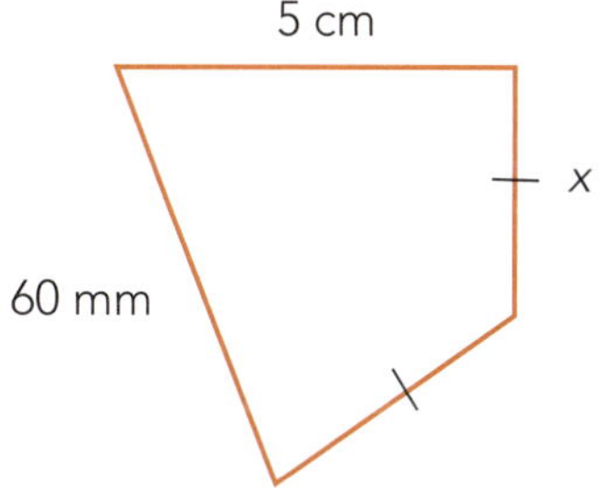

6 The perimeter of this triangle is 10.5 km. Find the length of the missing side.

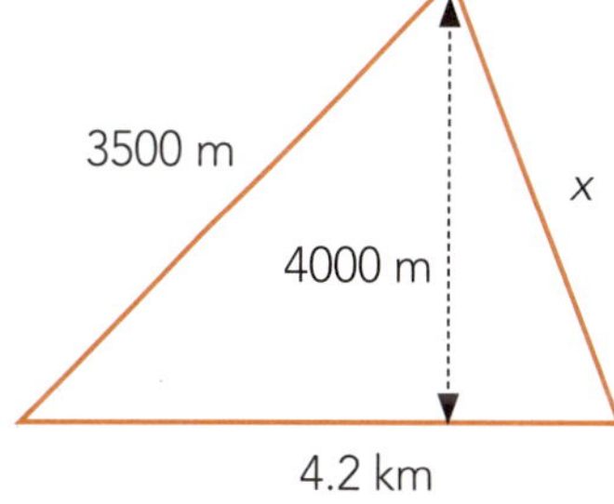

ISBN: 9780170447218

Circles

- The perimeter of a circle has a special term: **circumference**.
- π (pi) is about **3.14**, and represents the number of diameters needed to make up the length of the circumference.
- Because π is an irrational number, you will always need to **round your answers** appropriately, and indicate the number of decimal places.

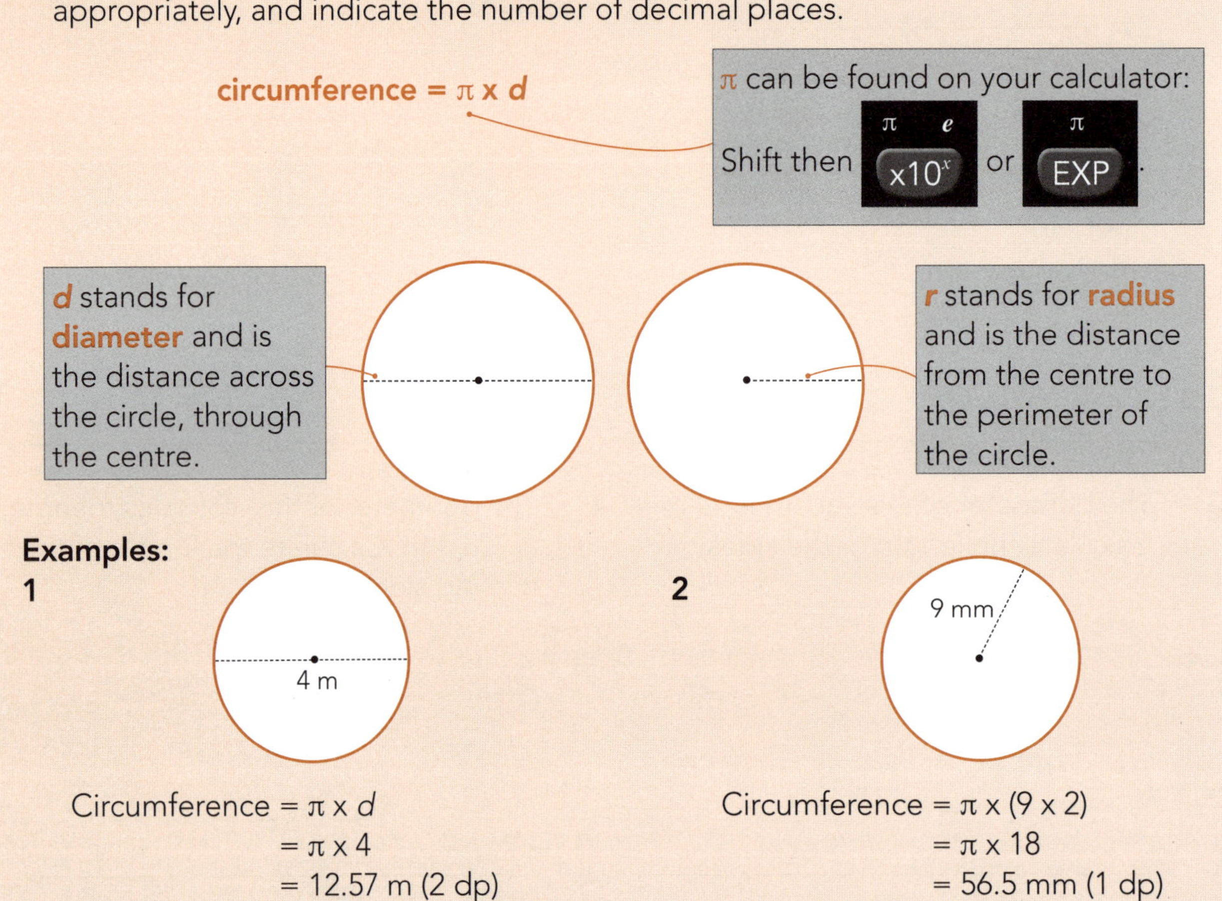

circumference = π x *d*

π can be found on your calculator: Shift then $\times 10^x$ or EXP.

d stands for **diameter** and is the distance across the circle, through the centre.

r stands for **radius** and is the distance from the centre to the perimeter of the circle.

Examples:

1 (4 m)

Circumference = π x *d*
= π x 4
= 12.57 m (2 dp)

2 (9 mm)

Circumference = π x (9 x 2)
= π x 18
= 56.5 mm (1 dp)

Calculate the circumferences of these circles.

1

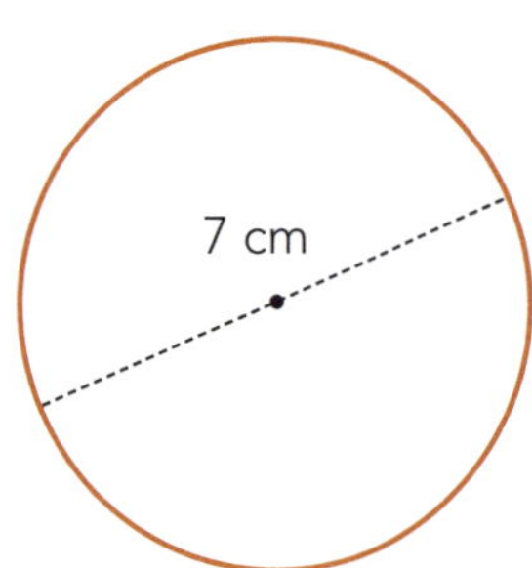

2

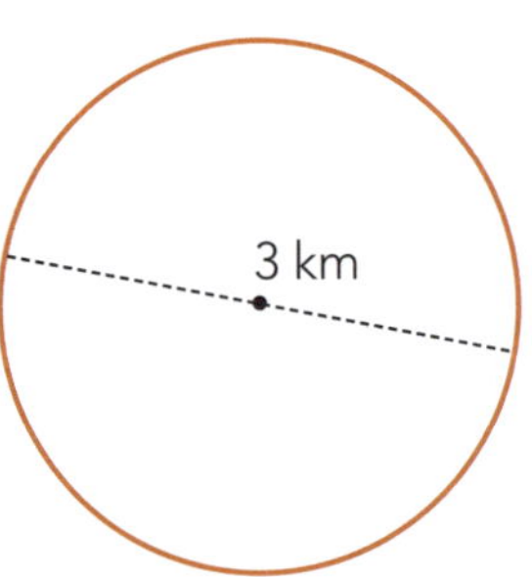

 ISBN: 9780170447218

3

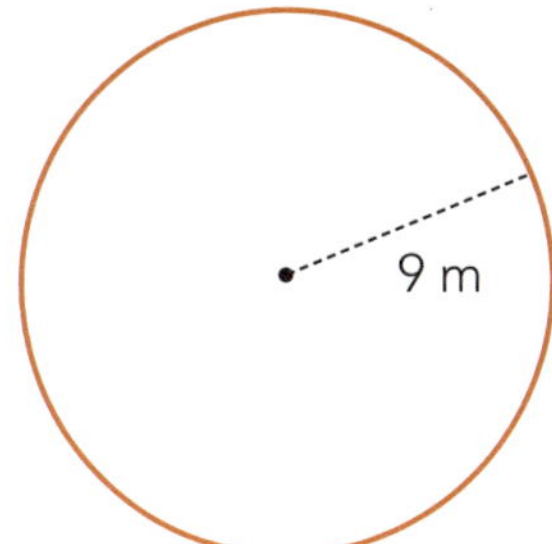

4

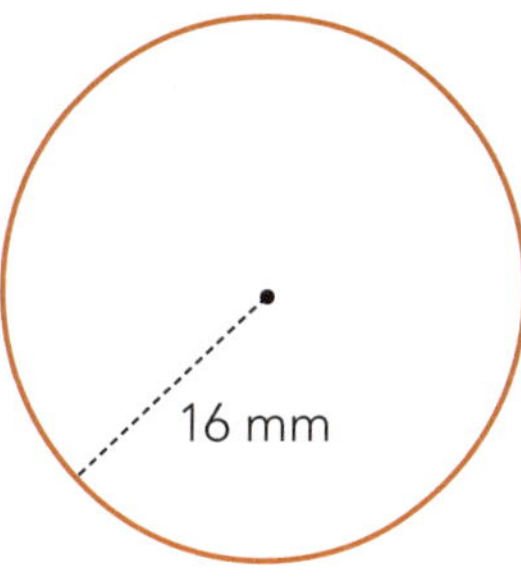

5

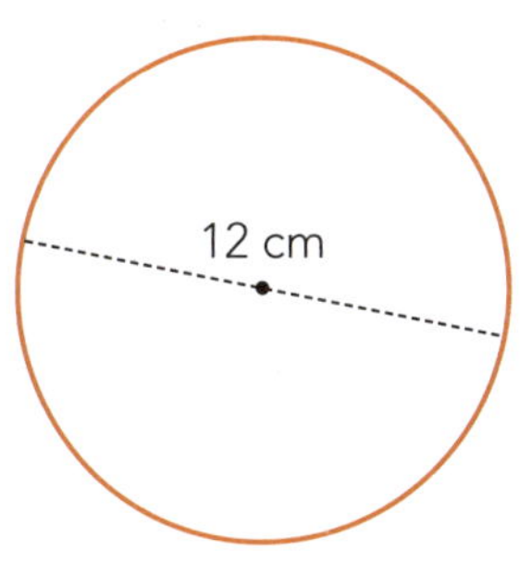

6

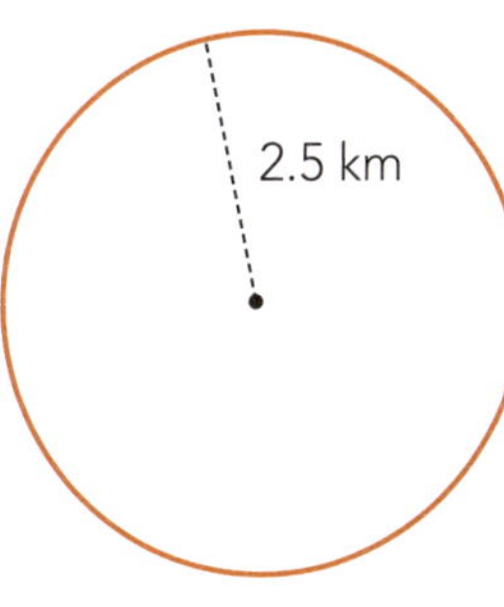

7

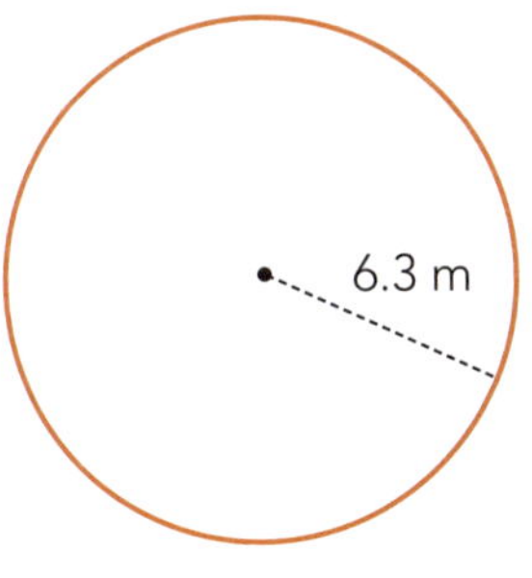

8

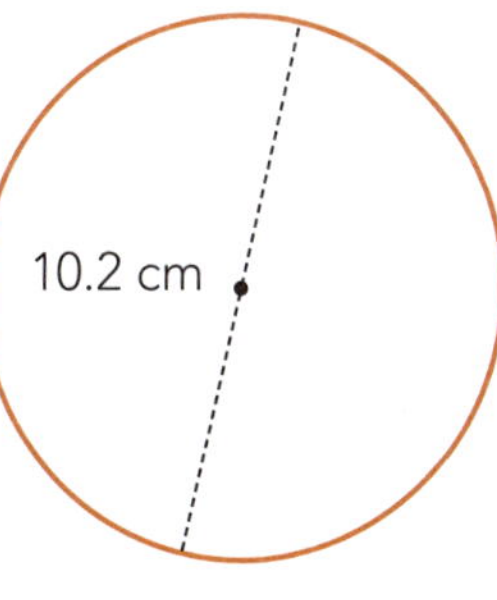

9 A circle has a diameter of 24 cm. Calculate its circumference.

10 A circle has a radius of 3 km. Calculate its circumference.

Parts of circles

Examples:

1 A semicircle, or half a circle.

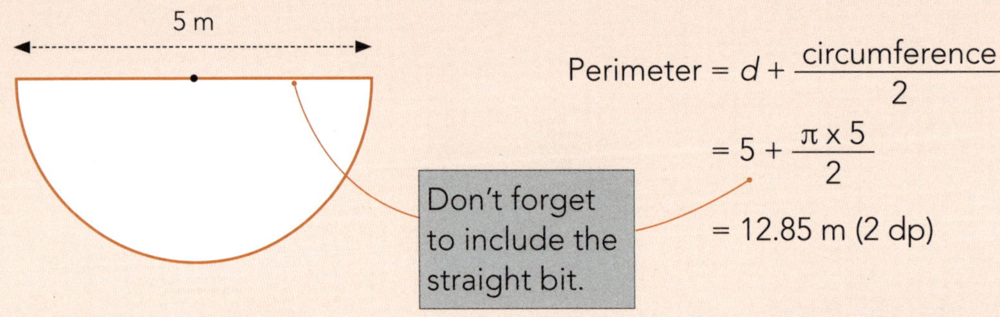

$$\text{Perimeter} = d + \frac{\text{circumference}}{2}$$

$$= 5 + \frac{\pi \times 5}{2}$$

$$= 12.85 \text{ m (2 dp)}$$

2 One quarter of a circle.

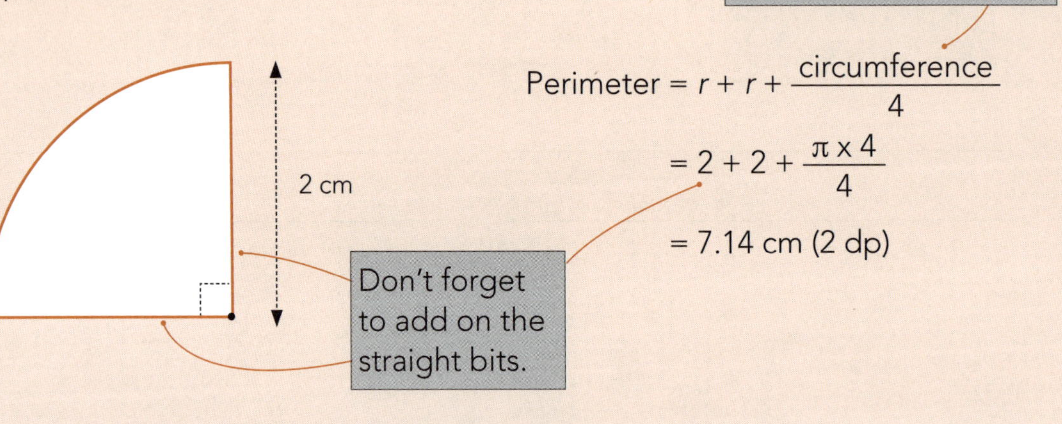

$$\text{Perimeter} = r + r + \frac{\text{circumference}}{4}$$

$$= 2 + 2 + \frac{\pi \times 4}{4}$$

$$= 7.14 \text{ cm (2 dp)}$$

Calculate the perimeters of these parts of circles.

1

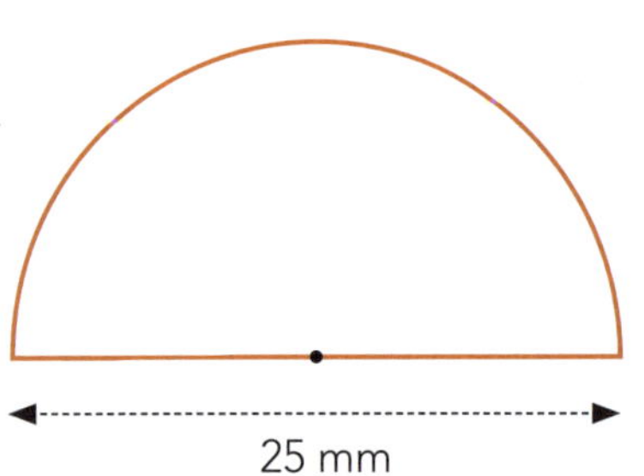

2

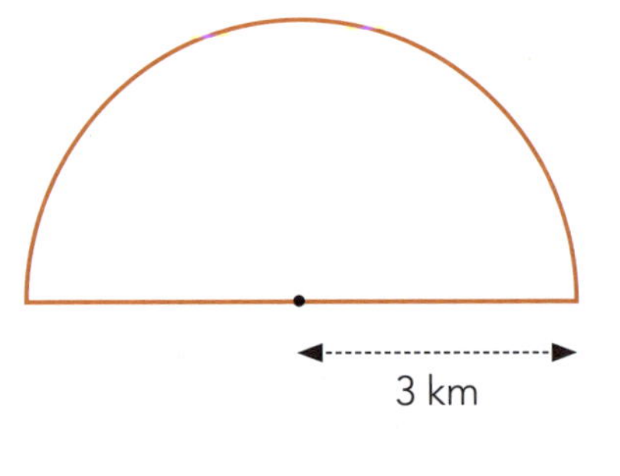

 ISBN: 9780170447218

3

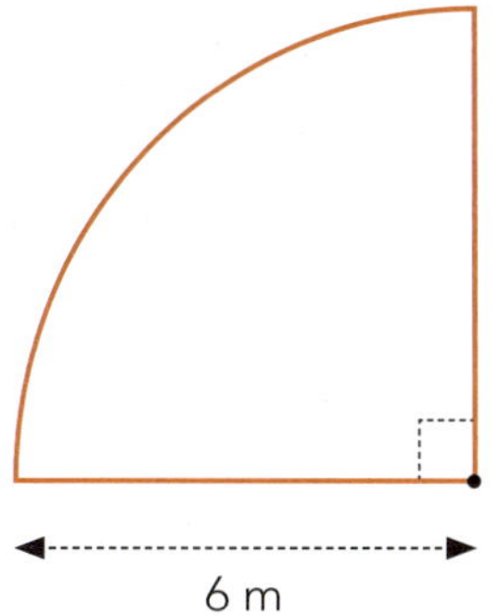

4

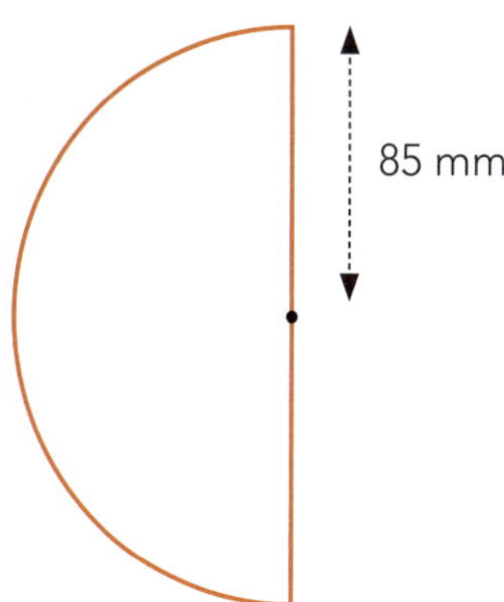

5

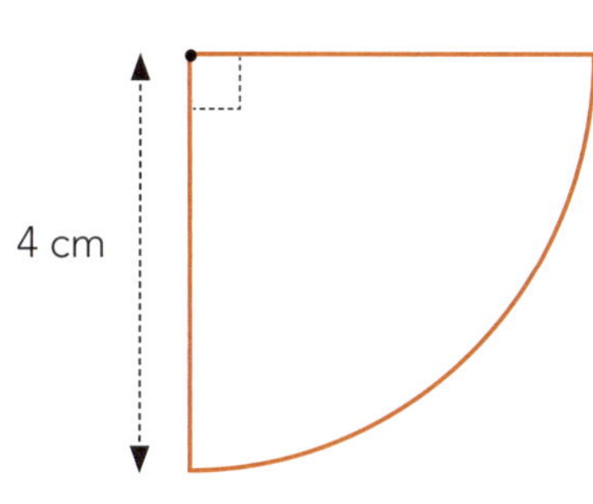

6

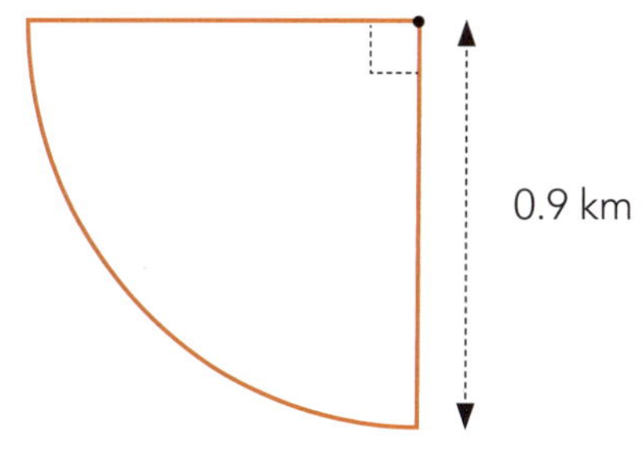

7

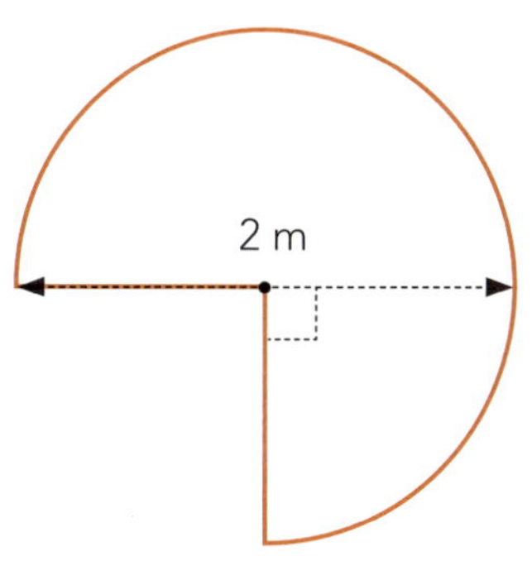

8

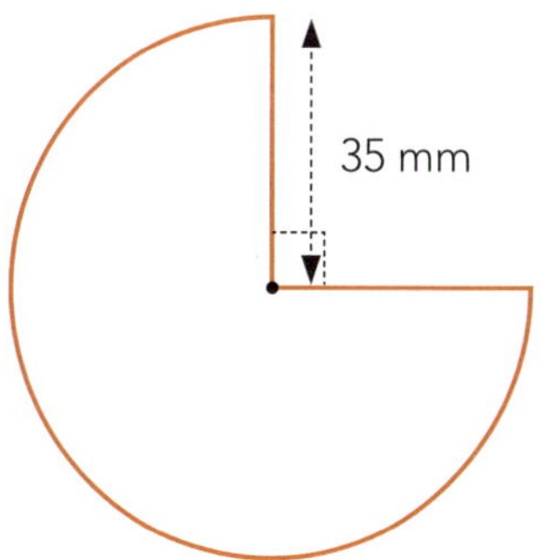

9 A semicircle that has a radius of 3 m.

10 A quarter circle that has a diameter of 10 cm.

Compound shapes

- A compound shape is one made up of **several 'basic' shapes**.
- Not all measurements may be written on diagrams, so you might need to calculate some.

Examples:

1

There is a value missing here.
You need to calculate it.
9 – 6 = 3 m

6 m
2 m
3 m
1 m
9 m

Perimeter = 9 + 3 + 6 + 2 + **3** + 1
= 24 m

2

There is a value missing here.
You need to calculate it.
15 – 7 = 8 cm

1 cm
3 cm
7 cm
15 cm
11 cm

Perimeter = 15 + 11 + **8** + 3 + 1
= 38 cm

Calculate the perimeters of these compound shapes.

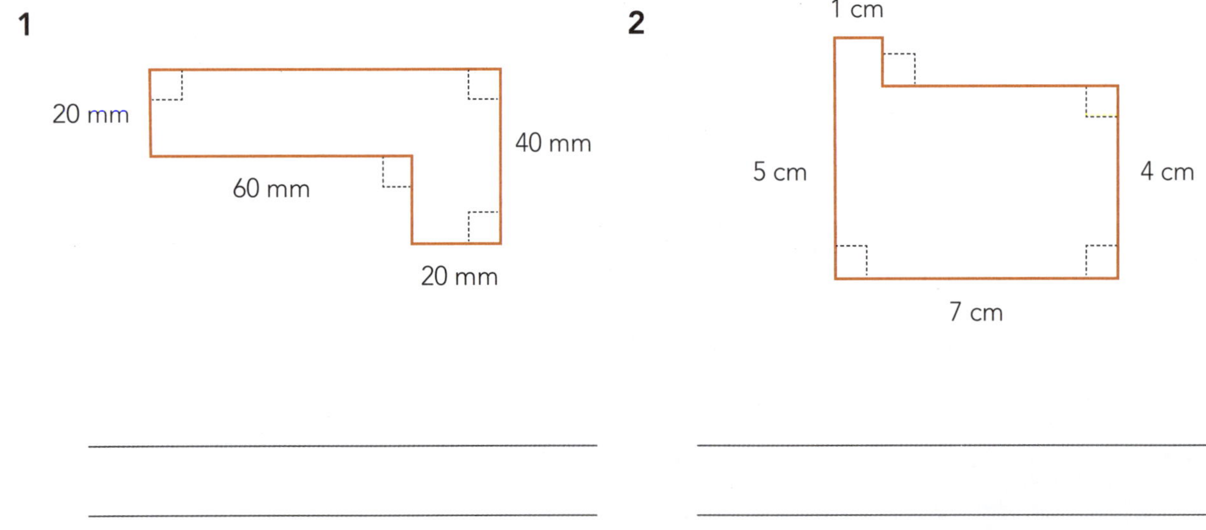

 ISBN: 9780170447218

3

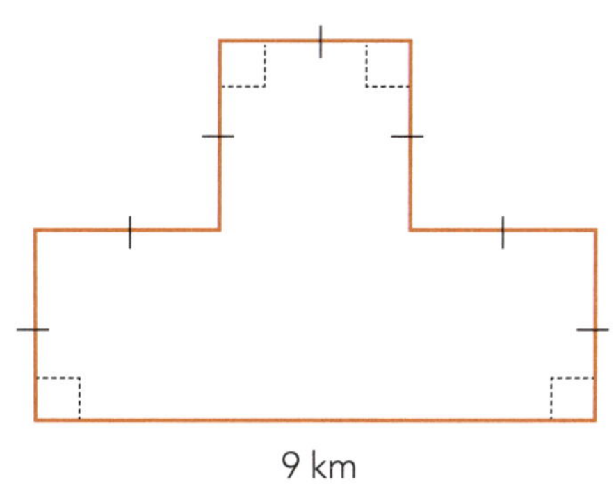

4

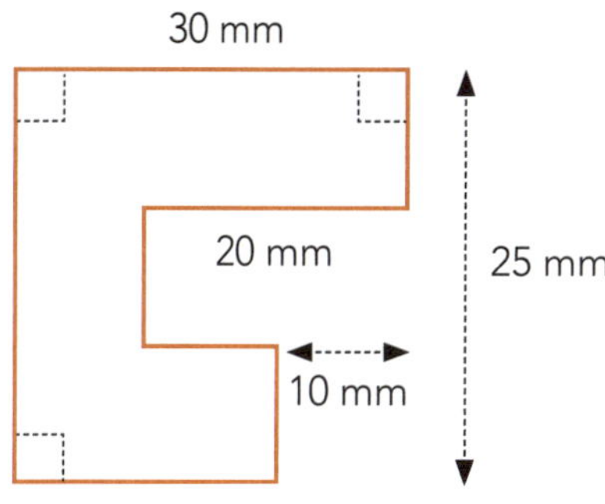

5

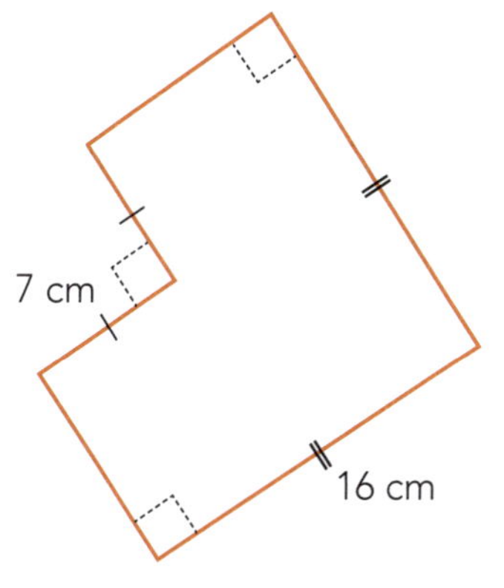

6

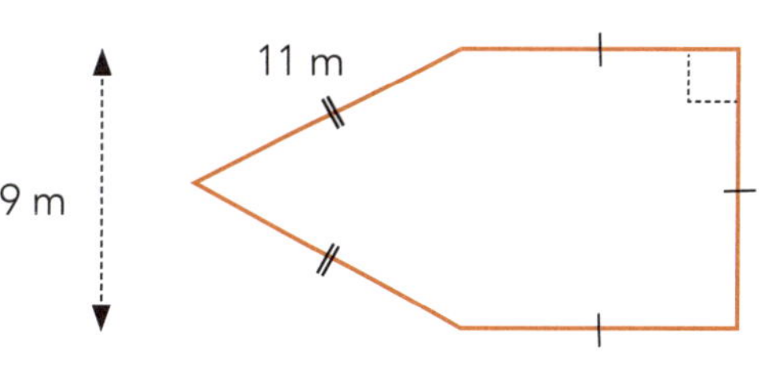

7

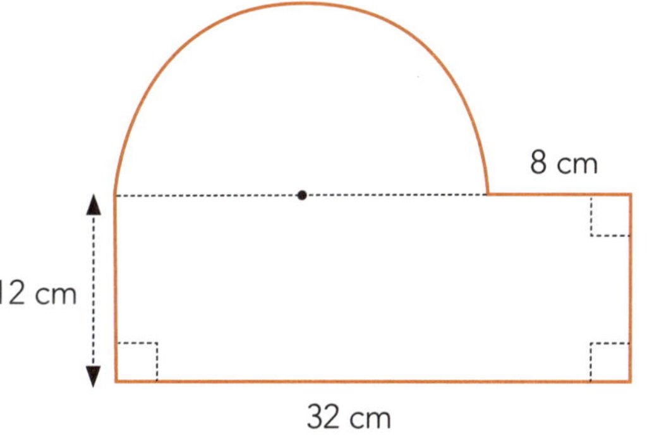

8

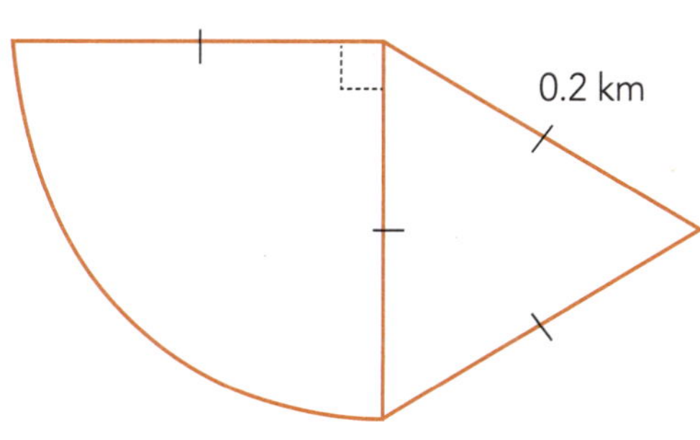

Word questions

Word questions are easier if you follow these steps:

Step 1: Identify the shape.
Step 2: Sketch a diagram.
Step 3: Add the measurements to the diagram.
Step 4: Calculate the perimeter.

Example: A rectangular cake measures 24 cm by 32 cm. Calculate the length of ribbon required to go round the cake (with no overlap).

Your diagram doesn't have to be perfect.

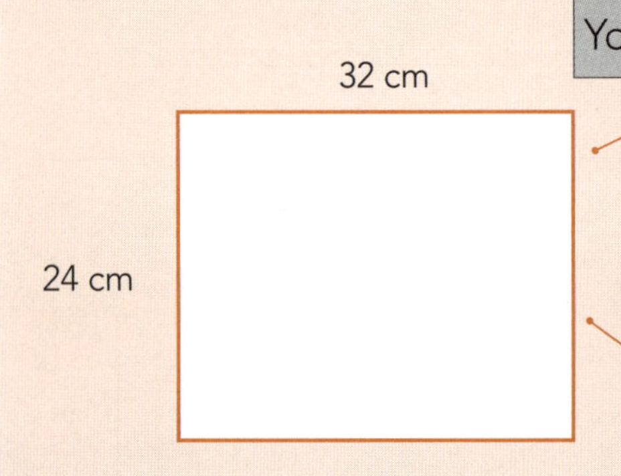

The cake is a rectangle, so opposite sides must be equal.

Ribbon length = 24 + 32 + 24 + 32

= 112 cm

Answer the following questions.

1 A pentagon-shaped table has a perimeter of 553 cm. How long is each side?

2 The sides of an equilateral triangle have a total length of 39 cm. How long is each side?

3 **a** Edward wants to fence a square paddock with sides 27.6 m long. What length of fencing will he need?

b If he used the same amount of fencing, but he used an existing fence to form one side of the square, how long would each side of the paddock be now?

 ISBN: 9780170447218

4 **a** A circular pool has a diameter of 4.33 m. What is the circumference of the pool?

b If the radius of the pool was increased by 20 cm, how much longer would the perimeter of the pool be?

5 **a** An 'L' shape is created using two rectangles. Its total height is 10 cm, and its total width is 7 cm. If each branch of the 'L' is 2 cm thick, calculate its perimeter.

b How would the perimeter change if the 'L' shape was still 10 cm by 7 cm, but the thickness of each branch was 3 cm?

c Find the perimeter of a 'T' shape with the same overall dimensions and with branches 3 cm thick.

d What is the perimeter if you reduce the branch width to 2 cm?

e Challenge: Explain why changing the branch width does not change the perimeter.

6 **a** A garden is created in the shape of a square plus a quarter circle. If sides of the square and the radius of the circle are both 2.5 m, calculate the perimeter of the bed.

b It was originally planned to be a rectangular bed measuring 5 m by 2.5 m. How much more edging would have been needed for a rectangular bed?

ISBN: 9780170447218

Challenge 2

Calculate the perimeter of each shape.

1

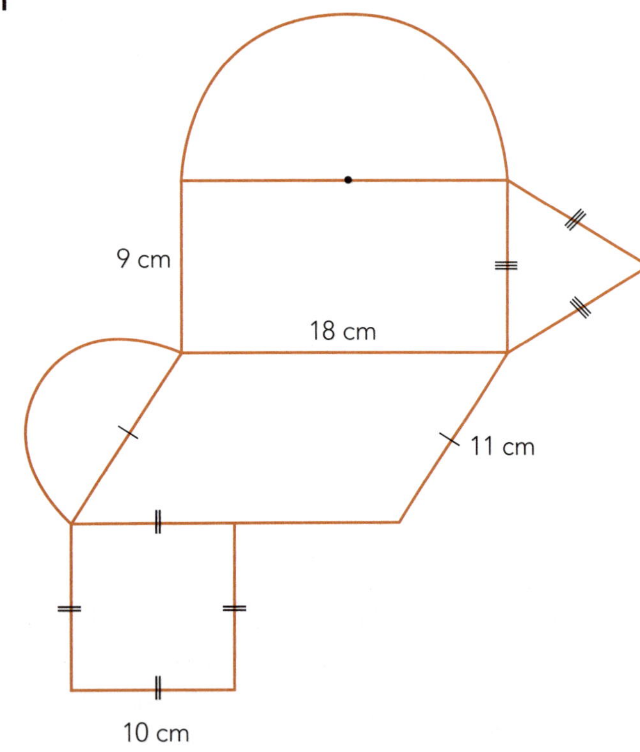

2

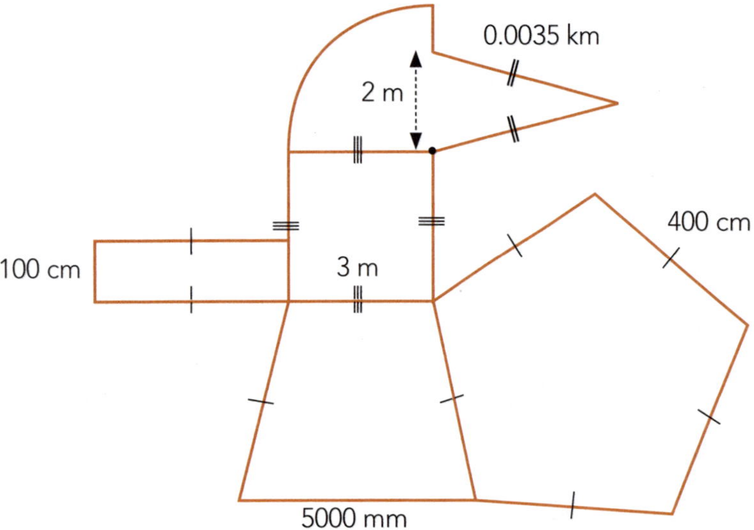

ISBN: 9780170447218

Area

Shapes on a grid

If you can **paint** it, it's area.

- The area is the size of a **flat surface** inside a two-dimensional (2D) shape.
- To calculate the area of shapes on grids, **count the number of squares** inside each.
- The shapes are drawn on a 1 cm by 1 cm grid.

Examples:

1 **2**

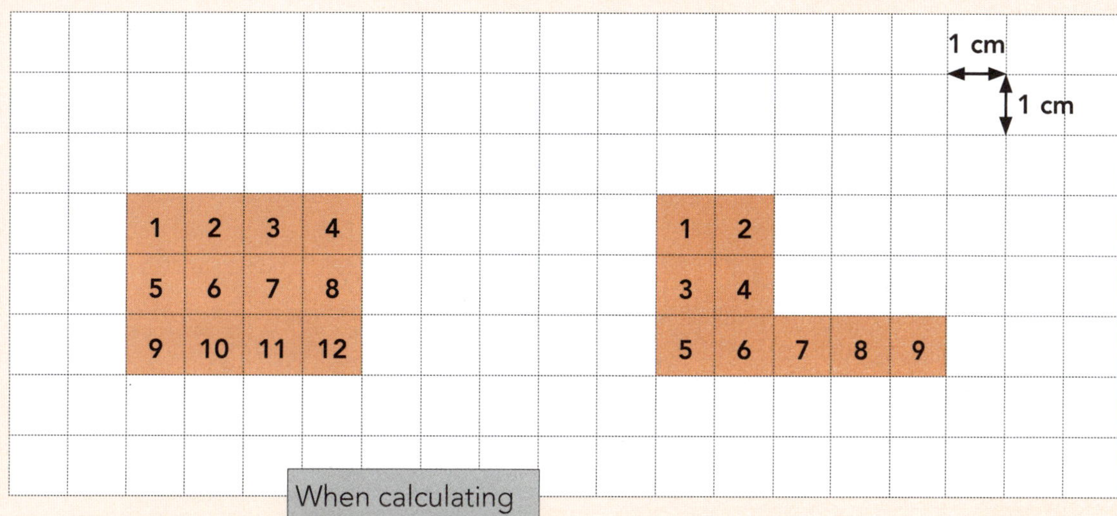

Area = 12 cm^2

When calculating area, the units have ^{2} after them.

Area = 9 cm^2

Find the areas of these shapes.

1

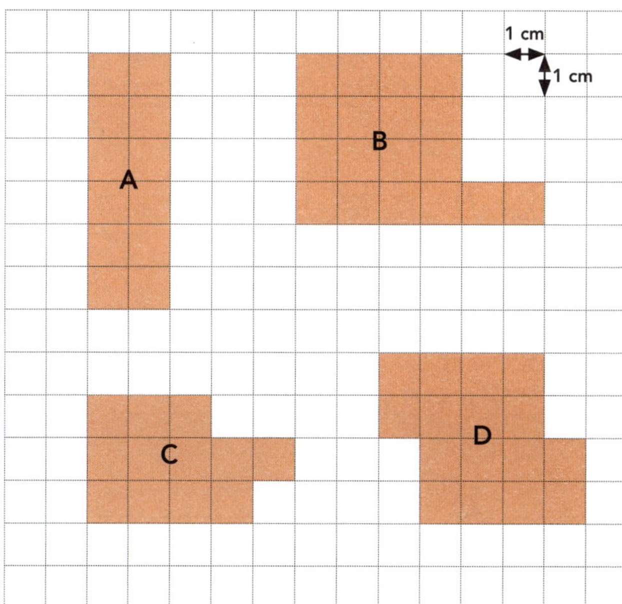

A = ______________________

B = ______________________

C = ______________________

D = ______________________

ISBN: 9780170447218

2

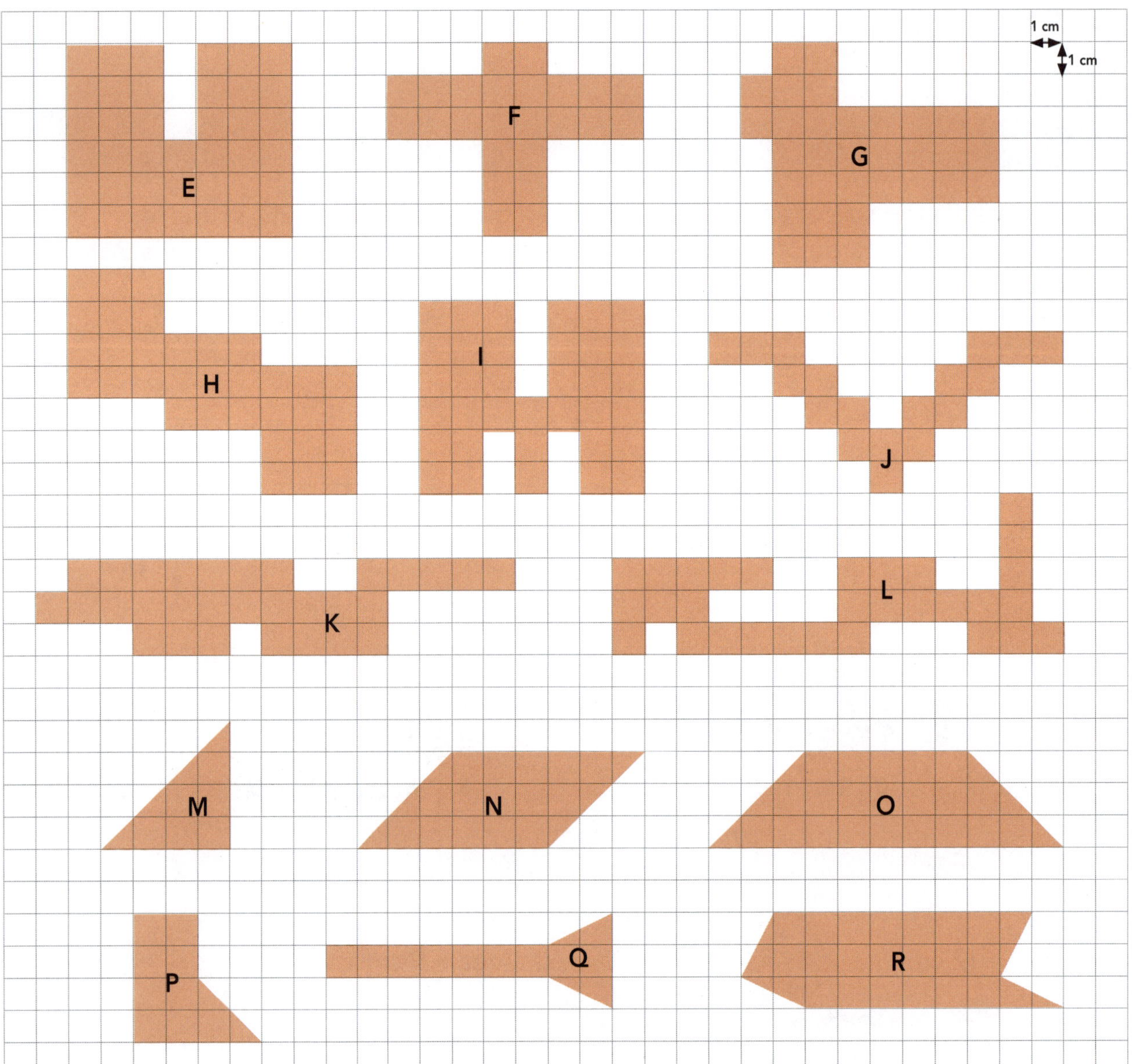

E = ______________________ L = ______________________

F = ______________________ M = ______________________

G = ______________________ N = ______________________

H = ______________________ O = ______________________

I = ______________________ P = ______________________

J = ______________________ Q = ______________________

K = ______________________ R = ______________________

ISBN: 9780170447218

Challenge 3

Join the dots to match each shape on the left with the approximate area on the right.

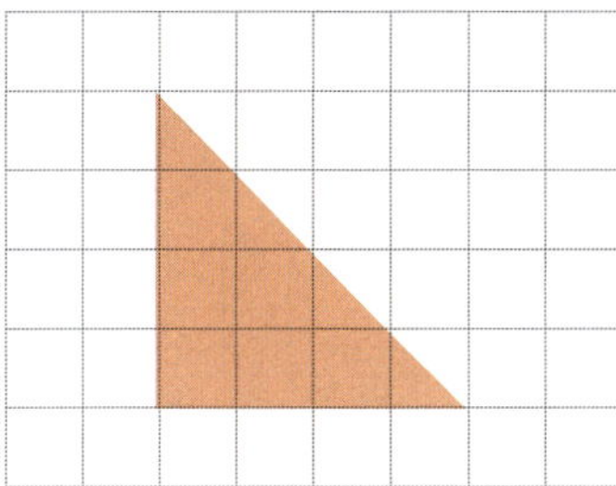 • • $12\ cm^2$

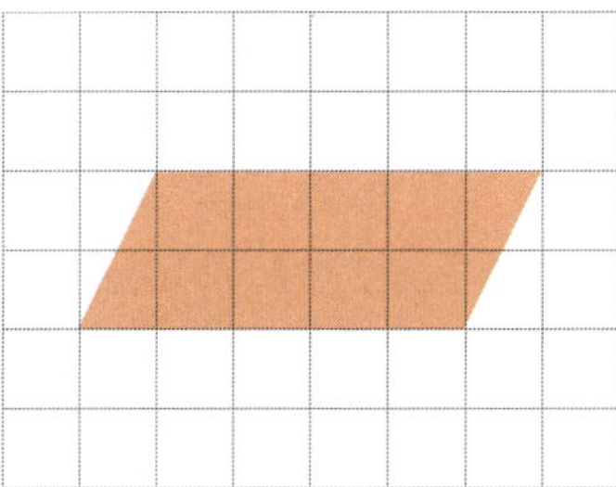 • • $16\ cm^2$

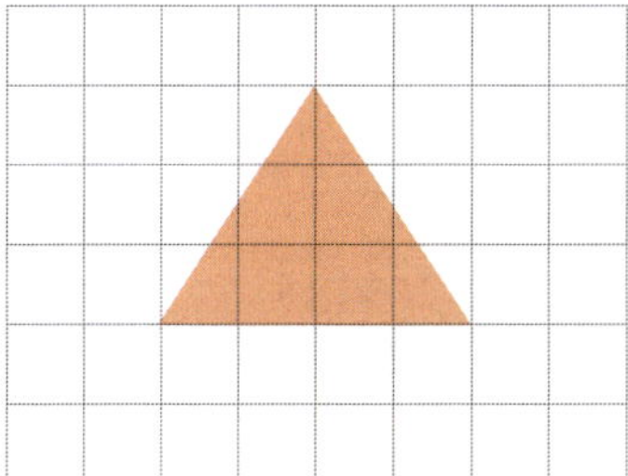 • • $10\ cm^2$

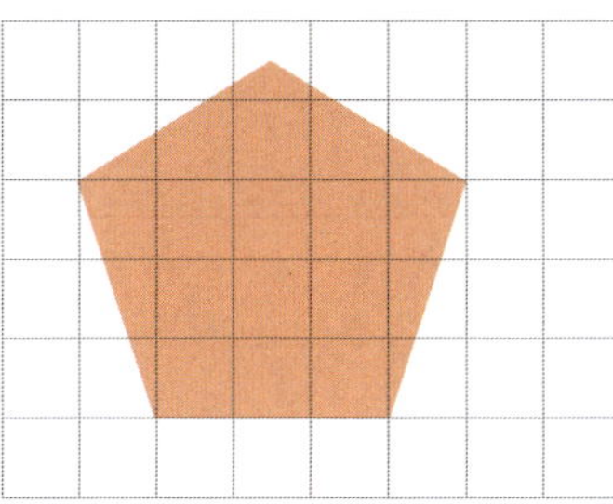 • • $8\ cm^2$

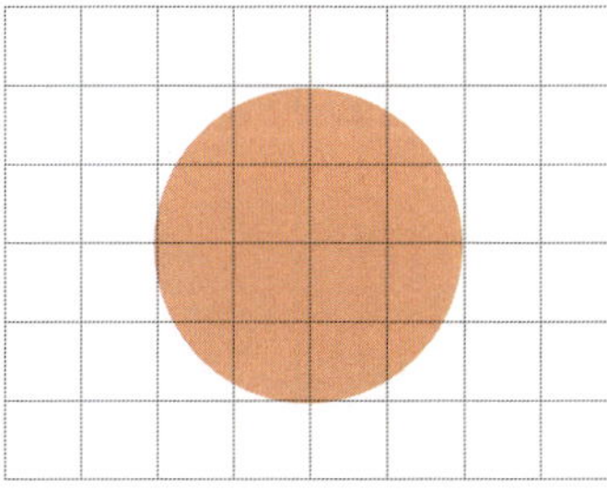 • • $6\ cm^2$

ISBN: 9780170447218

Quadrilaterals

Square and rectangle

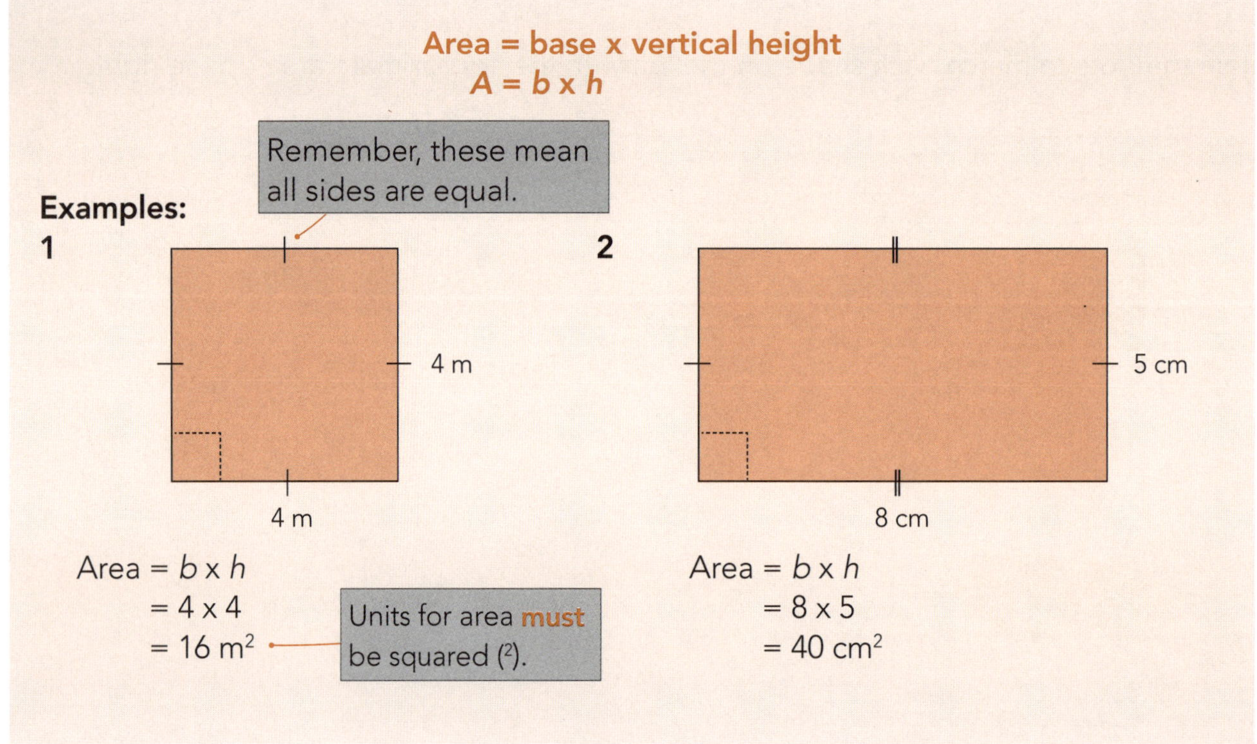

Calculate the areas of these squares and rectangles.

1

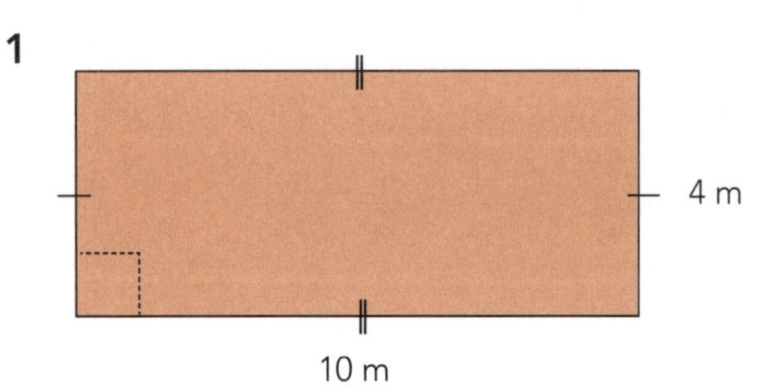

2

7 cm

7 cm

3

2 km

4

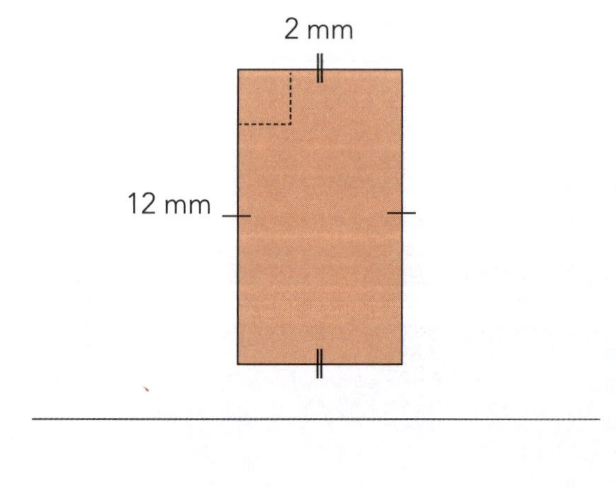

 ISBN: 9780170447218

5

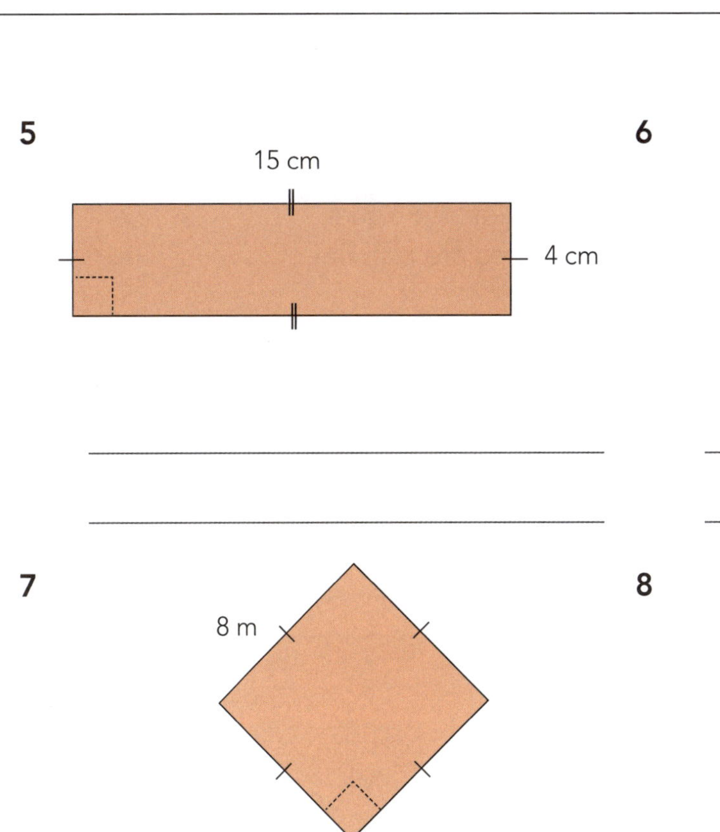

6

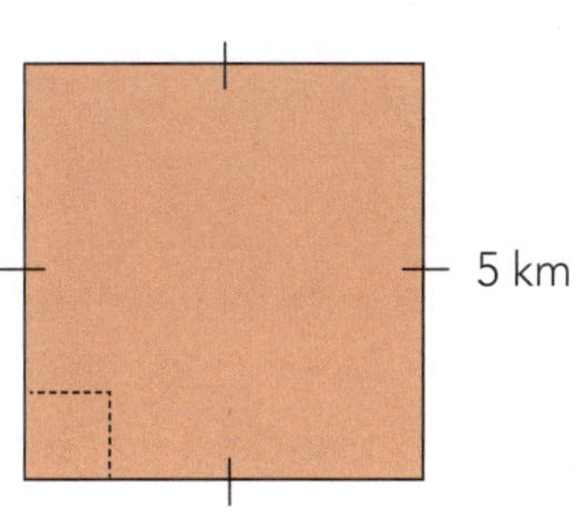

7

8

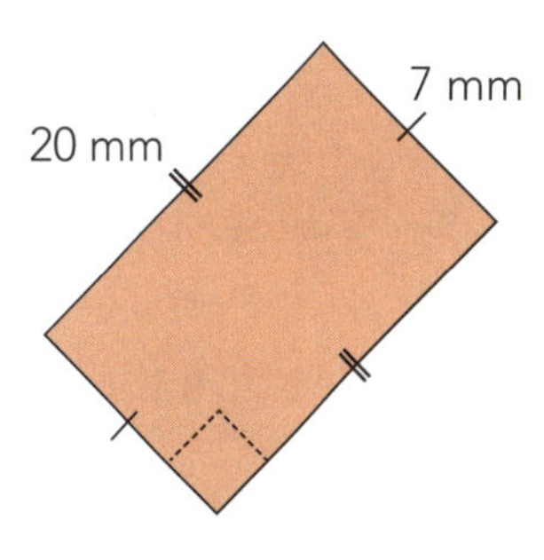

9

6.5 cm

5.5 cm

10

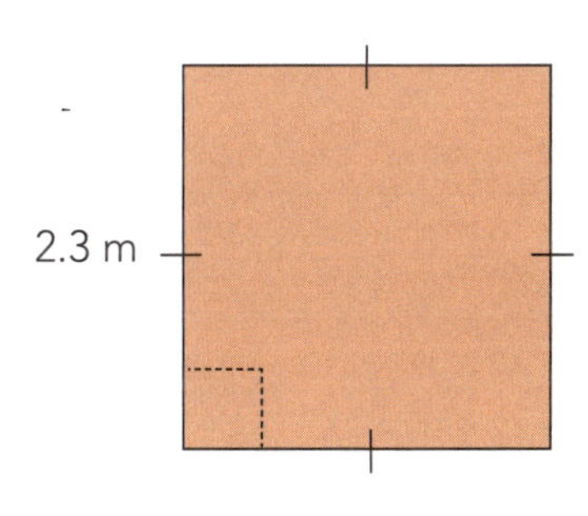

11

102.6 mm

24.3 mm

12

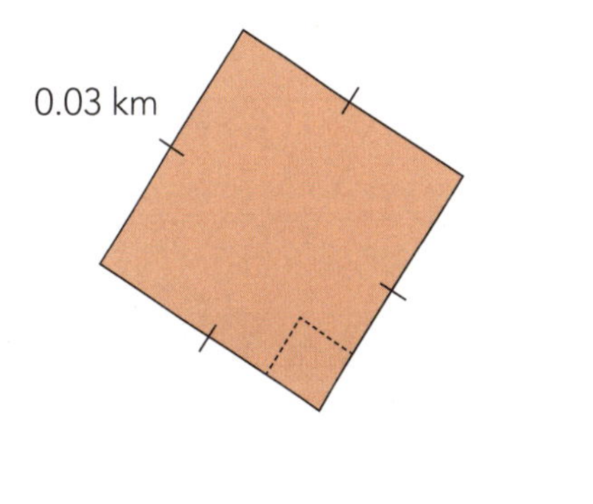

Parallelogram and rhombus

- A **parallelogram** has opposite sides that are parallel and equal.
- A **rhombus** has four equal sides, and opposite sides are parallel.

You can rearrange a parallelogram to look like a rectangle.

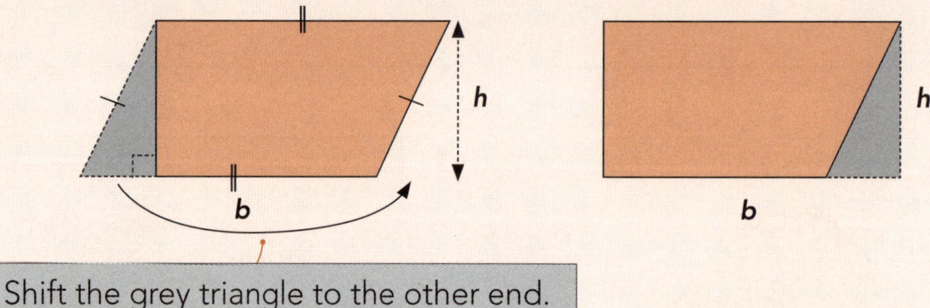

So the formula stays the same: **Area = base x vertical height**

$A = b \times h$

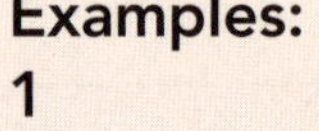

Examples:

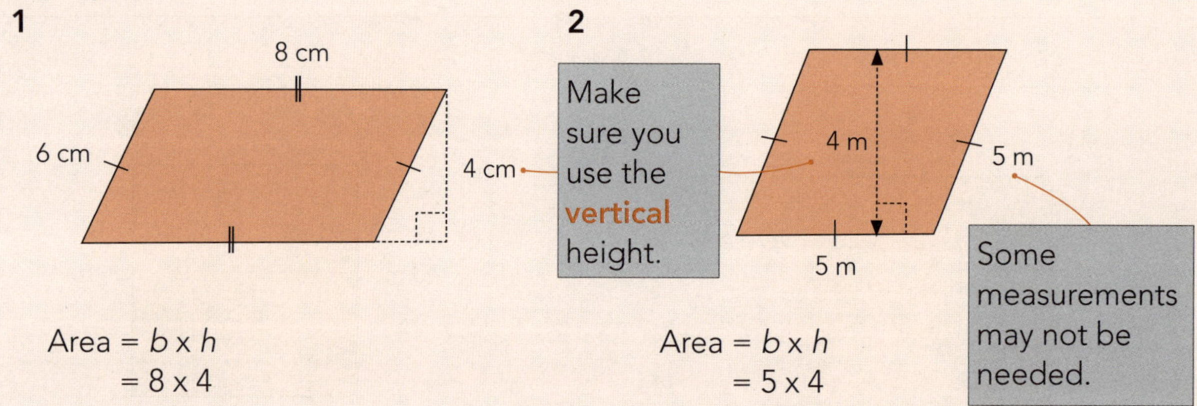

1

Area = $b \times h$
$= 8 \times 4$
$= 32$ cm^2

2

Area = $b \times h$
$= 5 \times 4$
$= 20$ m^2

Calculate the areas of these shapes.

1

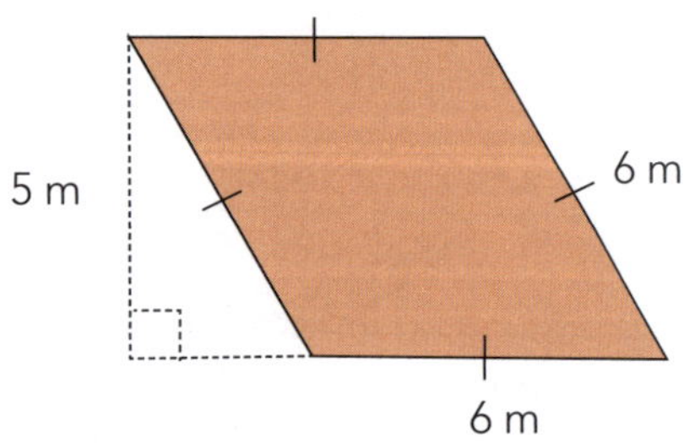

____

____

2

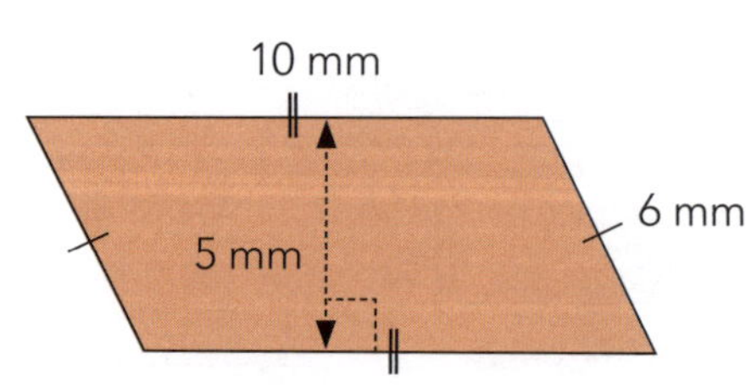

____

____

  ISBN: 9780170447218

3

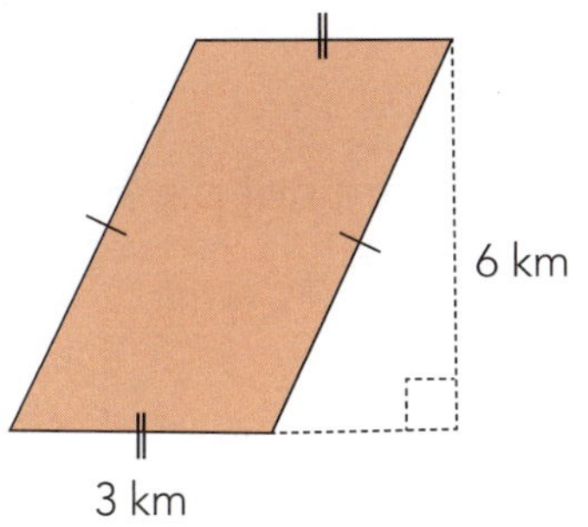

4

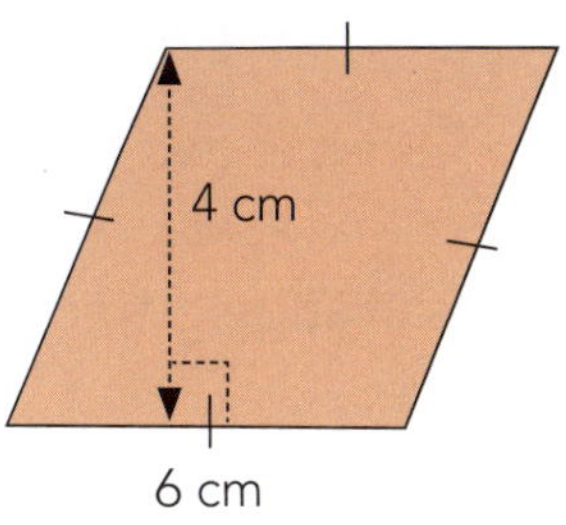

5

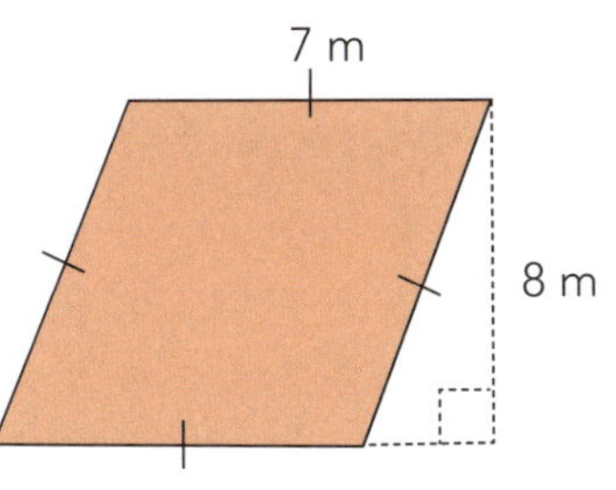

6

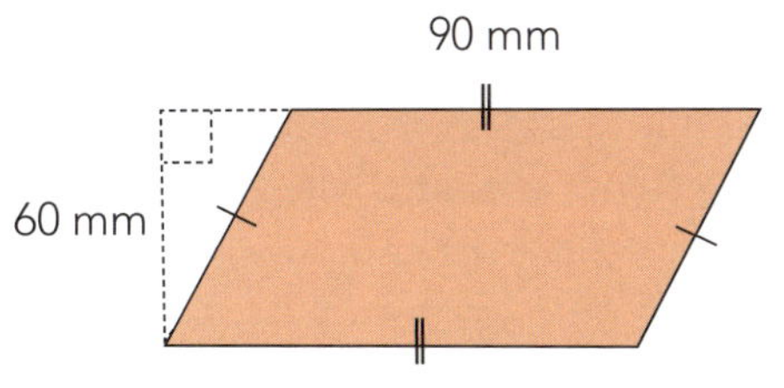

7

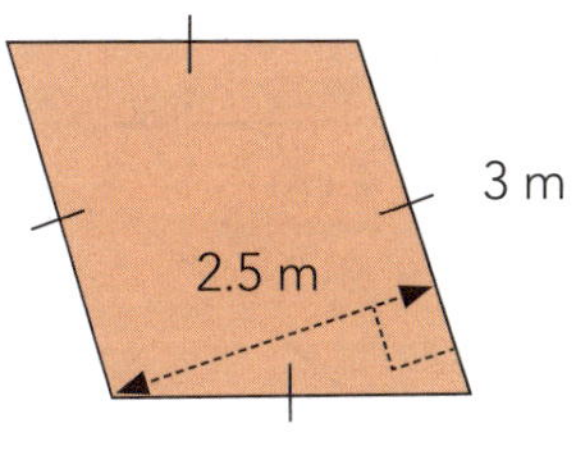

8

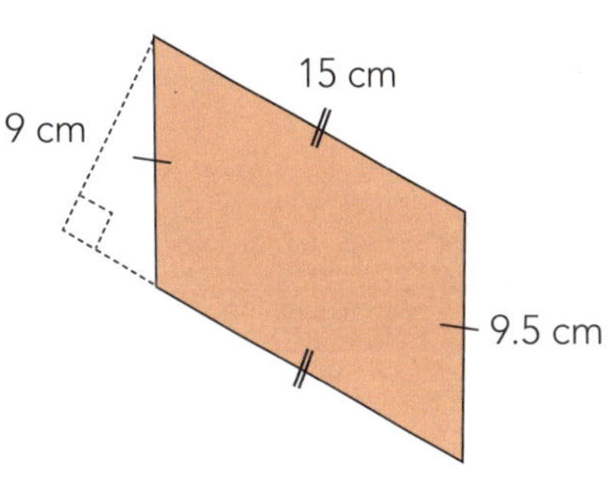

9

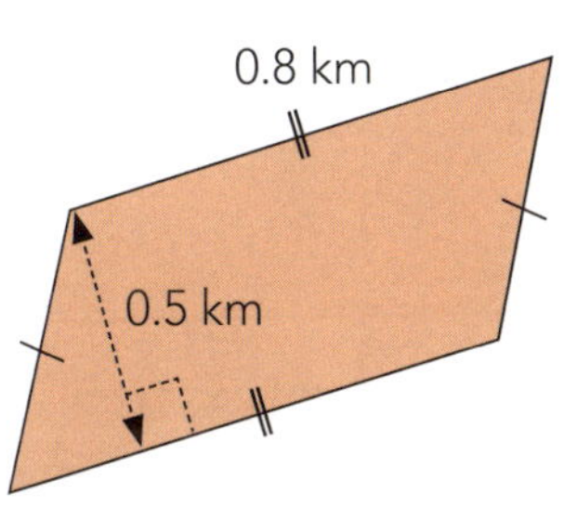

10

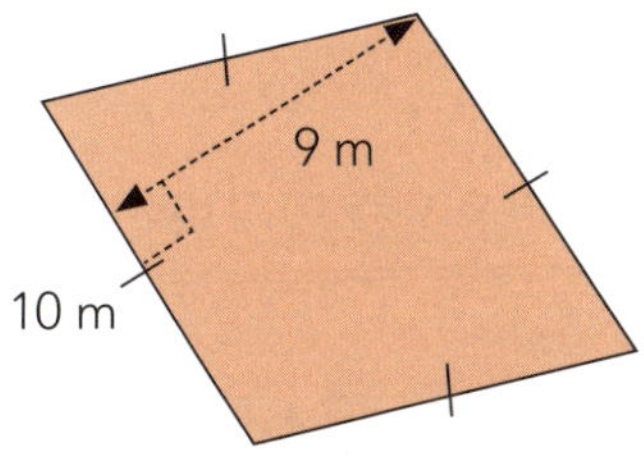

ISBN: 9780170447218

Trapezium

- A **trapezium** has two parallel sides; the other two sides are not parallel.

  You can rearrange a trapezium to look like a rectangle.

Shift the grey triangles to the top.

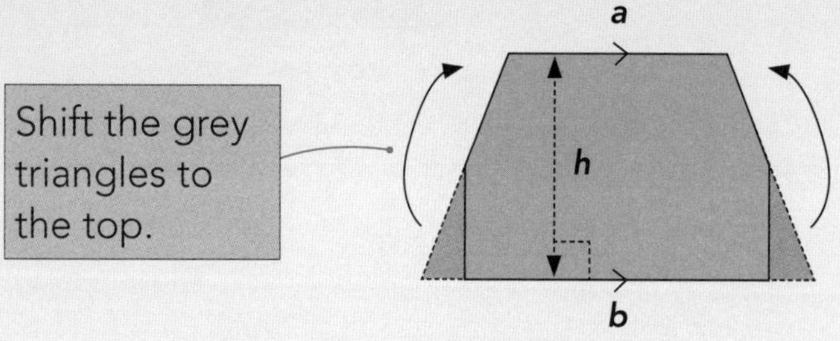

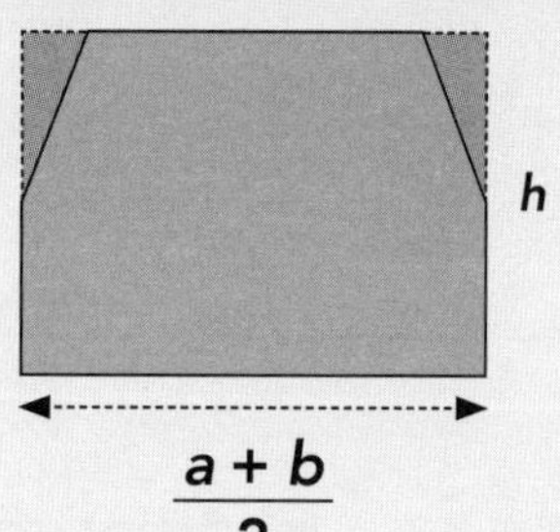

Area = (average of *a* and *b*) x vertical height

$$A = \frac{a+b}{2} \times h$$

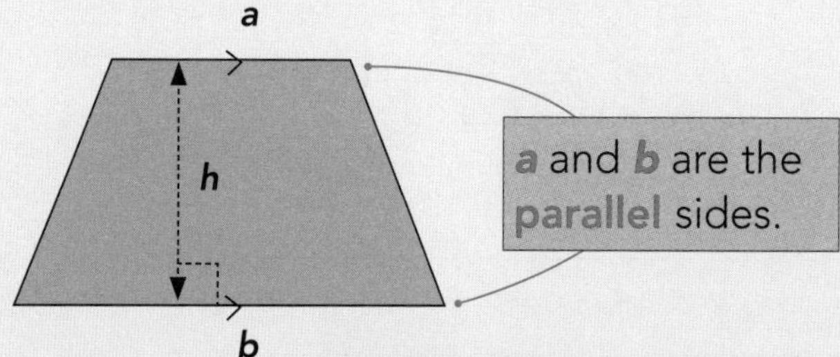

a and b are the parallel sides.

Examples:

1

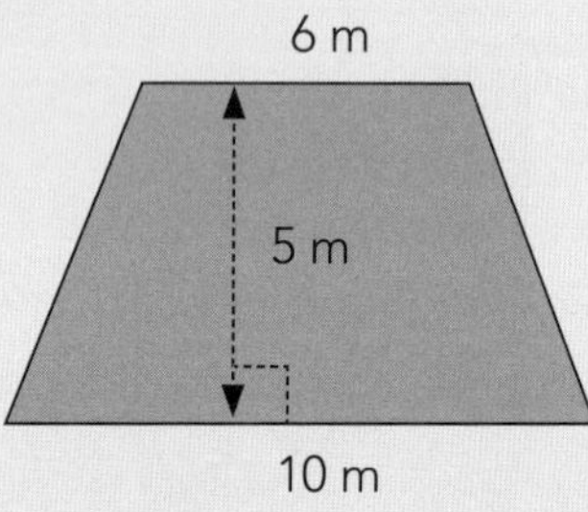

$$\text{Area} = \frac{a+b}{2} \times h$$

$$= \frac{6+10}{2} \times 5$$

$$= 40 \text{ m}^2$$

2

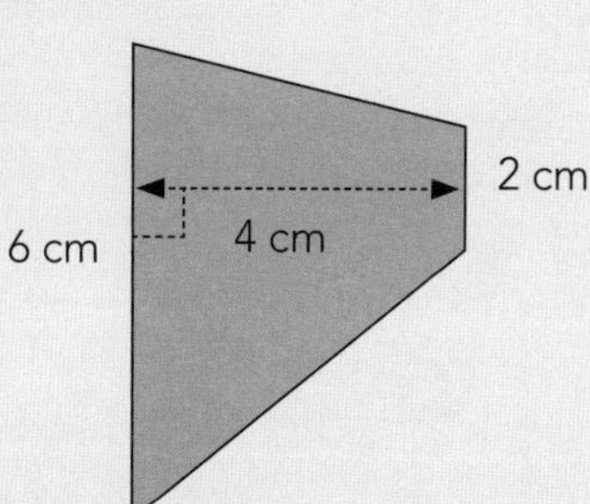

$$\text{Area} = \frac{a+b}{2} \times h$$

$$= \frac{6+2}{2} \times 4$$

$$= 16 \text{ cm}^2$$

Calculate the areas of these shapes.

1

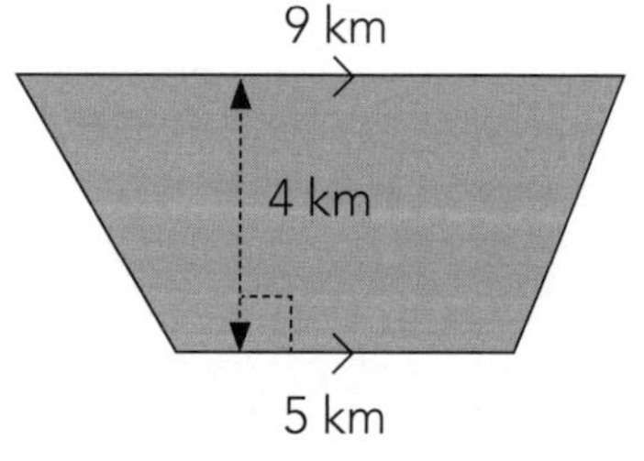

____

____

2

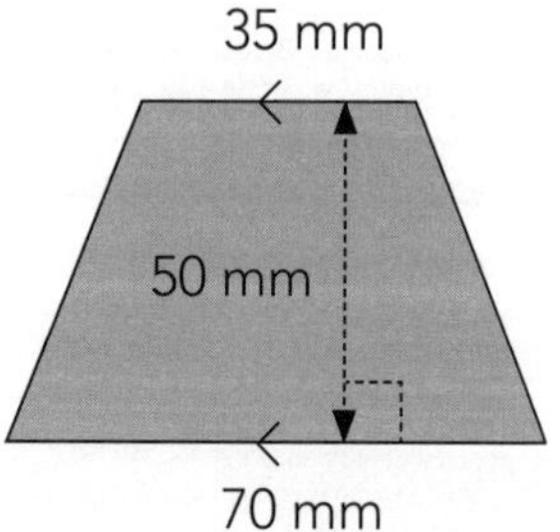

____

____

 ISBN: 9780170447218

3

9 cm
8 cm
13 cm

4

16 m
10 m
11 m

5

80 mm
25 mm
20 mm

6

0.8 km
0.5 km
0.9 km

7

24.2 cm
18.3 cm
12.5 cm

8

2.1 m
1.2 m
0.5 m

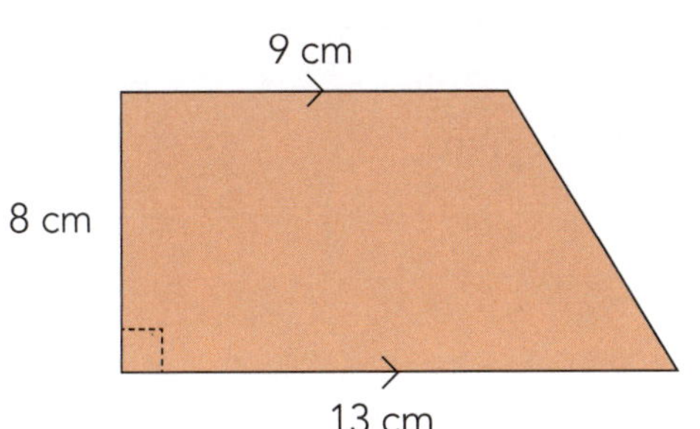

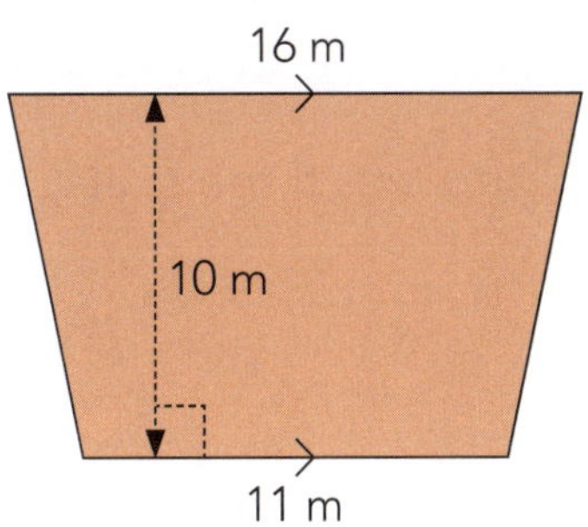

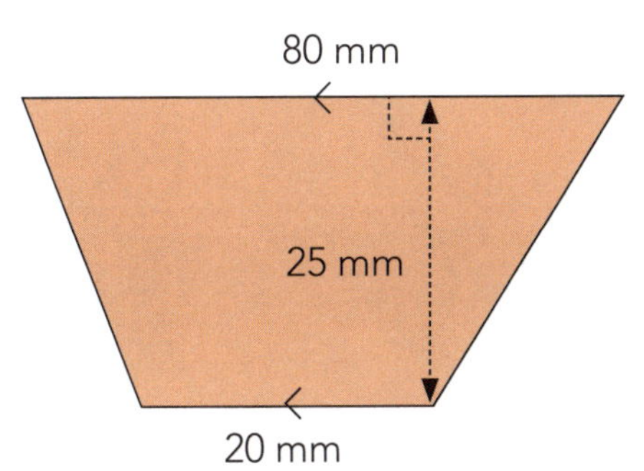

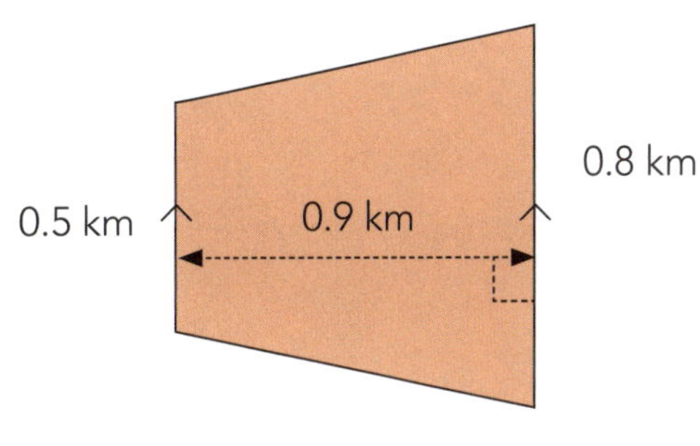

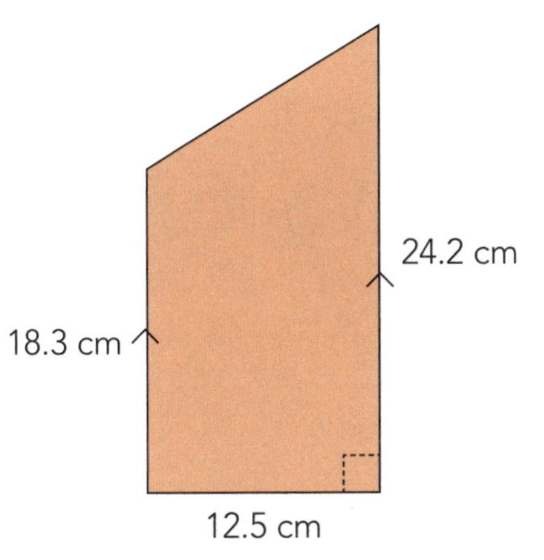

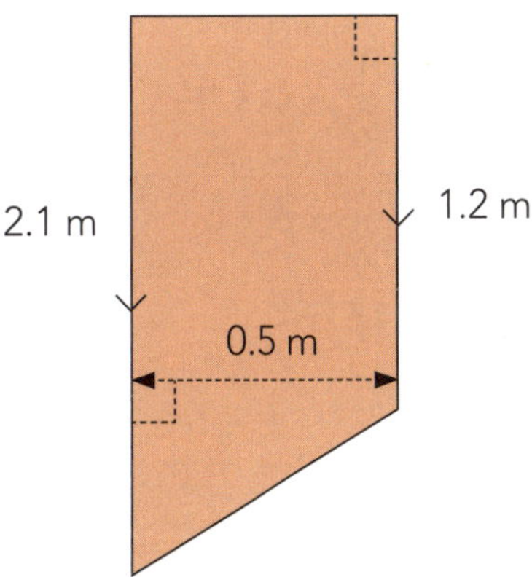

Triangles

- A **triangle** has three sides, and is half a rectangle or square.

$$\text{Area} = \frac{1}{2} \times \text{base} \times \text{vertical height}$$

$$A = \frac{1}{2} \times b \times h$$

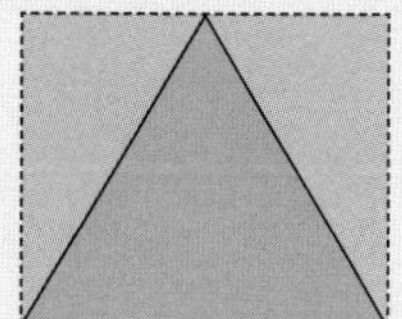

$$\text{Area} = \frac{1}{2} \times (\text{area rectangle}) = \frac{1}{2} \times \text{base} \times \text{height} = \frac{1}{2} \times b \times h$$

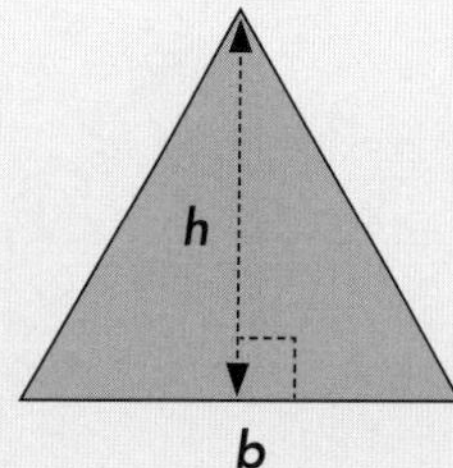

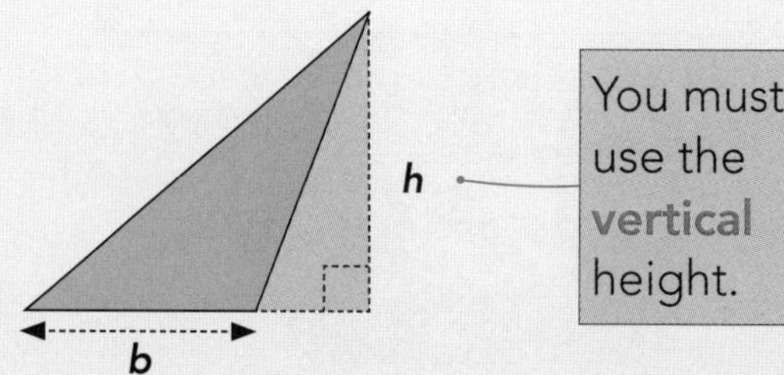

Examples:

1

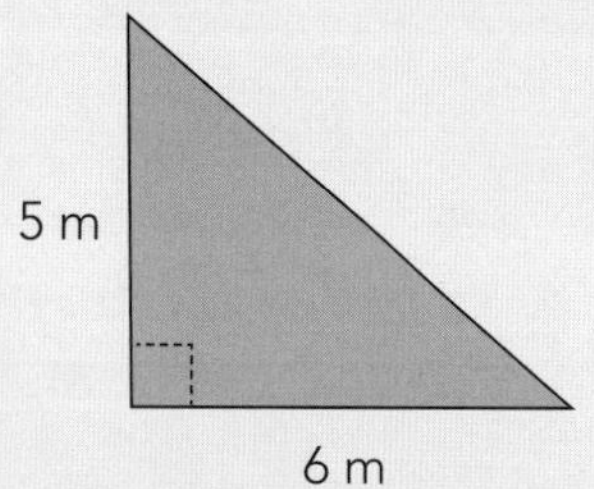

$$\text{Area} = \frac{1}{2} \times b \times h$$
$$= \frac{1}{2} \times 6 \times 5$$
$$= 15\ \text{m}^2$$

2

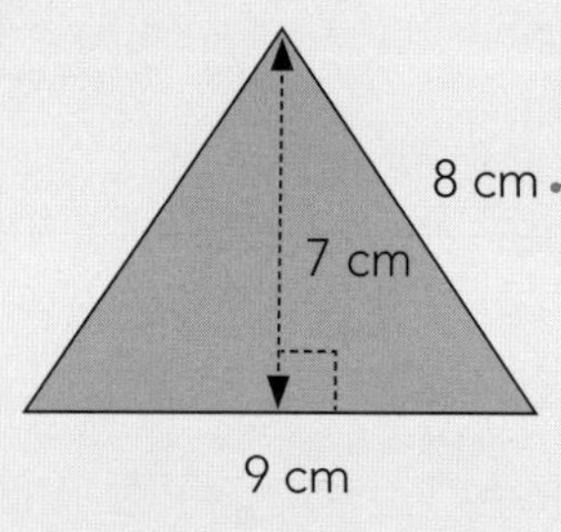

Some measurements may not be needed.

$$\text{Area} = \frac{1}{2} \times b \times h$$
$$= \frac{1}{2} \times 9 \times 7$$
$$= 31.5\ \text{cm}^2$$

Calculate the areas of these shapes.

1

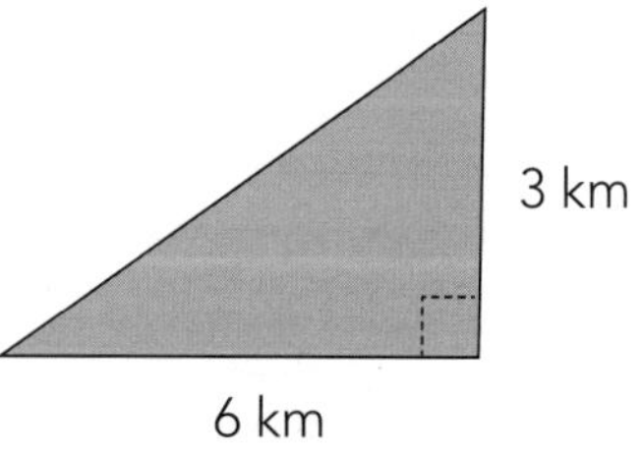

____

____

2

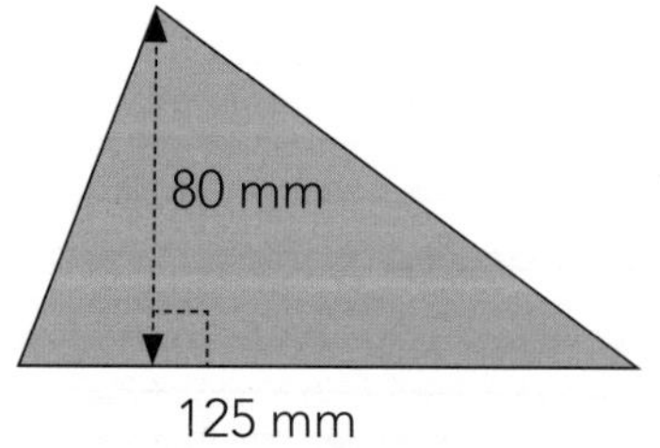

____

____

 ISBN: 9780170447218

3

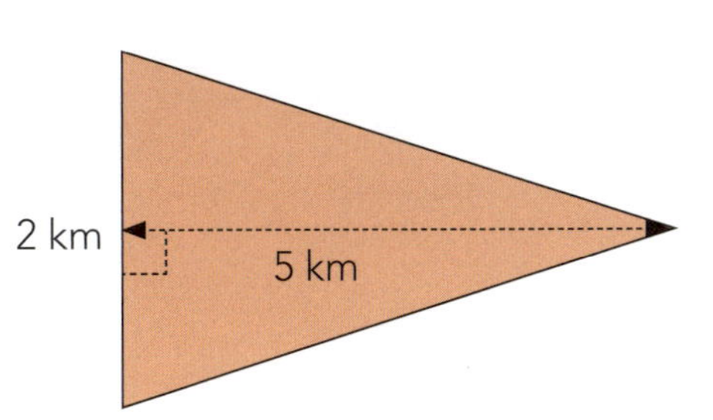

4

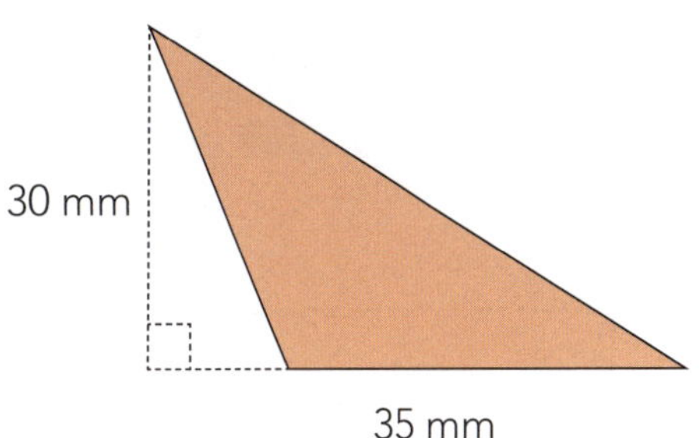

5

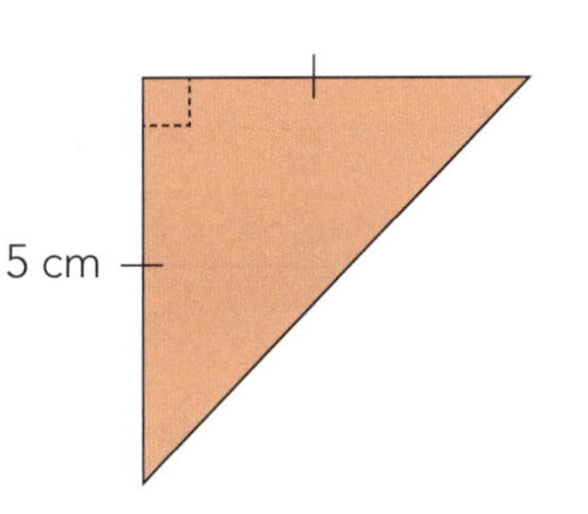

6

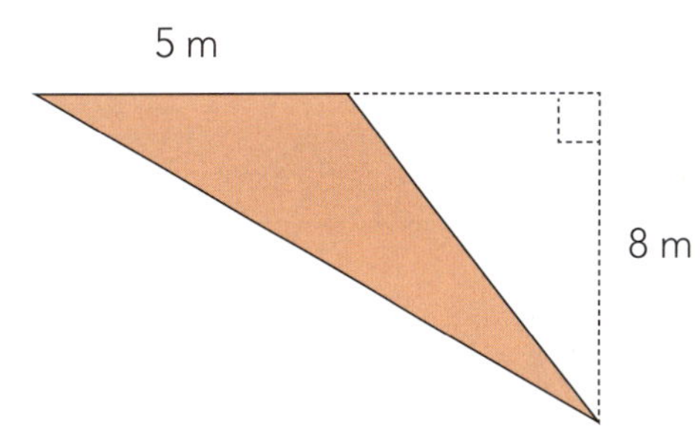

7

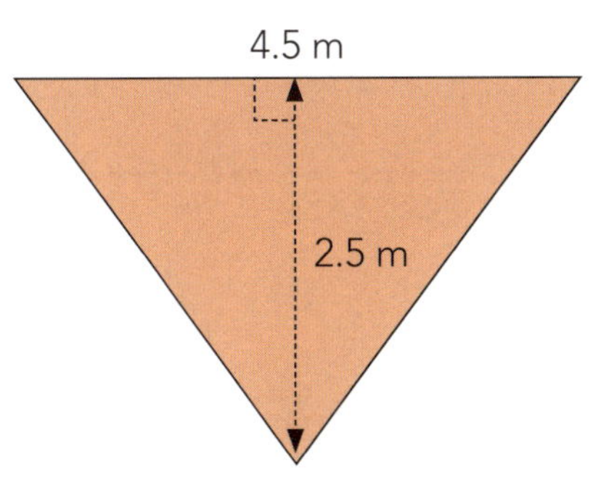

8

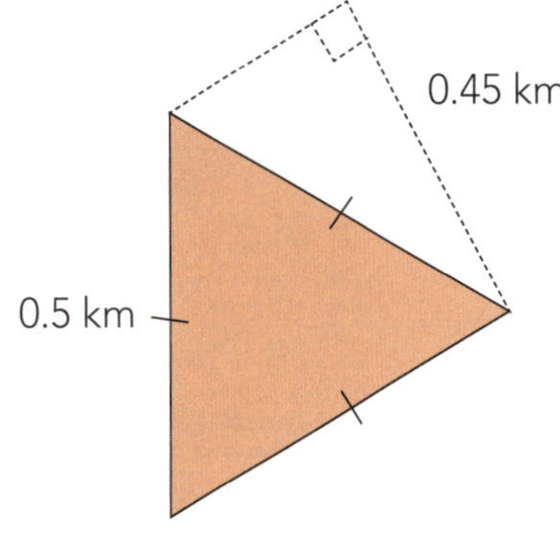

ISBN: 9780170447218

Mixing it up

Calculate the areas of these shapes.

1

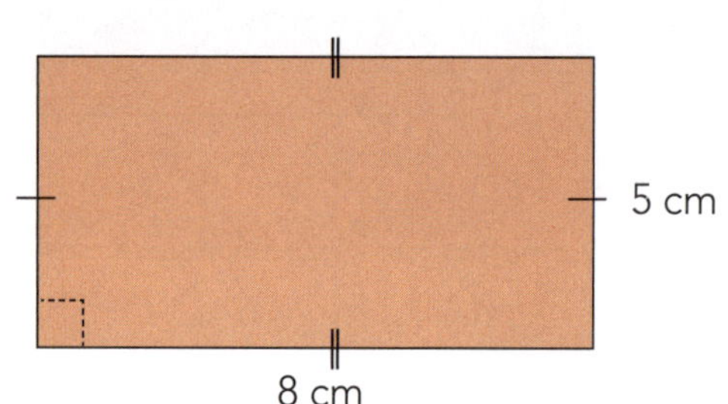

2

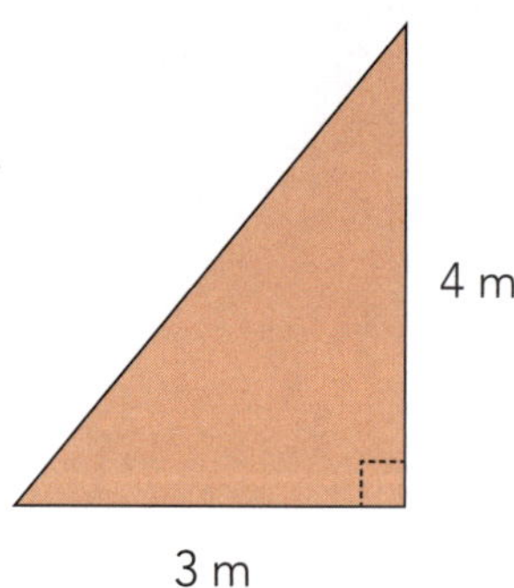

3

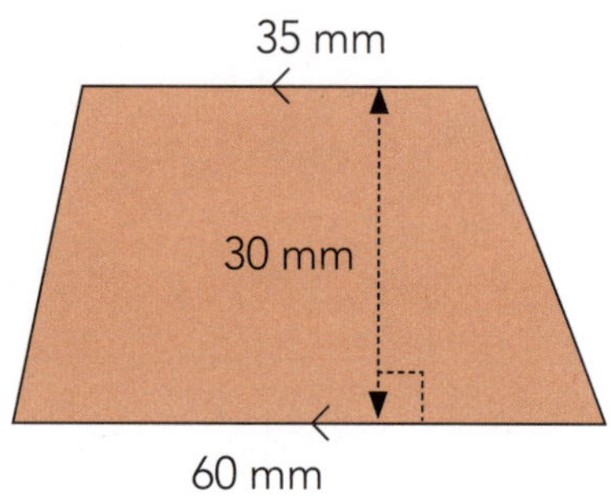

4

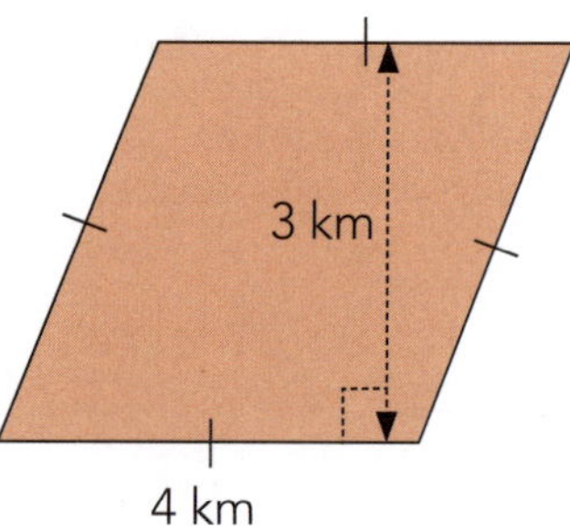

5

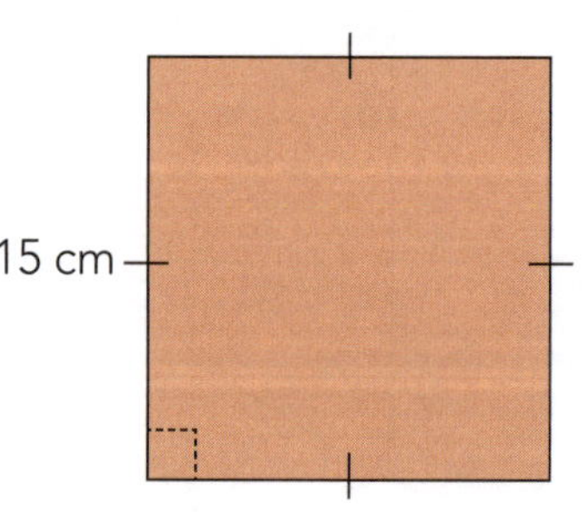

6

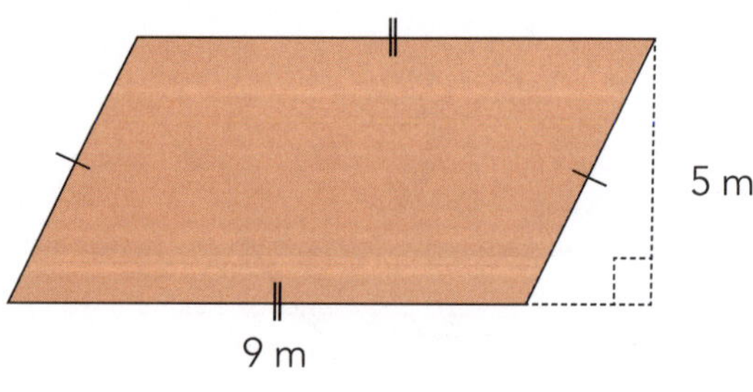

 ISBN: 9780170447218

7

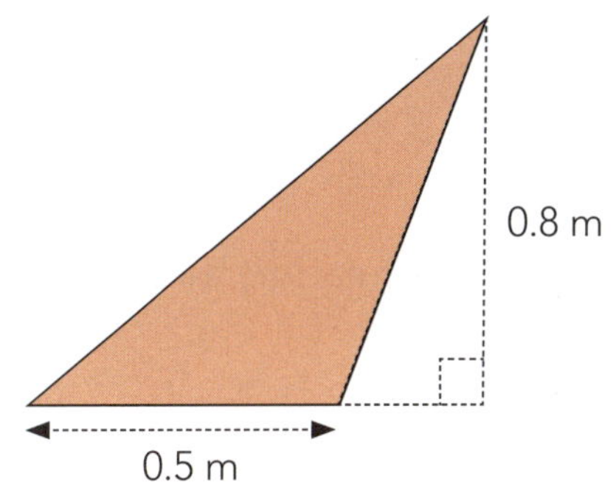

8

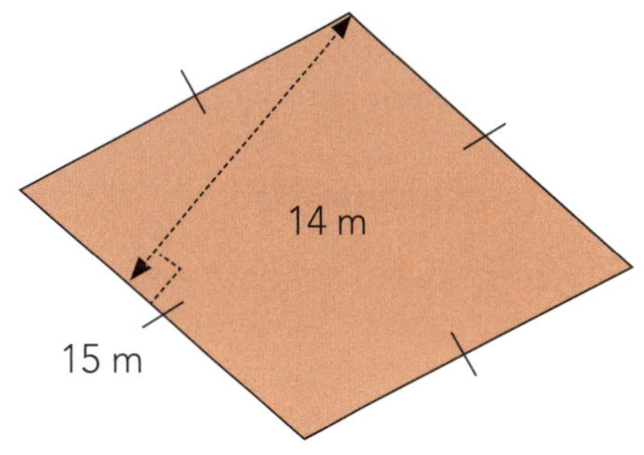

9

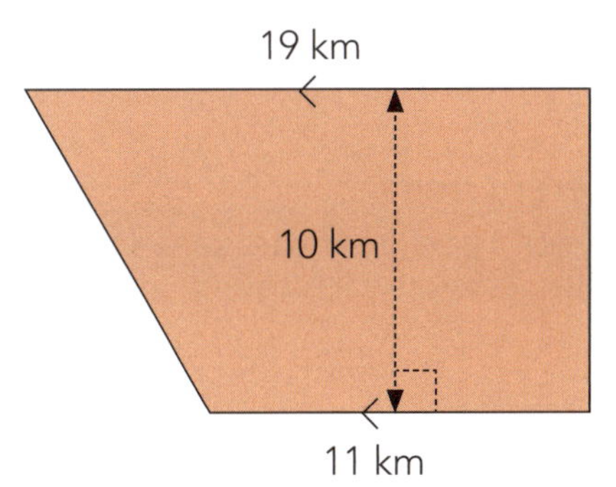

10

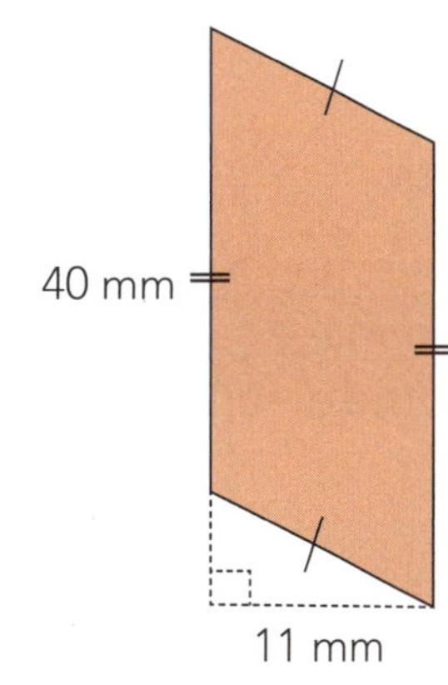

11

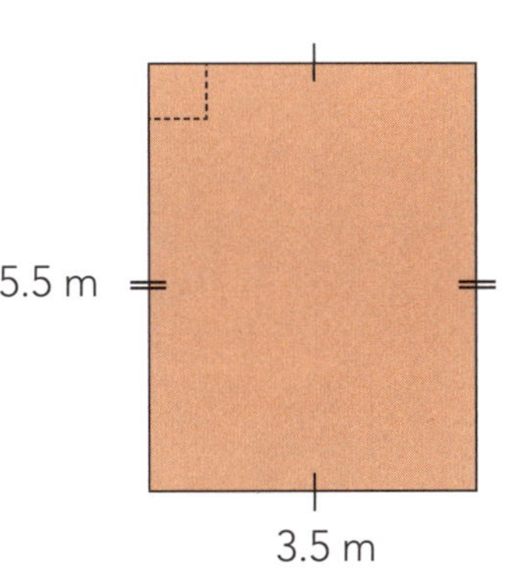

12

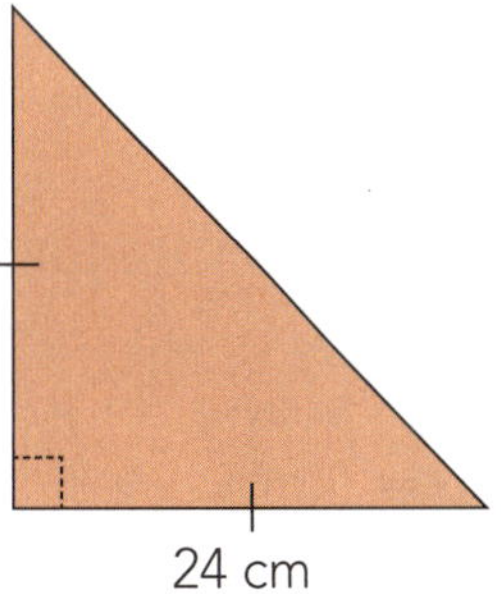

ISBN: 9780170447218

Things to look out for

Extra measurements

- There may be measurements that are not needed for calculating the area.

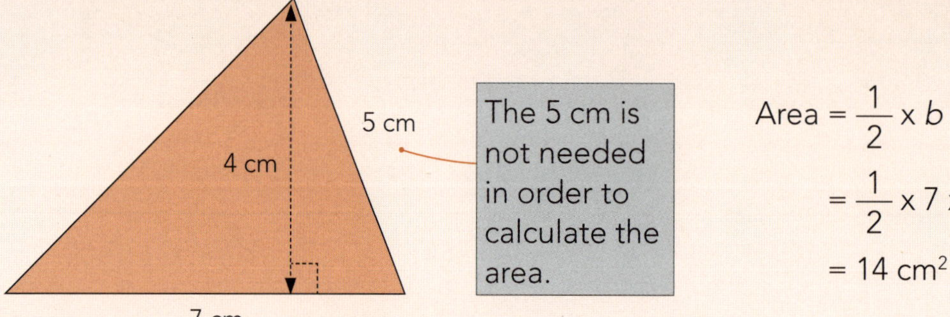

$$\text{Area} = \frac{1}{2} \times b \times h$$

$$= \frac{1}{2} \times 7 \times 4$$

$$= 14 \text{ cm}^2$$

Different units

- Some shapes may have measurements with different units.
- You need to make sure that all the information you need is in the same units before calculating the area.

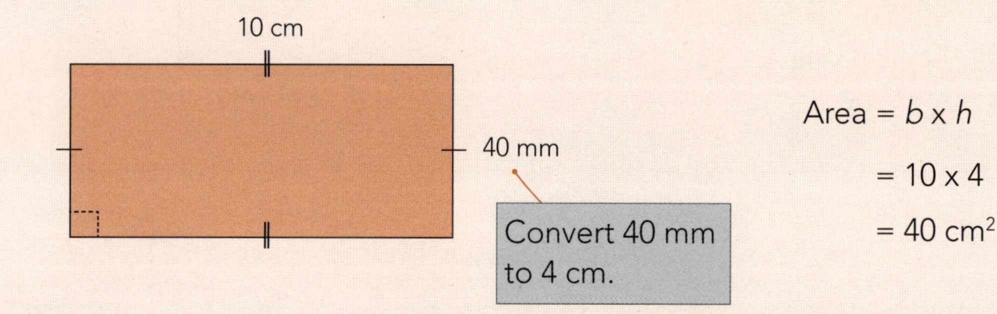

$$\text{Area} = b \times h$$

$$= 10 \times 4$$

$$= 40 \text{ cm}^2$$

Calculate the areas of the following shapes.

1 Write your answer in square kilometres (km^2).

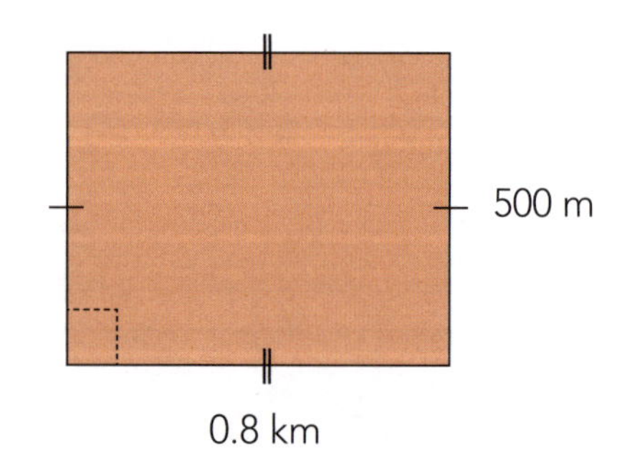

2

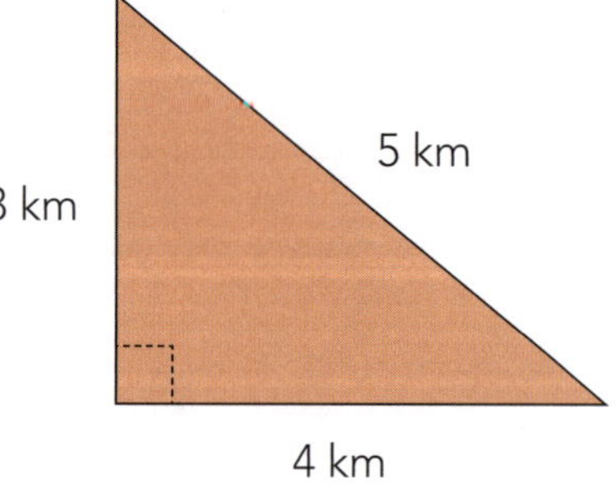

ISBN: 9780170447218

3

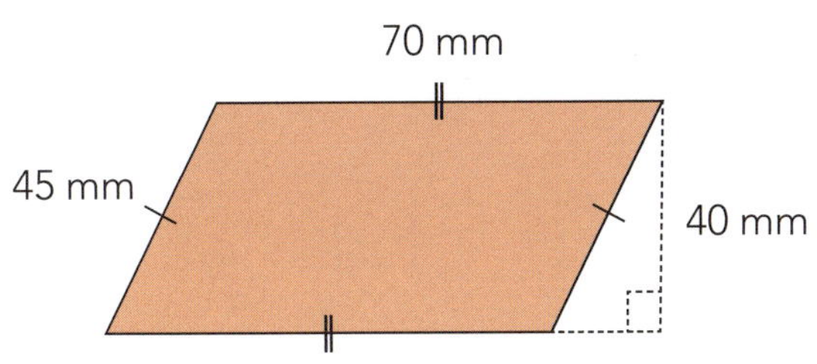

4 Write your answer in square centimetres (cm^2).

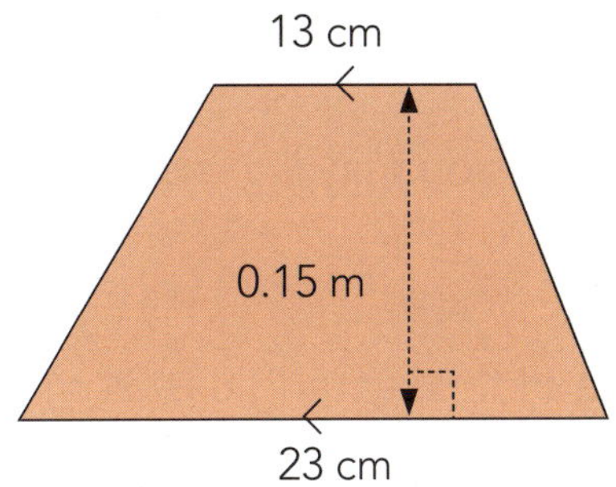

5 Write your answer in square kilometres (km^2).

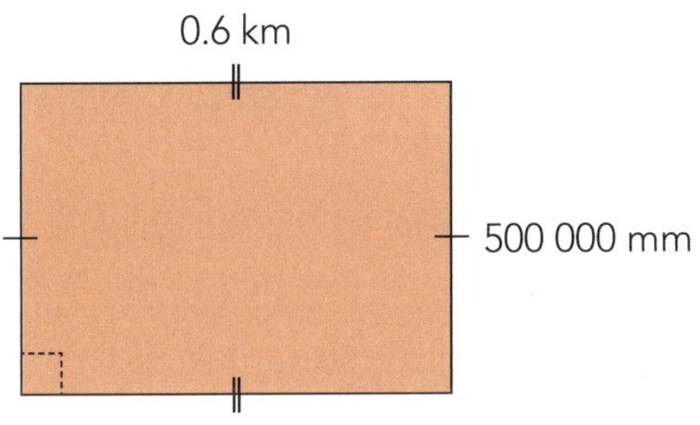

6 Write your answer in square metres (m^2).

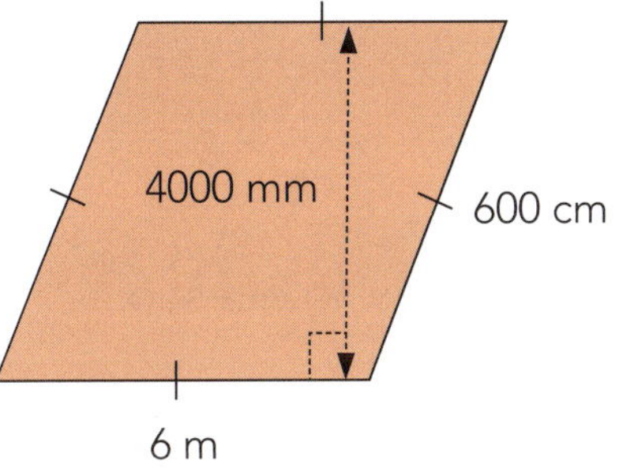

7 Write your answer in square metres (m^2).

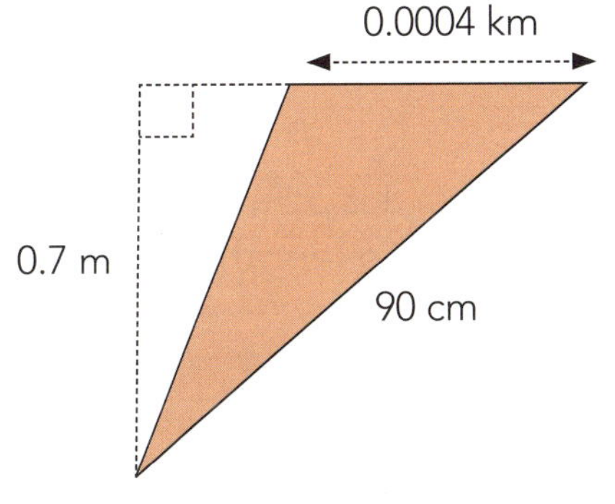

8 Write your answer in square metres (m^2).

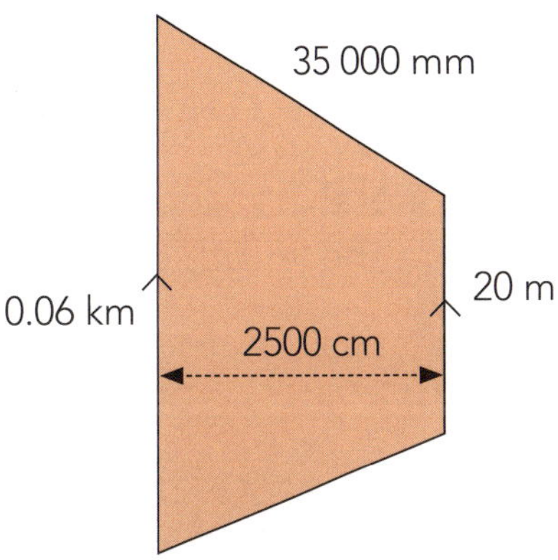

ISBN: 9780170447218

Challenge 4

- At times, you may be required to work 'backwards'.

Example:
The area of this rectangle is 24 m². Calculate the length of the base.

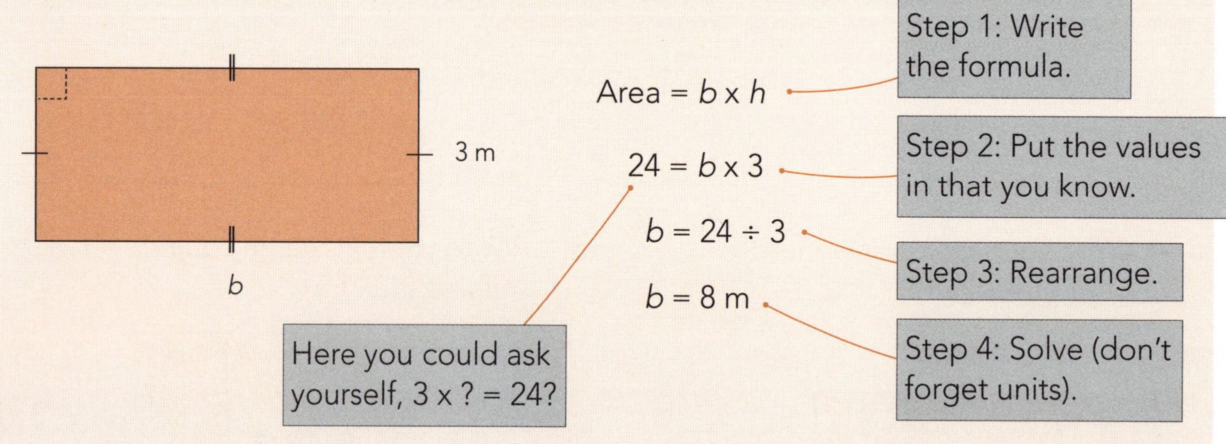

Answer the following questions.

1 The area of this rectangle is 16 cm². Calculate the length of side h.

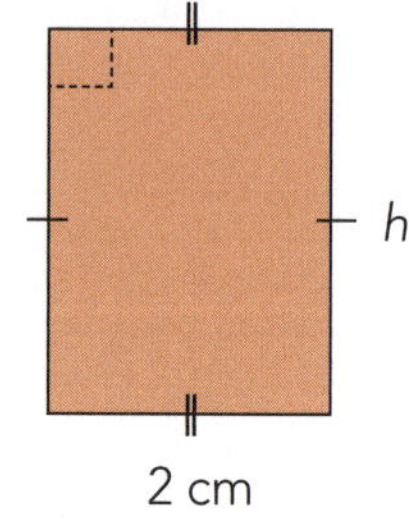

2 The area of this square is 36 m². Calculate the lengths of the sides.

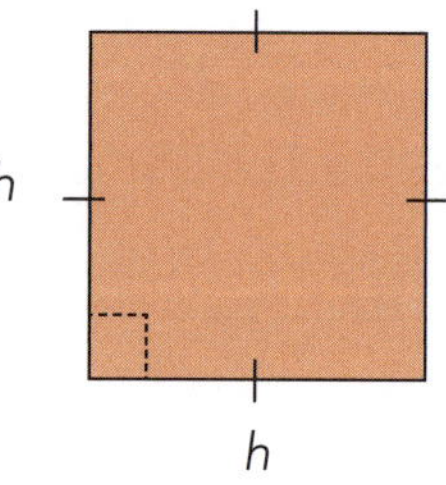

3 The area of this triangle is 14 km². Calculate the length of side h.

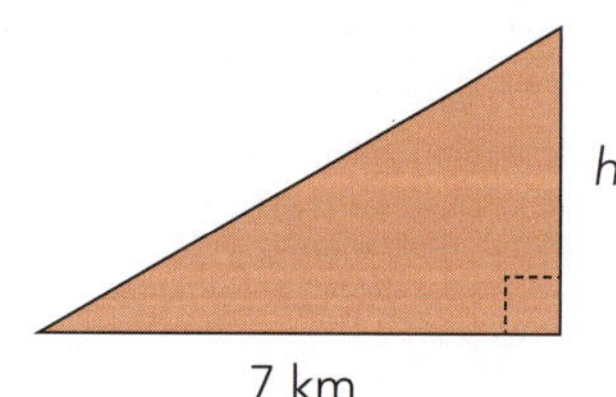

4 The area of this parallelogram is 3500 mm². Calculate the length of the base.

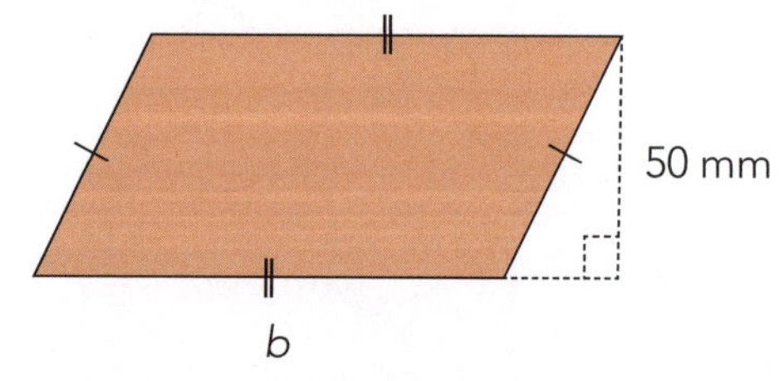

ISBN: 9780170447218

5 The area of this rhombus is 63 m^2. Calculate the length of h.

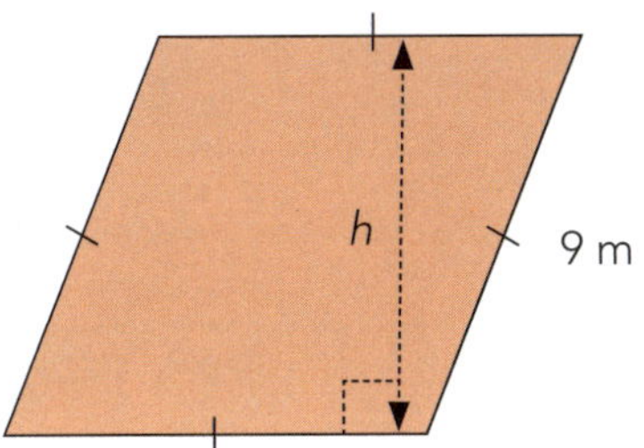

6 The area of this trapezium is 216 cm^2. Calculate its height.

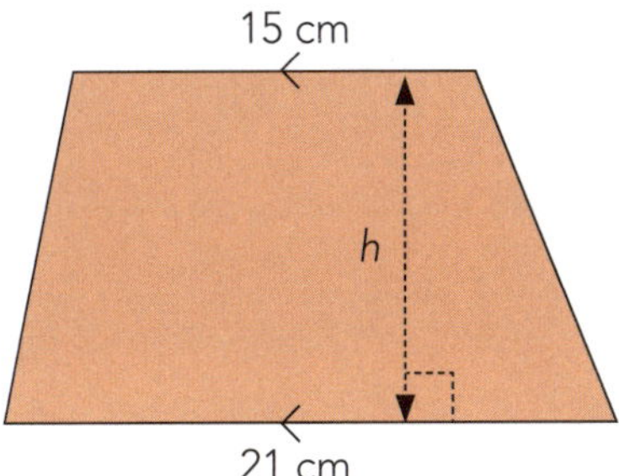

7 The area of this rectangle is 27 cm^2. Calculate the length of side b.

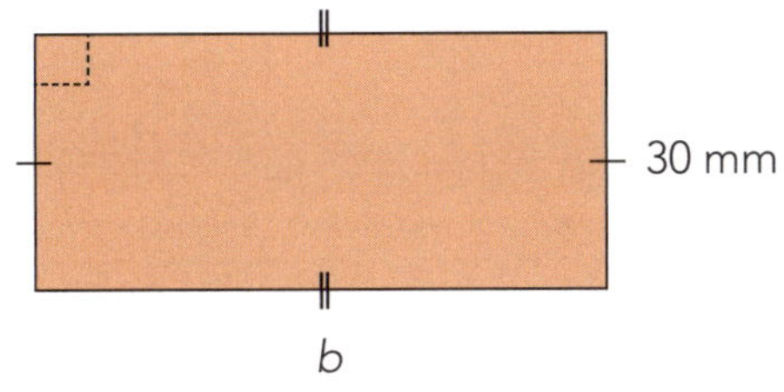

8 The area of this triangle is 15 km^2. Calculate the length of the base.

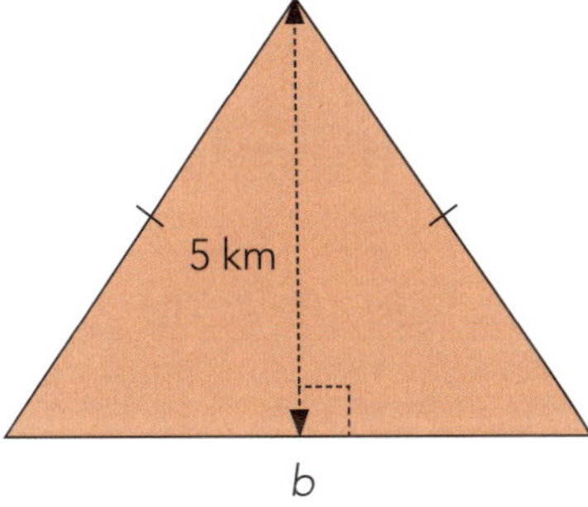

9 The area of this trapezium is 30 m^2. Calculate the length of b.

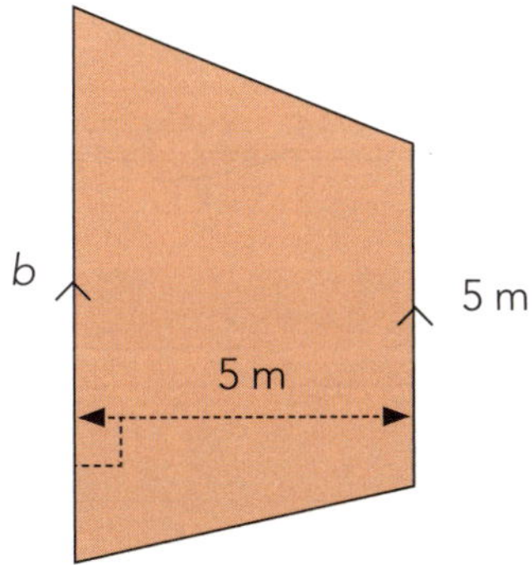

10 The area of this parallelogram is 1 200 000 000 mm^2. Calculate the length of h. (Hint: Do your working in mm.)

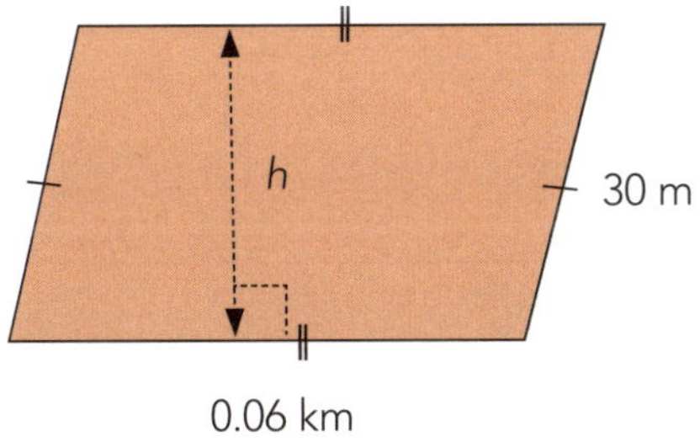

ISBN: 9780170447218

Circles

Area = π x radius²

$$A = \pi r^2$$

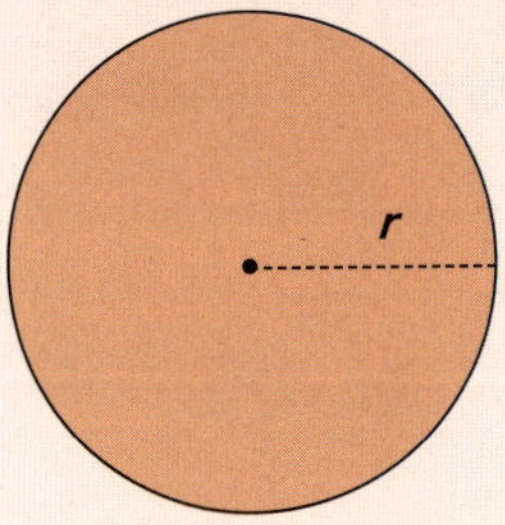

r

Examples:

1

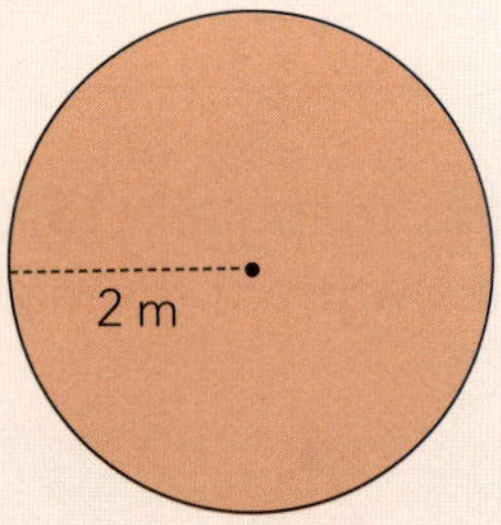

2 m

Area = πr^2
$= \pi \times 2^2$
$= 12.57\ m^2$ (2 dp)

2

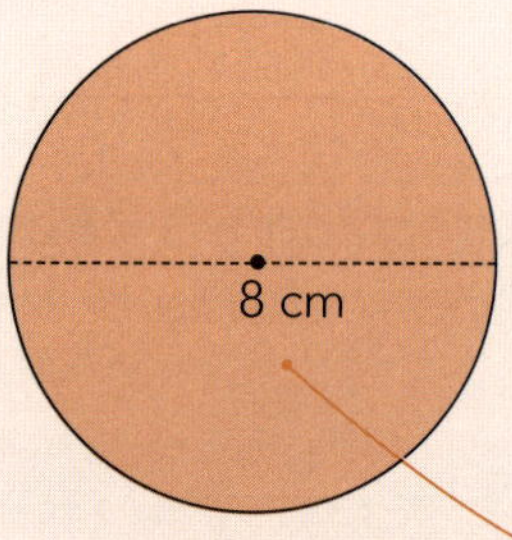

8 cm

Area = πr^2
$= \pi \times 4^2$
$= 50.27\ cm^2$ (2 dp)

If you are given the diameter, then halve it to get the radius.

Calculate the areas of these circles.

1

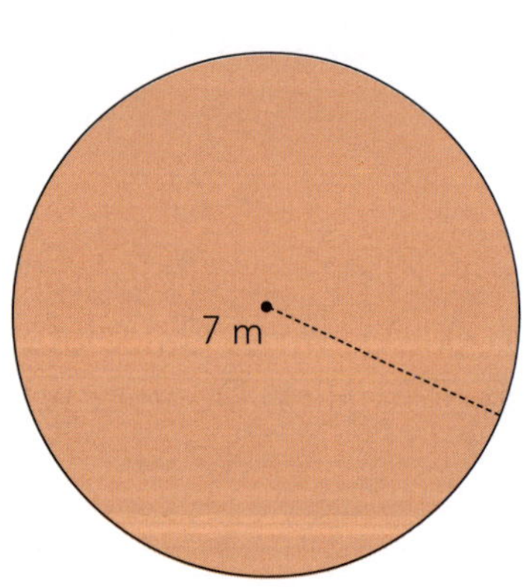

2

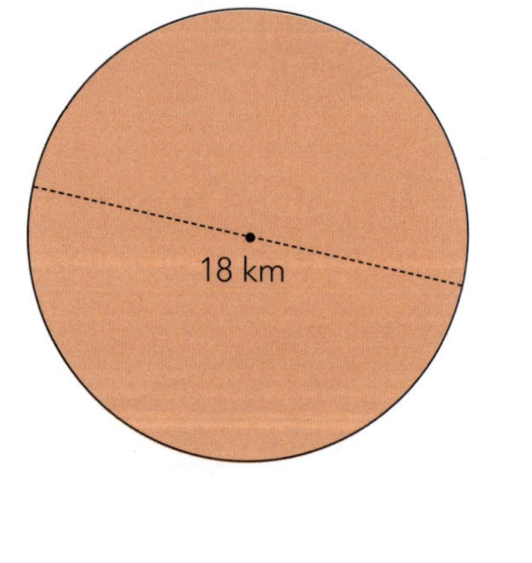

 ISBN: 9780170447218

3

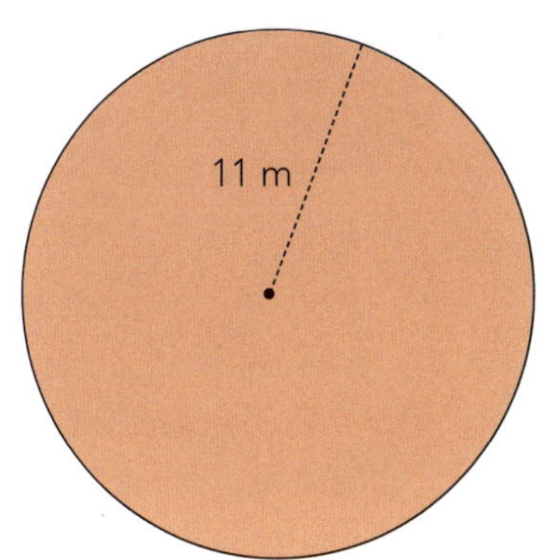

4

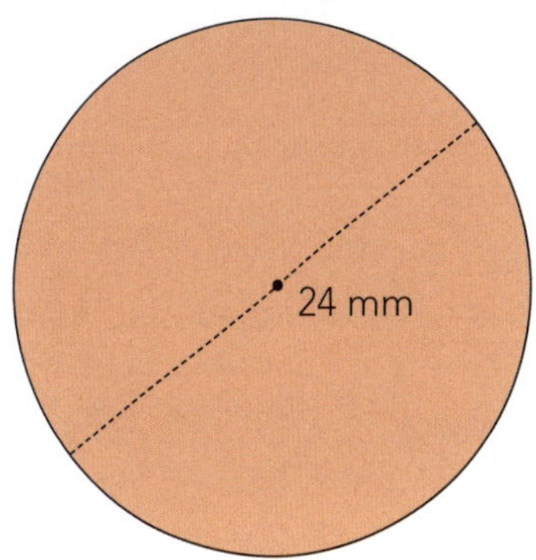

5

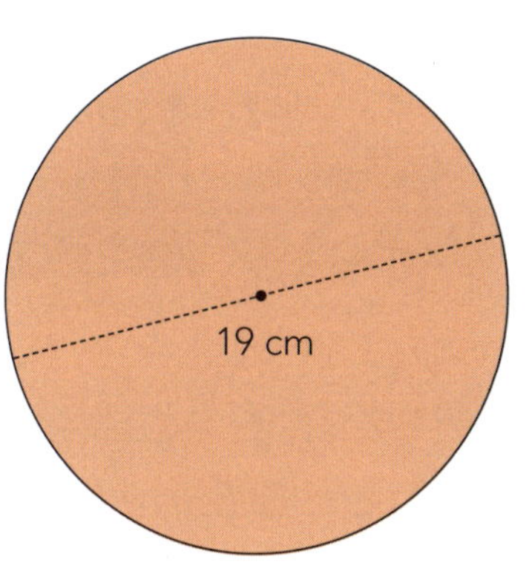

6

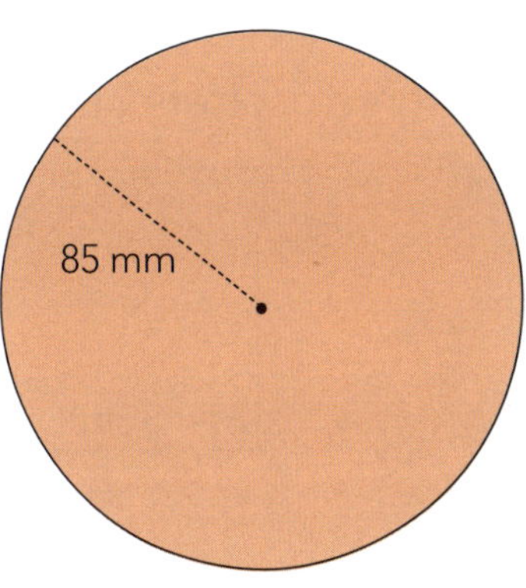

7

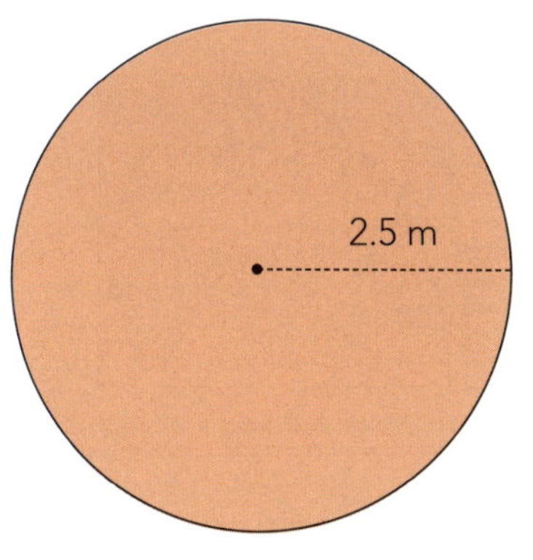

8

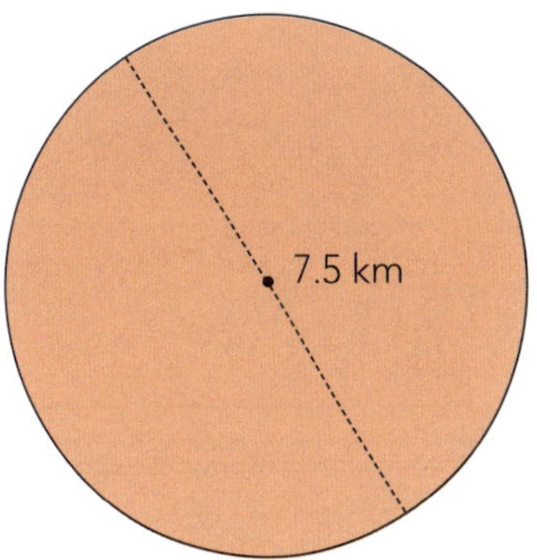

ISBN: 9780170447218

Parts of circles

Area = π x radius ^{2}

Examples:

1 This is a semicircle, also known as half a circle.

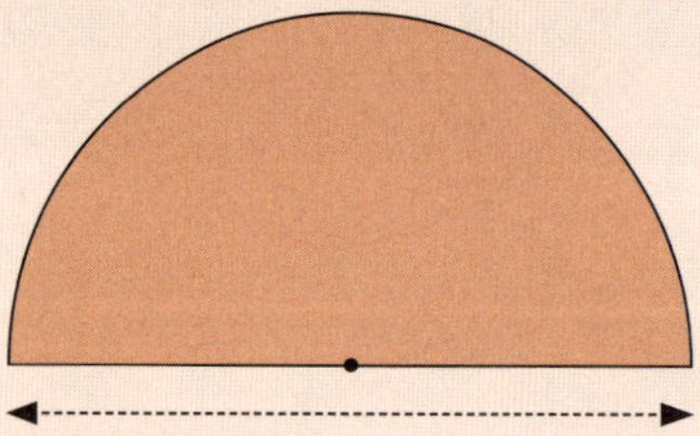

6 m

Find the area of **half** a circle.

$$\text{Area} = \frac{1}{2} \times \pi \times r^2$$

$$= \frac{1}{2} \times \pi \times 3^2$$

$$= 14.14 \text{ m}^2 \text{ (2 dp)}$$

Remember to halve the diameter.

2 This is three quarters of a circle.

5 cm

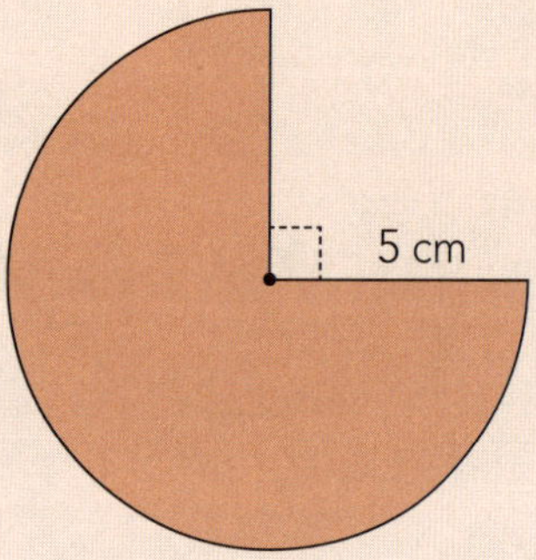

Find the area of **three quarters** of a circle.

$$\text{Area} = \frac{3}{4} \times \pi \times r^2$$

$$= \frac{3}{4} \times \pi \times 5^2$$

$$= 58.90 \text{ cm}^2 \text{ (2 dp)}$$

Calculate the areas of these shapes.

1

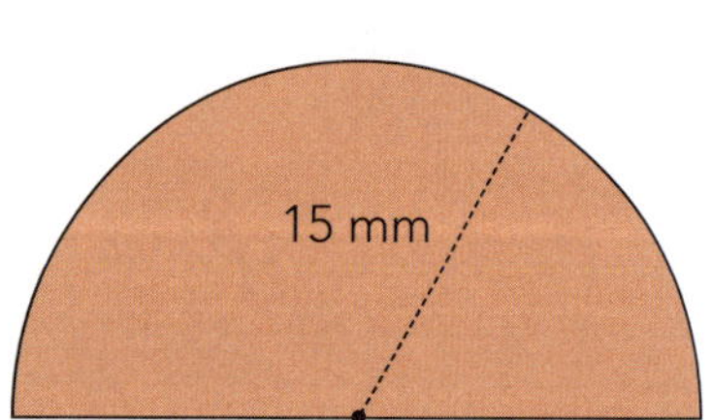

2

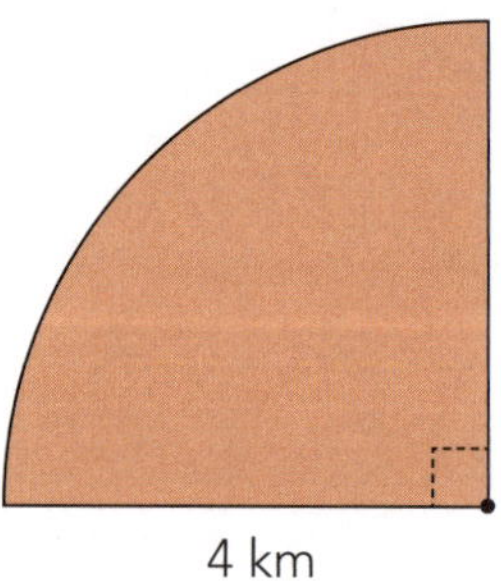

 ISBN: 9780170447218

3

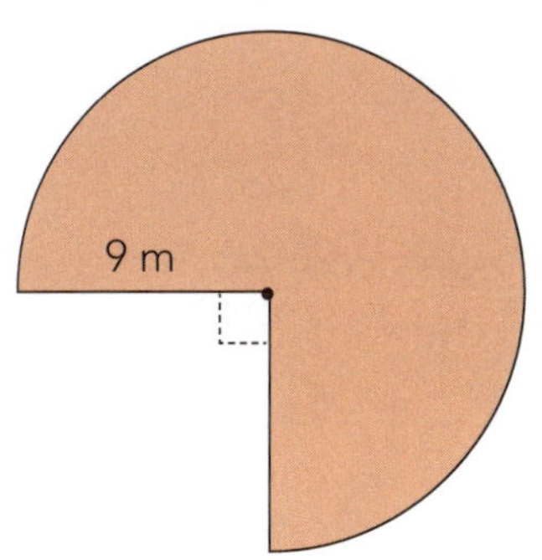

4

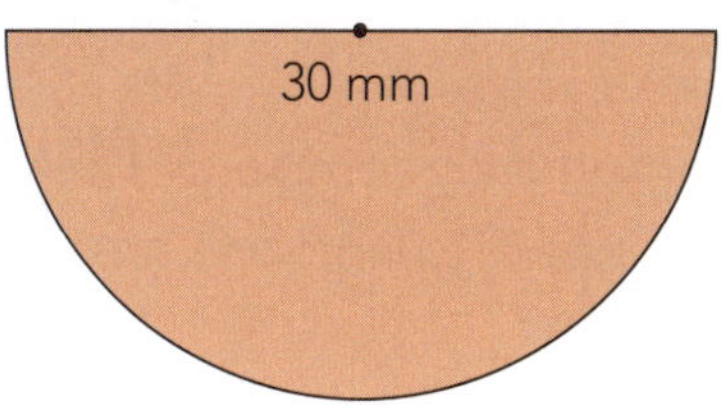

5

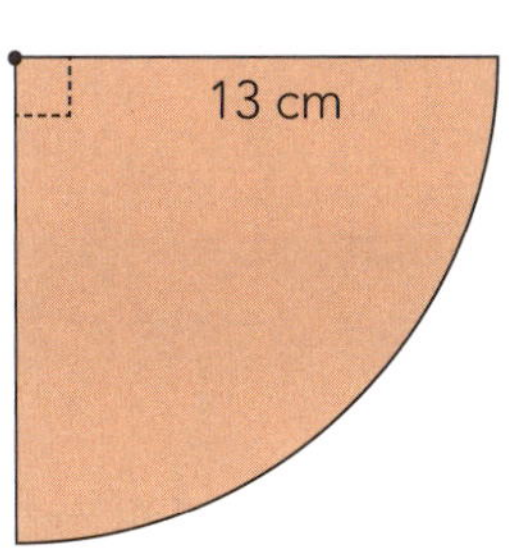

6 The diameter of this shape is 2.4 km.

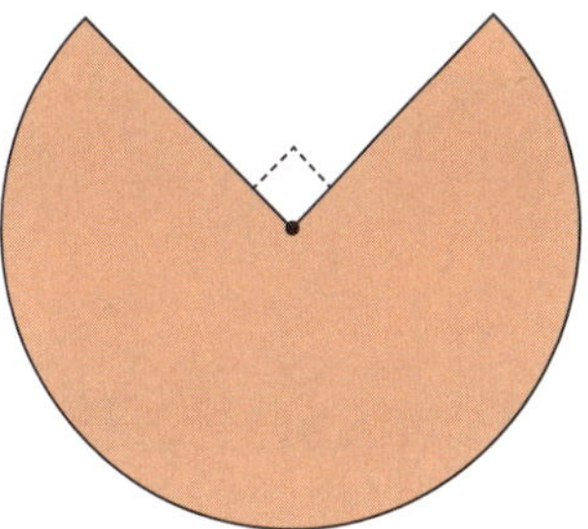

7 This is a third of a circle.

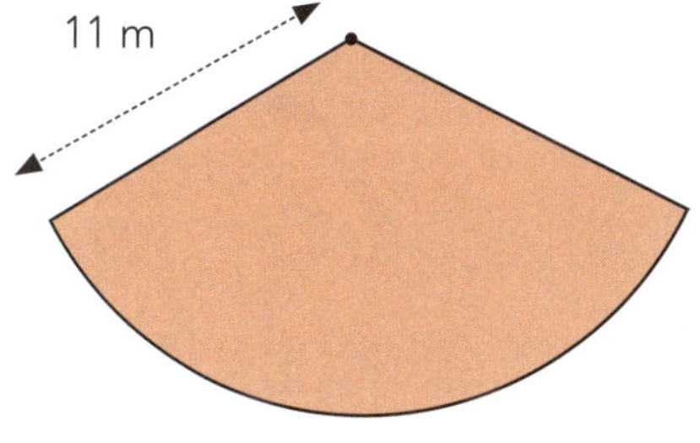

8 This is five sixths of a circle.

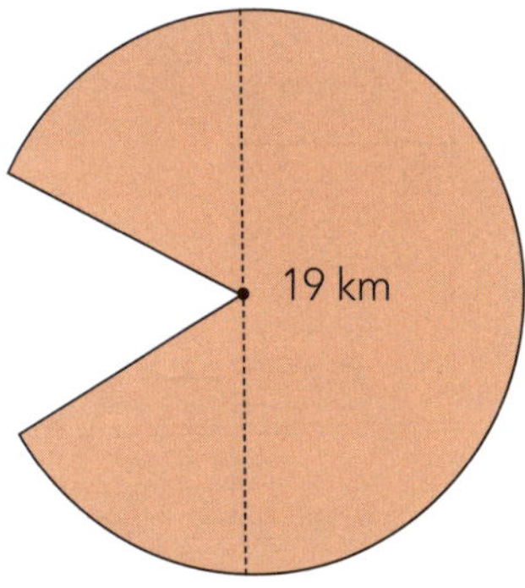

ISBN: 9780170447218

Compound shapes

- Remember, compound shapes are shapes that are made up of **other simple shapes**.
- You need to find the areas of the simple shapes and then **add** them together.

Examples:

1

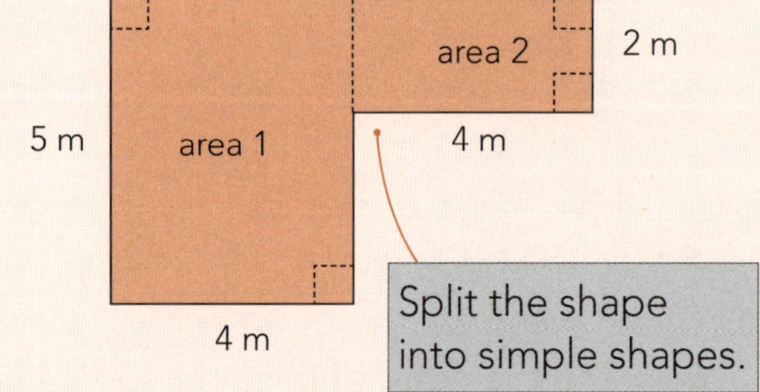

Area = (area 1) + (area 2)

= (4 x 5) + (4 x 2)

= 20 + 8

= 28 m^2

Calculate the two areas and add them together.

2

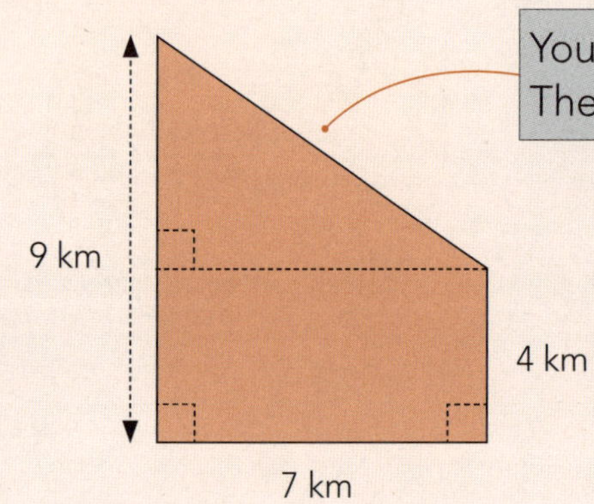

You may need to calculate some values. The height of the triangle is 9 – 4 = 5 km.

Area = (triangle) + (rectangle)

$= (\frac{1}{2} \times 5 \times 7) + (7 \times 4)$

= 17.5 + 28

= 45.5 km^2

Calculate the areas of these shapes.

1

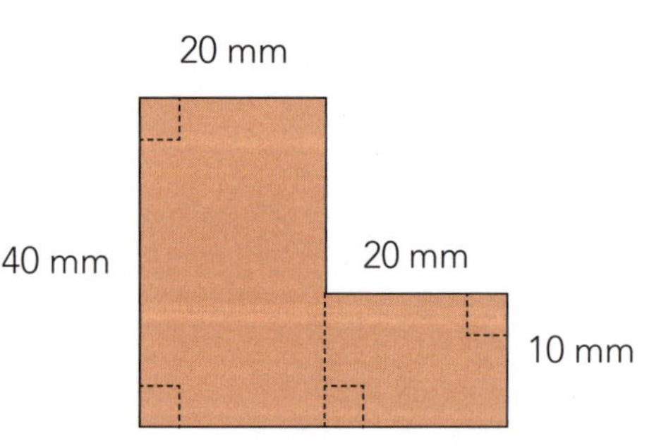

2

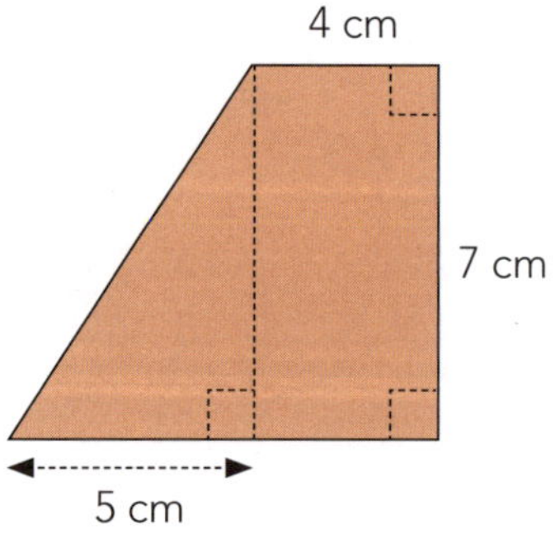

 ISBN: 9780170447218

3

3 m
9 m
9 m
6 m

4

4 km
5 km
3 km
7 km

5

8 cm
9 cm

6

10 mm
22 mm

7

4.5 m
4 m

8

12 cm
2 cm
10 cm
10 cm
4 cm
18 cm

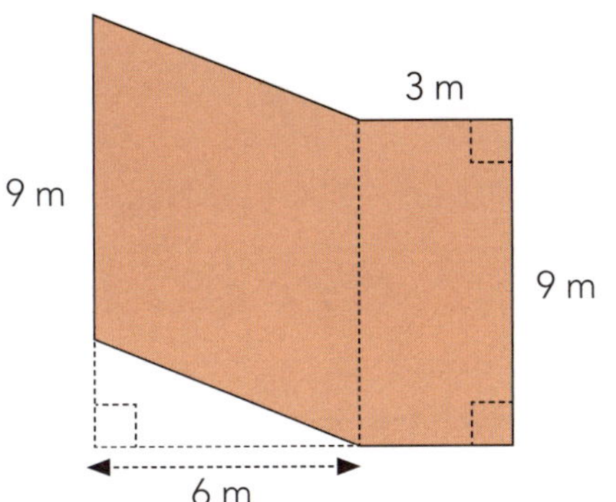

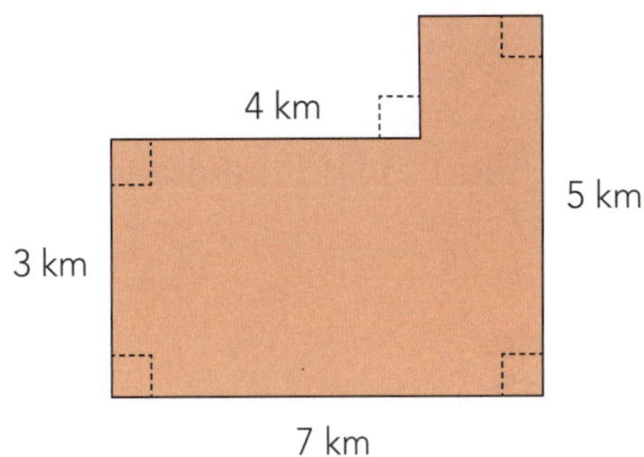

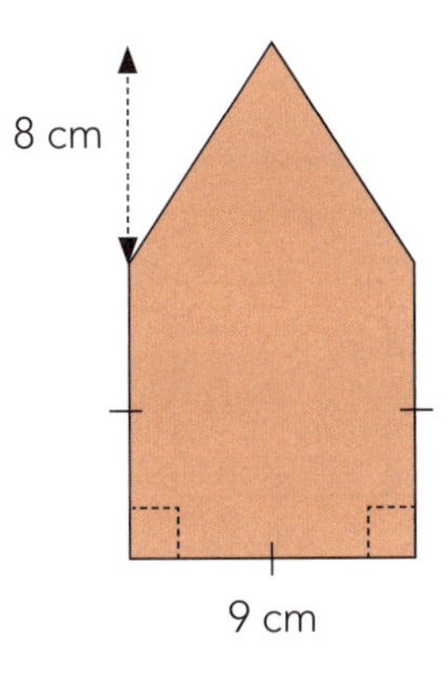

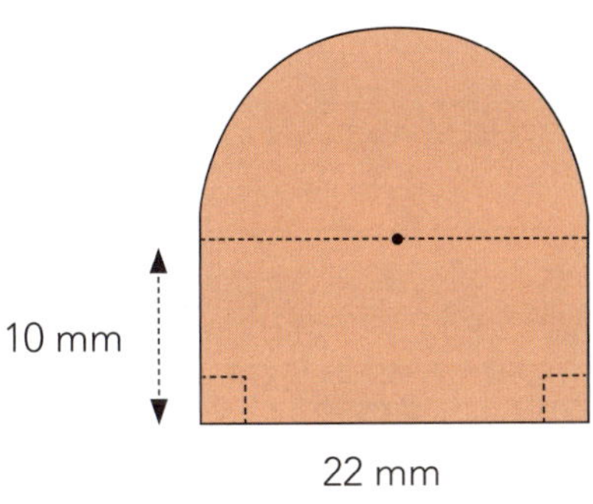

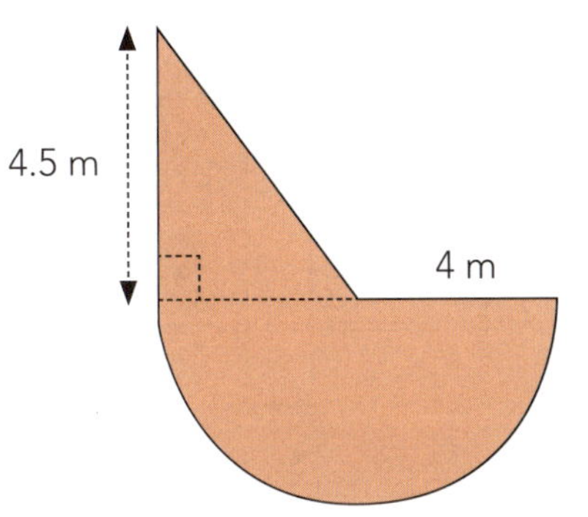

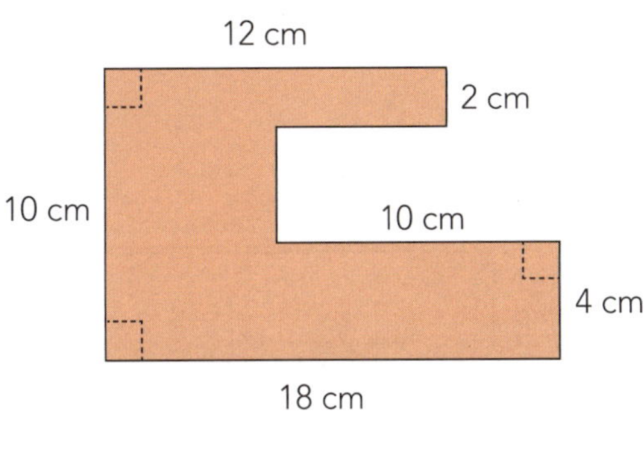

Shapes with holes

- You need to find the areas of the simple shapes and then **subtract** one from the other.

Example:

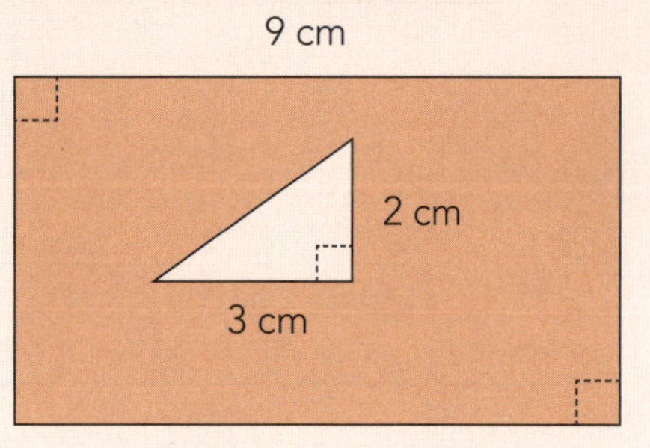

Shaded area = (rectangle) – (triangle)

$= (9 \times 5) - (\frac{1}{2} \times 3 \times 2)$

$= 45 - 3$

$= 42\ cm^2$

Calculate the two areas and subtract one from the other.

Calculate the shaded areas of these shapes.

1

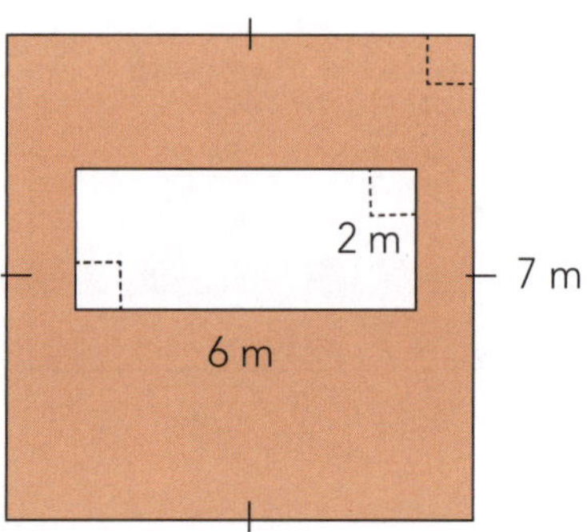

2

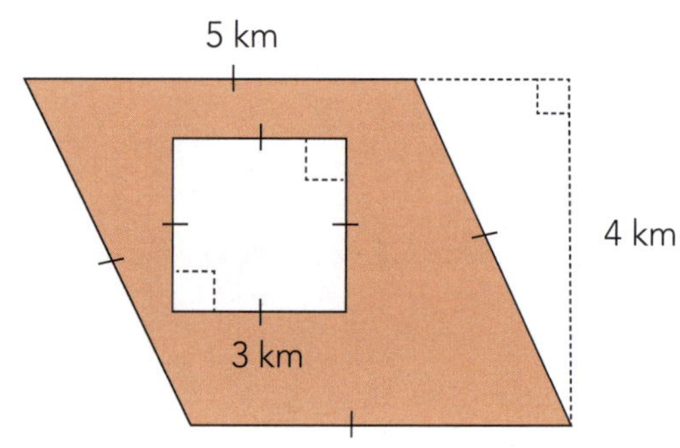

3

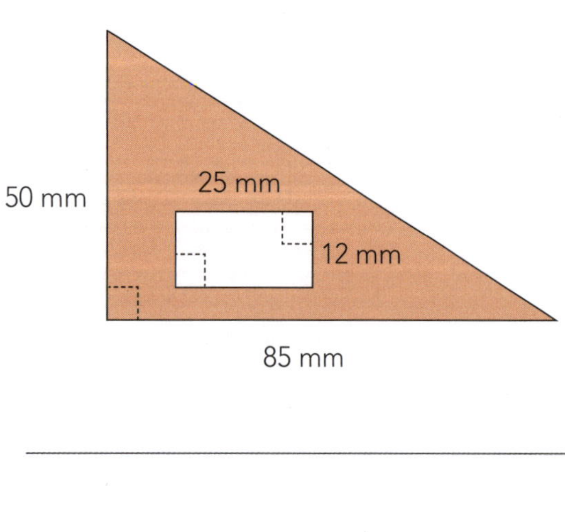

4

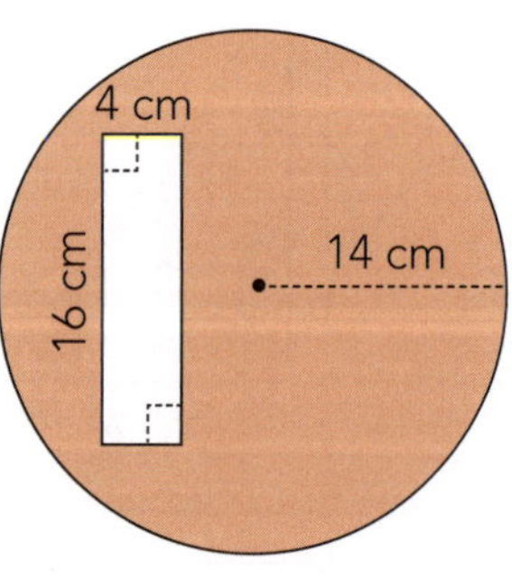

 ISBN: 9780170447218

5

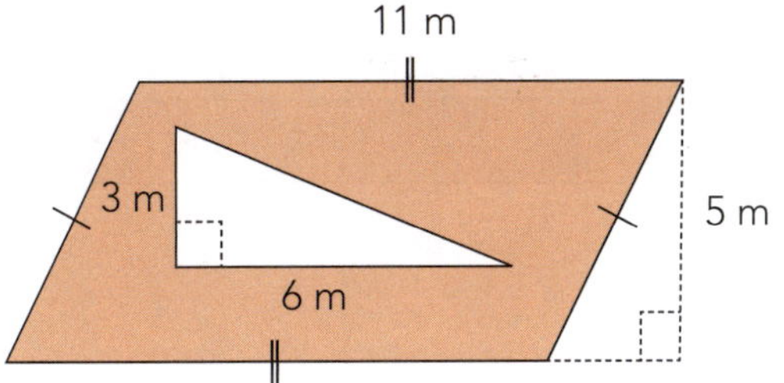

6

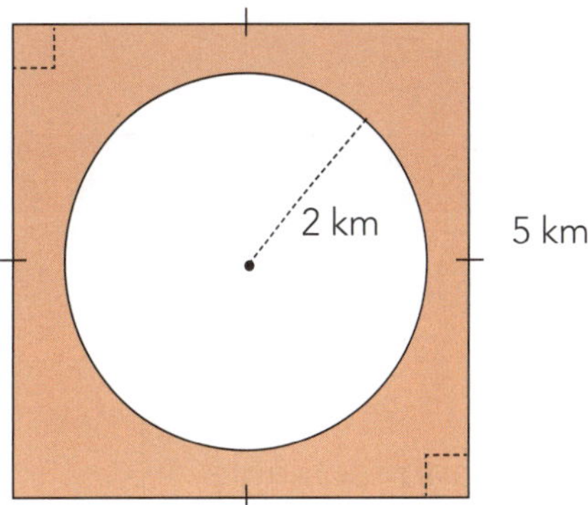

7

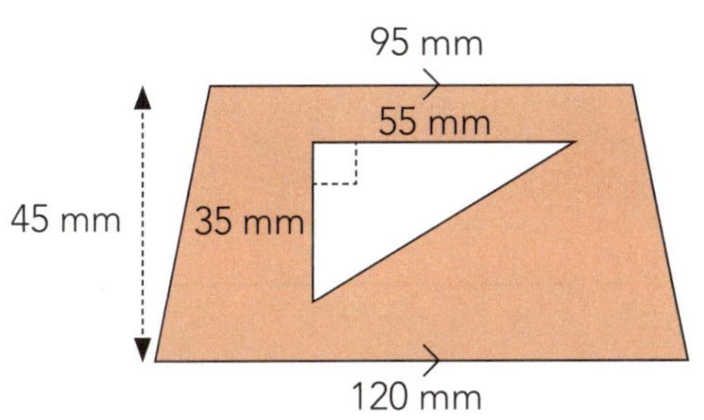

8

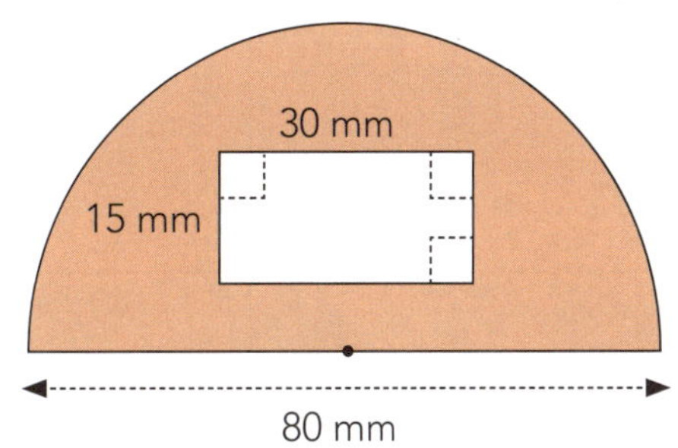

9 Write your answer in square centimetres (cm^2).

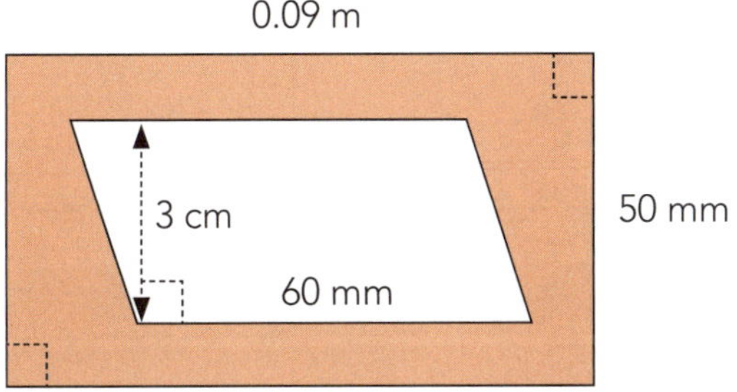

10 Write your answer in square metres (m^2).

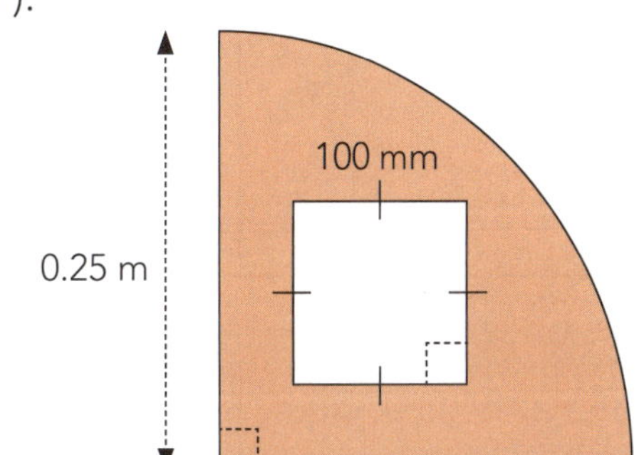

ISBN: 9780170447218

Summary

Shape	Picture	Formula
Square and rectangle		$A = b \times h$
Parallelogram and rhombus		
Trapezium		
Triangle		
Circle		

ISBN: 9780170447218

Word questions

Answer the following questions. Don't forget to sketch a diagram first.

1 A bedroom measures 3.2 m by 4.1 m. What is the area of the bedroom?

2 Kylie is cutting off a corner of her rectangular lawn to form a triangular area for the chickens. One of the short sides of the triangle must be 2.25 m long. If the area needs to be 9 m^2, how long is the other short side?

3 **a** Edward needs to fence a paddock for his horse. The area of grass must be at least 60 m^2. If the length of the paddock is 8 m, what would be its minimum width?

b What would be your answer if the hay shed, which has an area of 12 m^2, occupies one corner?

4 **a** A circular pool has a diameter of 4.33 m. Calculate its area.

b How much does the area change if the pool's radius is increased by 20 cm?

ISBN: 9780170447218

5 **a** Remember the 'L' shape created using two rectangles? Its total height was 10 cm and its total width 7 cm. If each branch of the 'L' is 2 cm thick, calculate its area.

b Does the area change if the 'L' shape was still 10 cm by 7 cm, but the thickness of each branch was 3 cm? By how much?

6 **a** Remember the garden created in the shape of a square plus a quarter circle? The sides of the square and the radius of the circle were all 2.5 m. Calculate the area of the bed.

b It was originally planned to be a rectangular bed measuring 5 m by 2.5 m. How much smaller than the rectangular bed is the area in part **a**?

7 **a** The end wall of a building is in the shape of a trapezium. Its sloping sides both measure 5 m, the floor is 21 m long, the ceiling is 15 m and its vertical height is 4 m. Calculate the area of this side of the building.

b The architect decided to put a circular window in this wall. Its diameter would be 2 m. Calculate the area of the wall that will need to be painted.

 ISBN: 9780170447218

Challenge 5

A decorative strip based on a tukutuku pattern has been designed to go along one side of a school hall.

- It is to be made up of a series of panels that look like these:

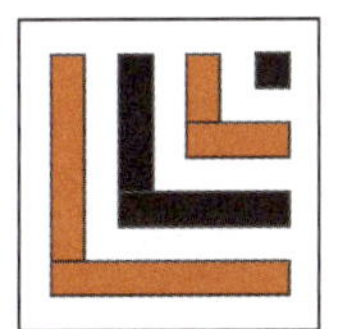 and 

- The dimensions on both panel designs are the same, and shown on the diagram at right.

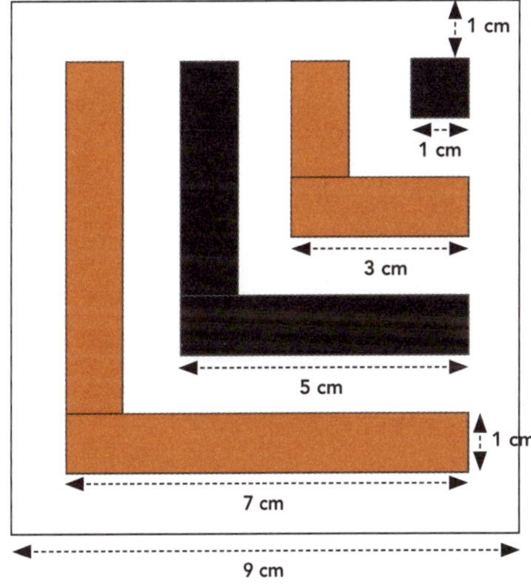

1 Calculate the areas of each colour in each panel design.

a

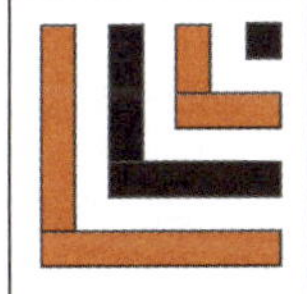

Black	
Orange	
White	

b

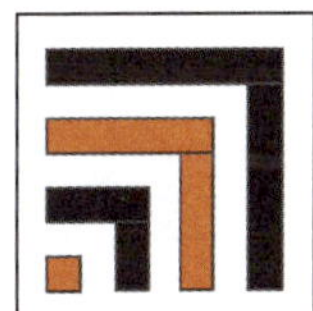

Black	
Orange	
White	

2 If there are equal numbers of both panel designs, calculate the percentage of each colour in the entire strip.

	Area	Percentage
Black		
Orange		
White		

Volume

Cuboids with cube blocks

If you can **fill** it, it's volume.

- The volume of a three-dimensional (3D) shape is the amount of **space** the shape occupies.
- A **cuboid** is a box shape, e.g. a shoebox.
- A **cube** is a box shape where all the dimensions are equal, e.g. a die.
- Each block represents 1 cm³.

Volume = height x width x depth

$V = h \times w \times d$

Example:

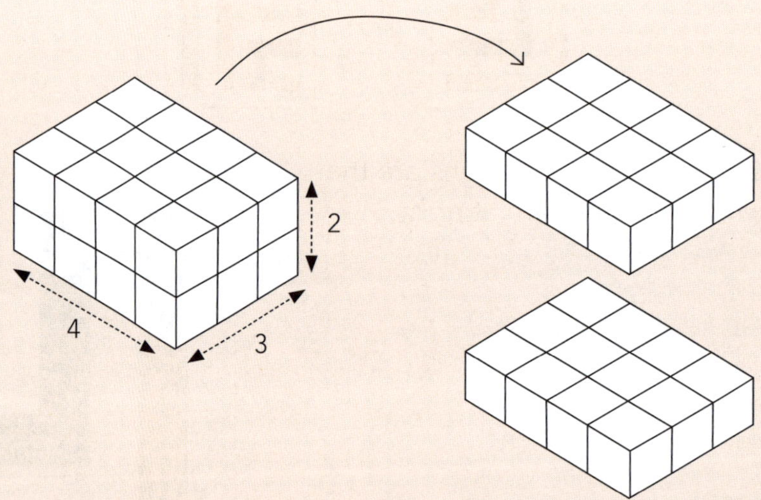

Volume = number of layers x number of blocks in one layer

= 2 x 4 x 3

= 24 cm³

This is the same as **height x width x depth**.

When calculating volume, the units must be cubed (³).

Calculate the volumes of these cuboids. The small blocks are 1 cm cubes.

1

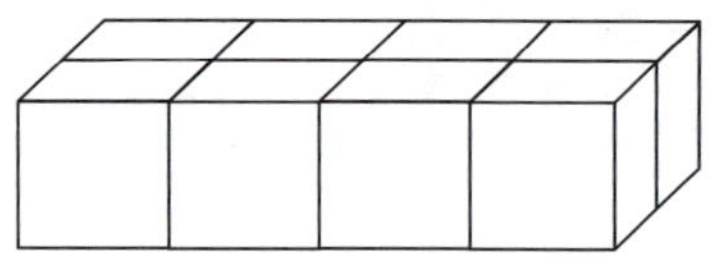

Volume = $h \times w \times d$

= ____________

= ____________

2

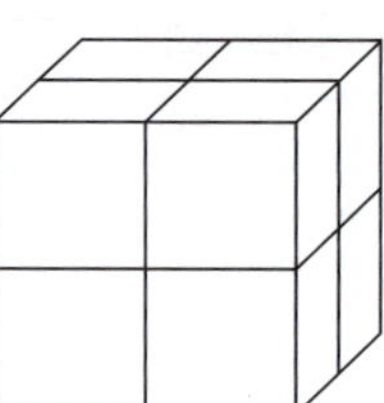

____

____

 ISBN: 9780170447218

3

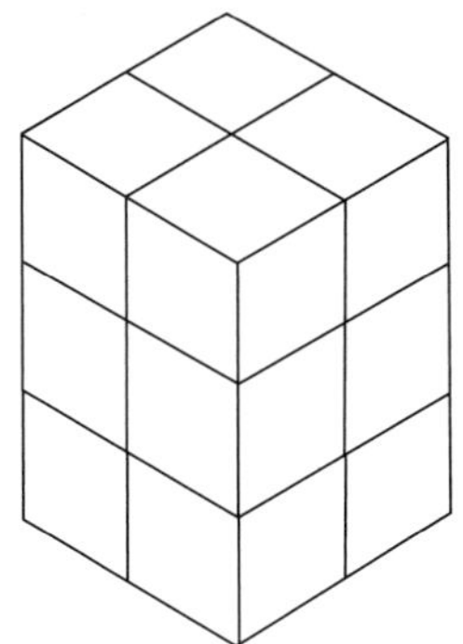

4

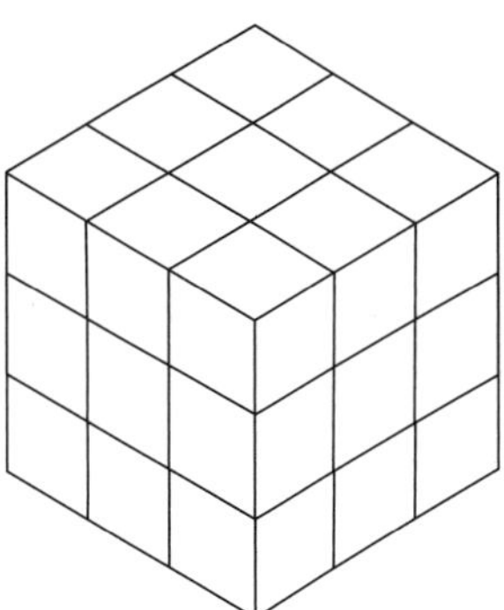

5

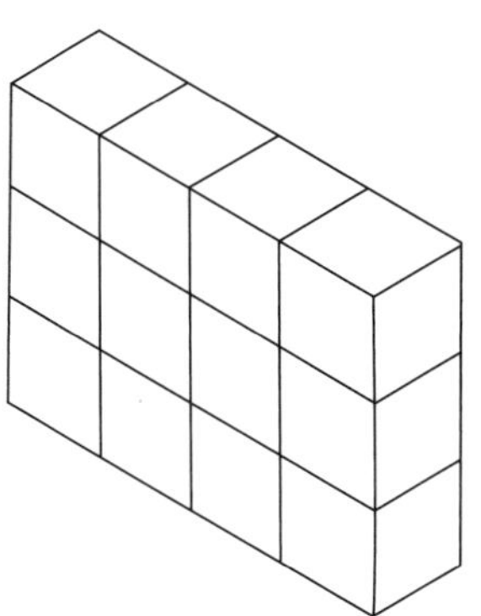

6

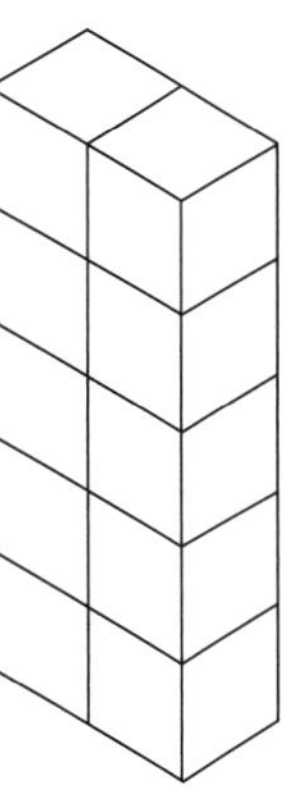

7

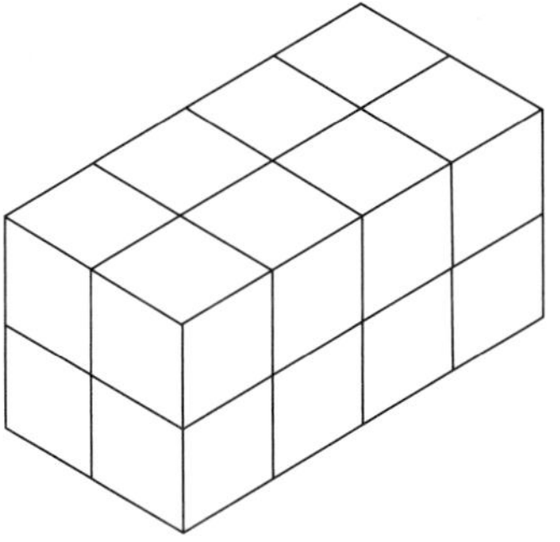

8

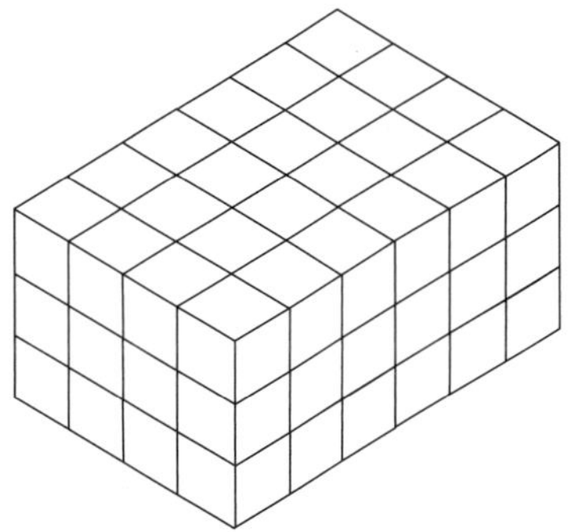

ISBN: 9780170447218

Cuboids

- Remember, a **cuboid** is a box shape.

Volume = height x width x depth

$V = h \times w \times d$

Examples:

1

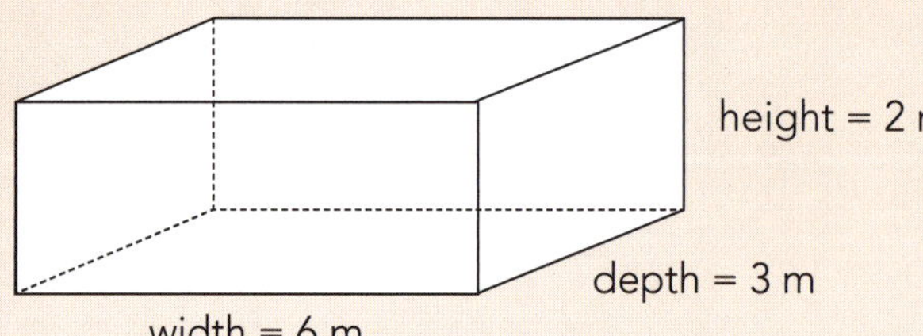

Volume = $h \times w \times d$

$= 2 \times 6 \times 3$

$= 36\ m^3$

2 Another way to think about it is to find the area of the 'face' and multiply it by the depth.

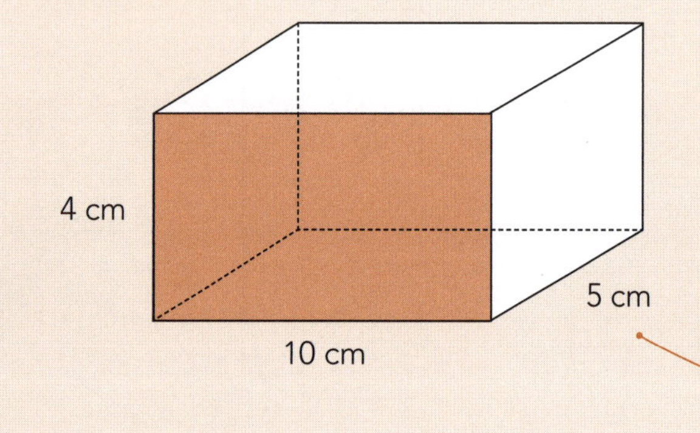

Volume = **area of face** x d

$= (4 \times 10) \times 5$

$= (40) \times 5$

$= 200\ cm^3$

Area of the face is **40 cm²**, which is multiplied by the depth (5 cm).

Calculate the volumes of these cuboids.

1

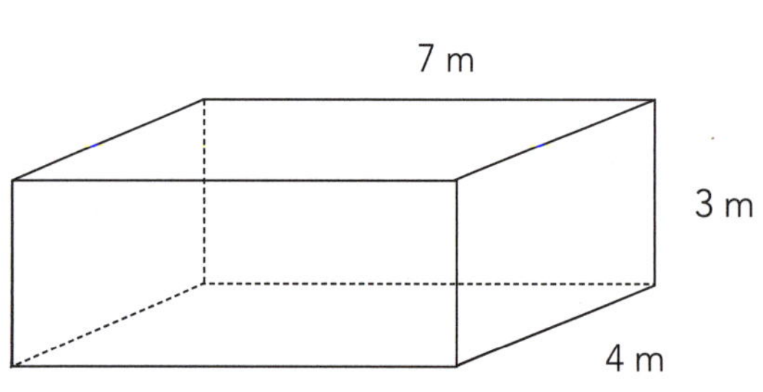

____

____

2

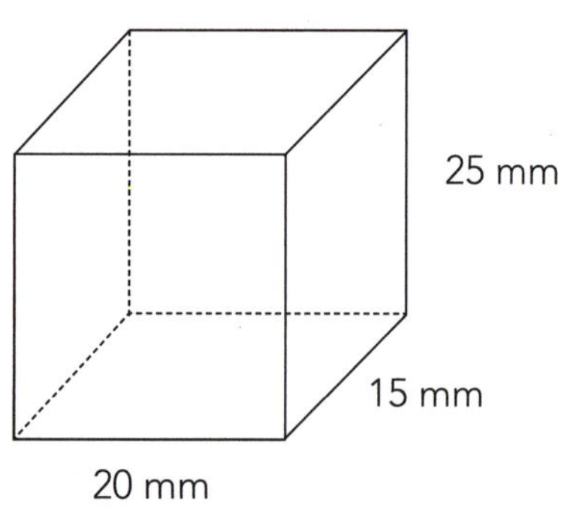

____

____

 ISBN: 9780170447218

3

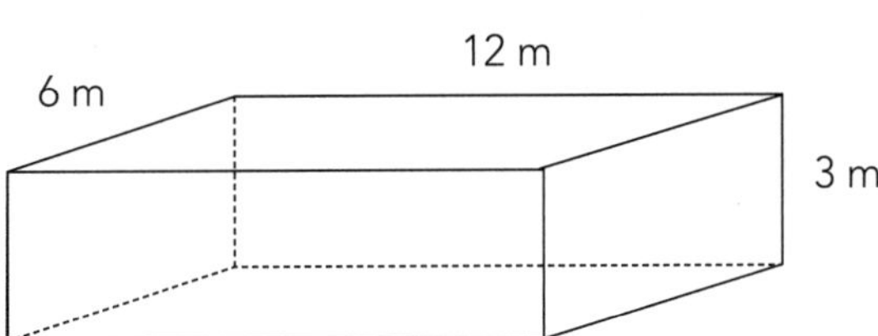

4

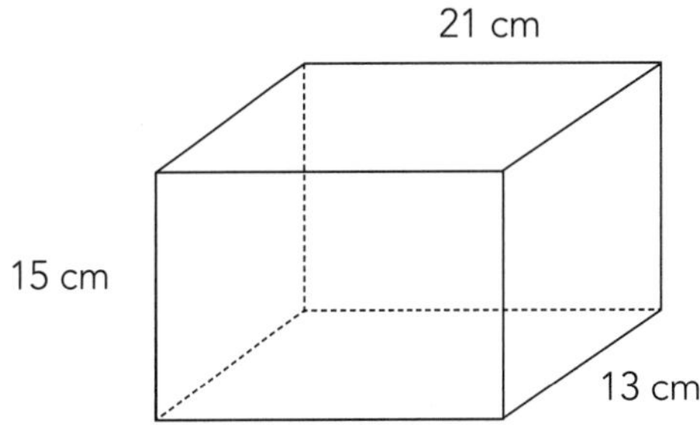

5 This is a cube.

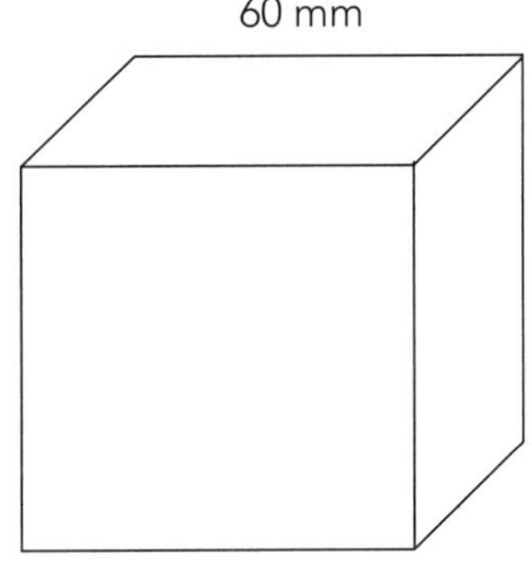

6

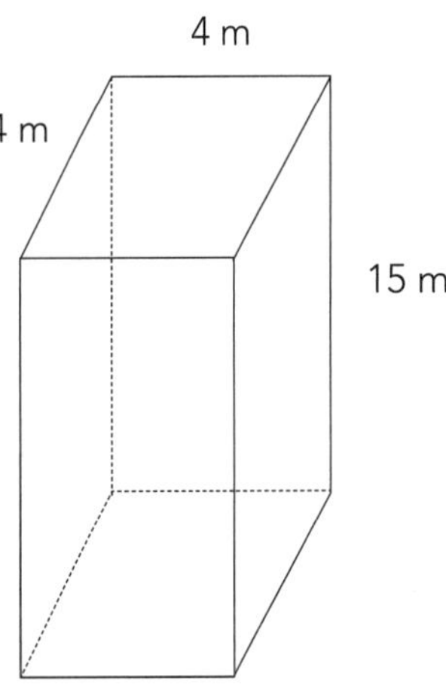

7

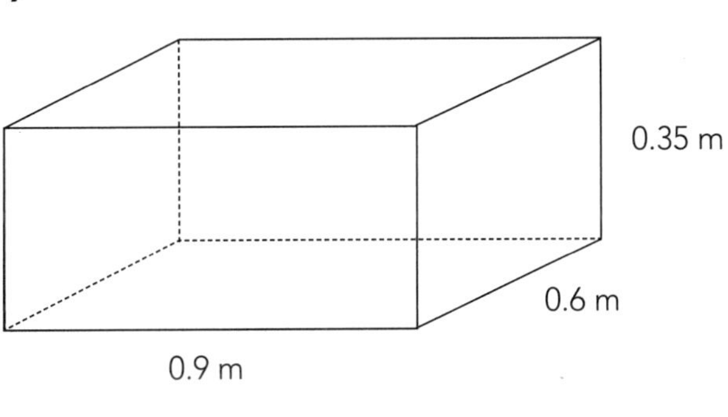

8

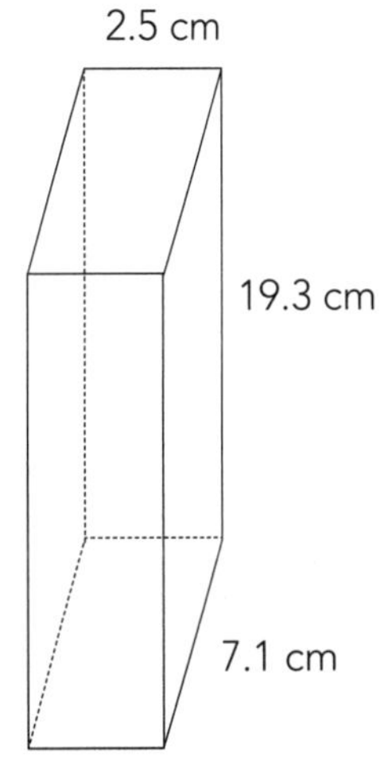

Compound shapes with cube blocks

- Shapes made up of several cuboids are called **compound cuboids**.
- We can find the volume of a compound cuboid by splitting it into simple cuboids, and then counting the cubes.

Volume = height x width x depth

$V = h \times w \times d$

Example:

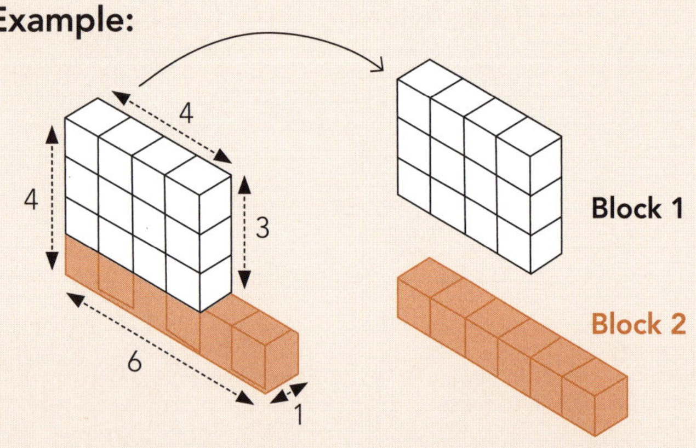

Volume = **Block 1** + **Block 2**
= 3 x 4 x 1 + 1 x 6 x 1
= 12 + 6
= 18

Notice that the answer is the same if the split is done like this:

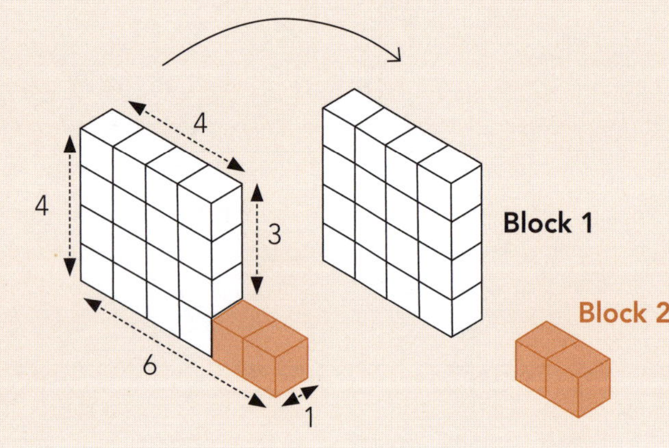

Volume = **Block 1** + **Block 2**
= 4 x 4 x 1 + 1 x 2 x 1
= 16 + 2
= 18

Calculate the volumes of these shapes. Numbers **1**–**4** are made up of two cuboids.

1

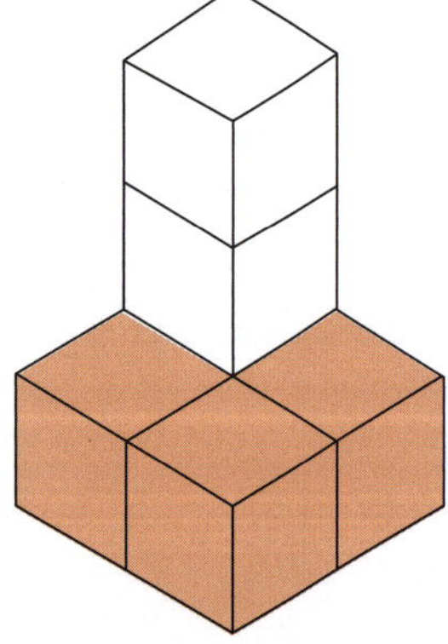

____

____

2

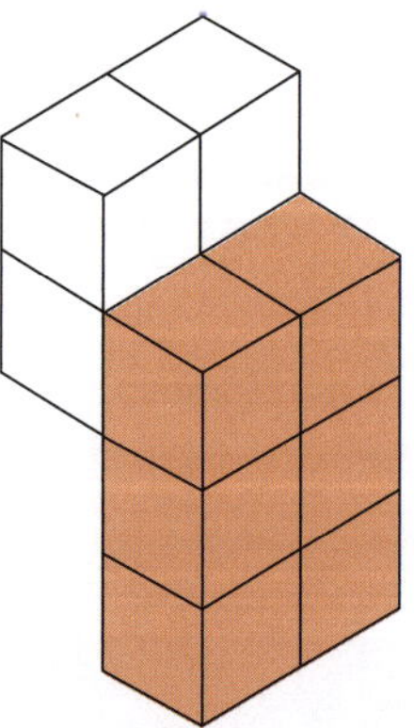

____

____

 ISBN: 9780170447218

3

4

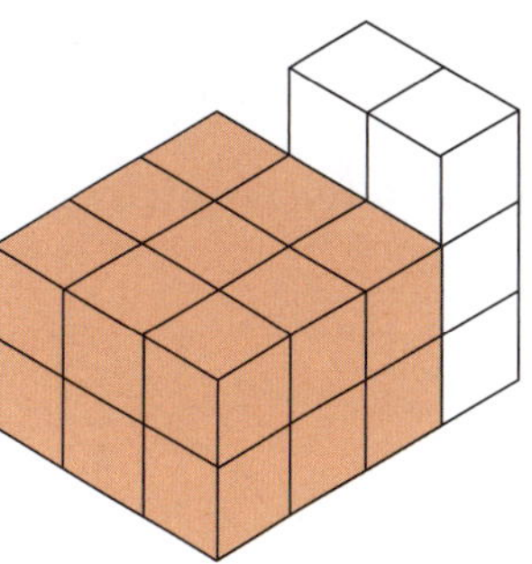

Numbers **5** to **8** are made up of three cuboids.

5

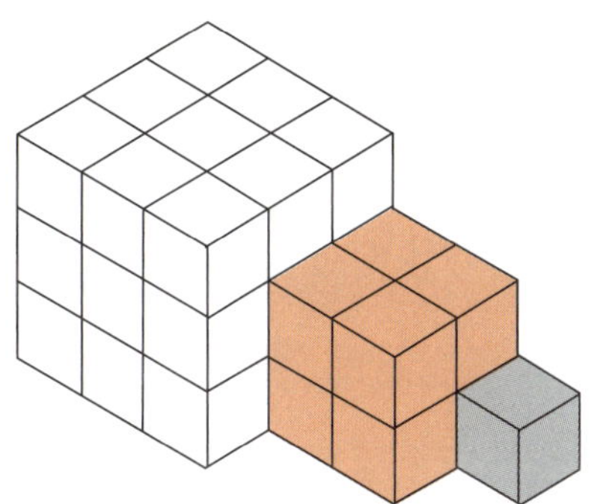

6

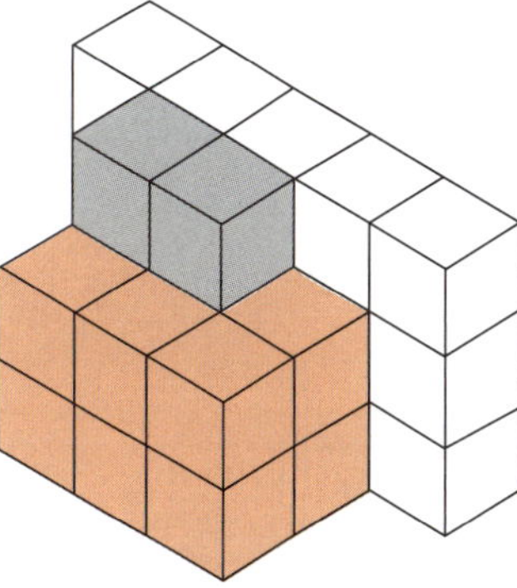

7

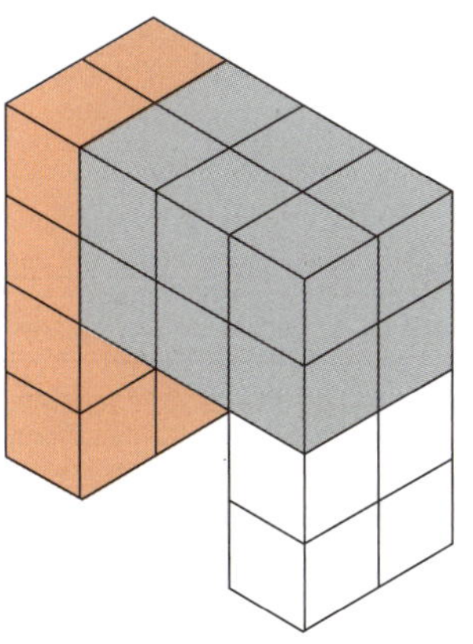

8

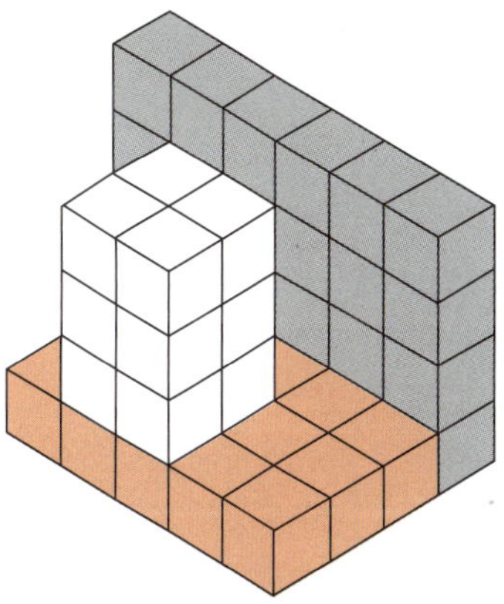

ISBN: 9780170447218

Compound cuboids

- There are two methods for finding the volume of a compound cuboid.

Volume = height x width x depth

$V = h \times w \times d$

Example: We can find the volume of a compound cuboid by either:

1 splitting it into simple cuboids, and then calculating the volume of each one

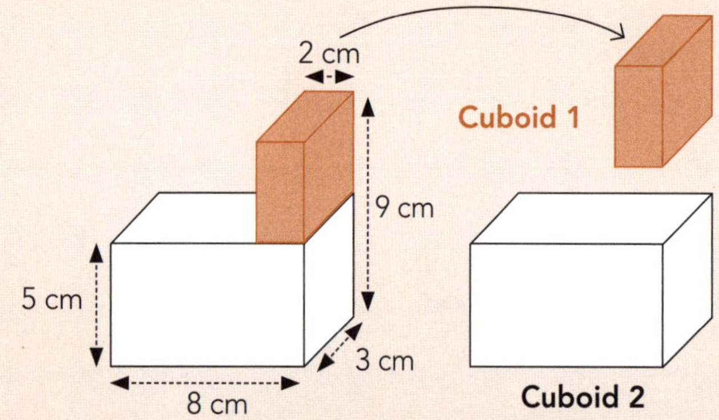

Volume = **Cuboid 1** + **Cuboid 2**

= (4 x 2 x 3) + (5 x 8 x 3)

= 24 + 120

= 144 cm^3

or 2 finding the area of a face and multiplying by the depth.

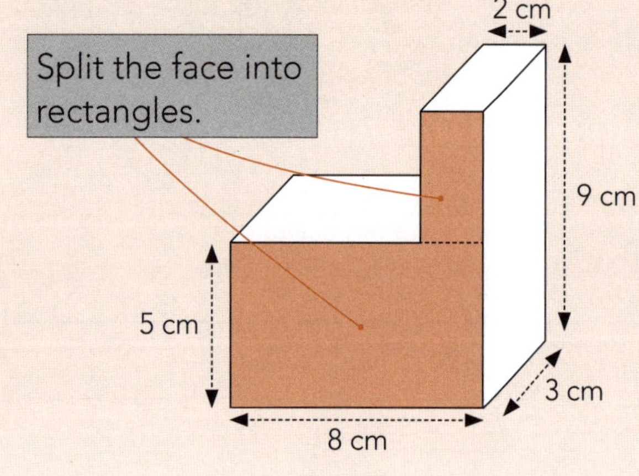

Volume = **area of face** x *d*

= ((5 x 8) + (4 x 2)) x d

= (40 + 8) x 3

= 48 x 3

= 144 cm^3

Calculate the volumes of these compound cuboids.

1

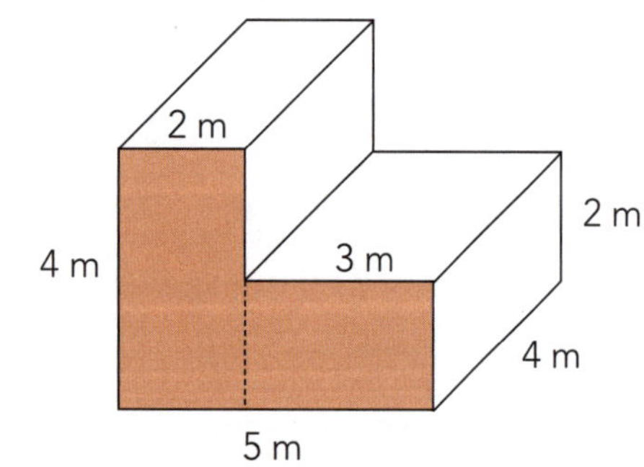

____

____

2

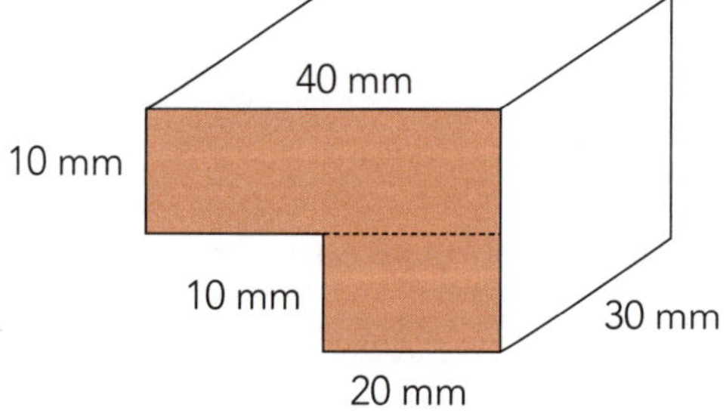

____

____

 ISBN: 9780170447218

3

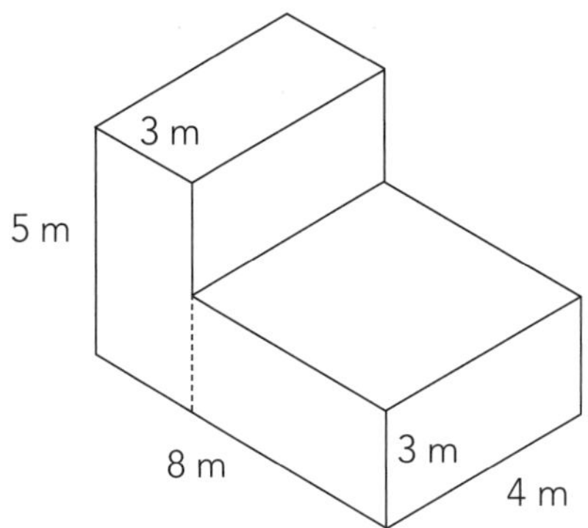

4

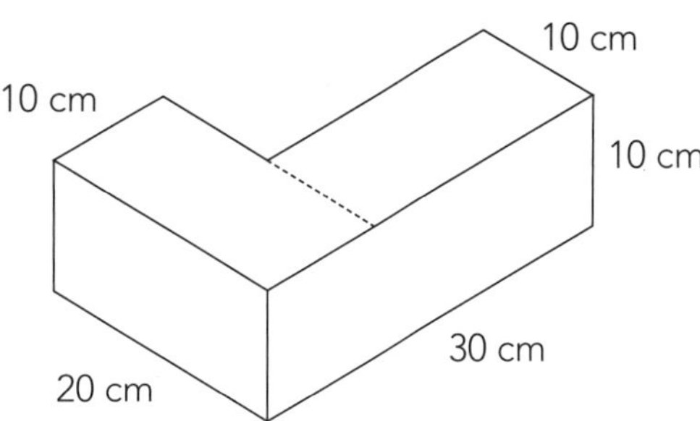

5

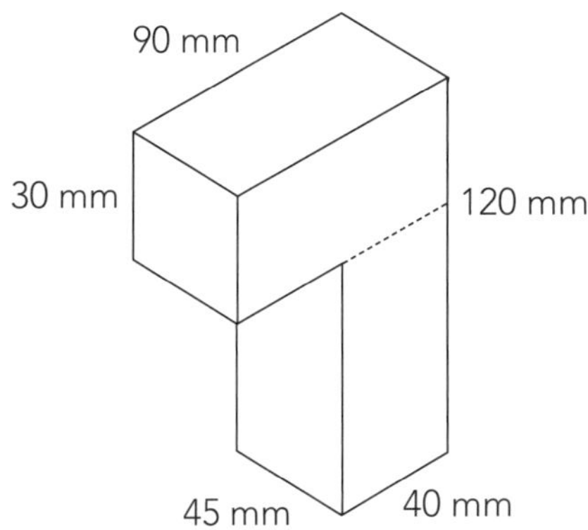

6

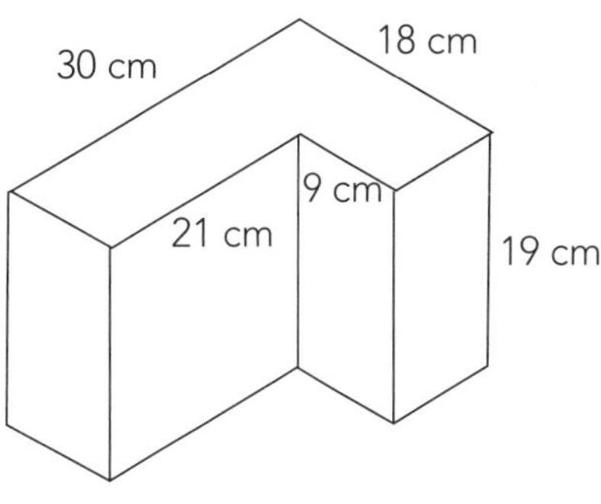

7 Write your answer in cubic metres (m^3).

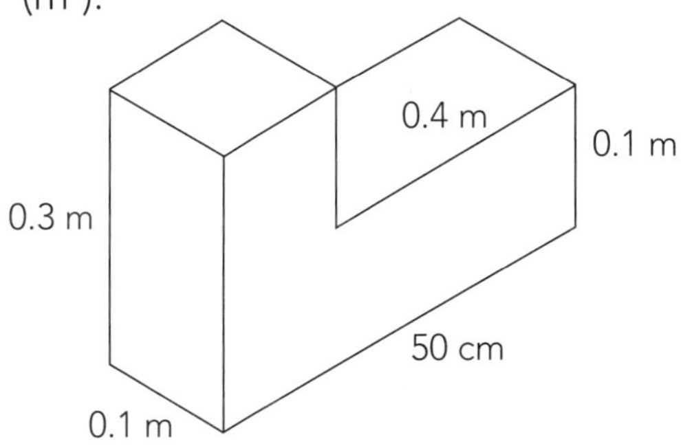

8

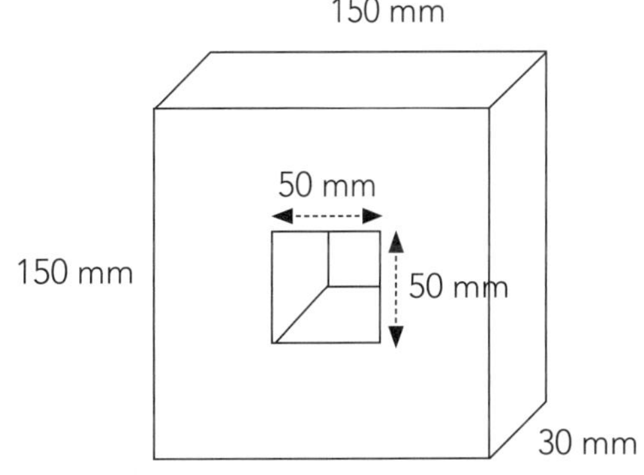

ISBN: 9780170447218

One-litre challenge

- One litre is equivalent to 1000 cm^3.
- This is a cube that contains exactly one litre.

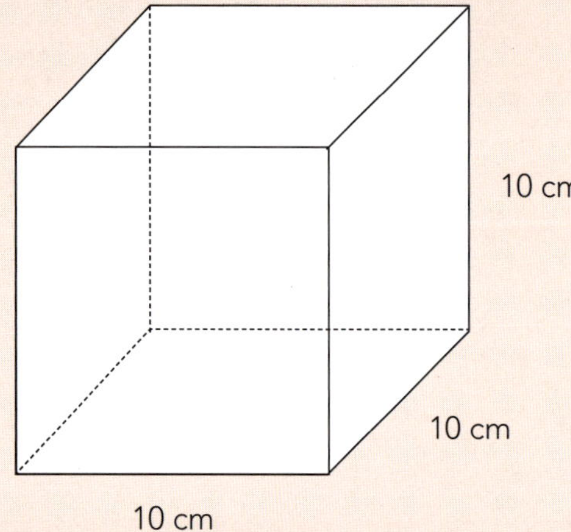

Volume = height x width x depth
= 10 x 10 x 10
= 1000 cm^3

- However, litres come in all shapes and sizes. Think about food and drink packaging.

Calculate the missing measurements required to make these cuboids exactly 1 L (1000 cm^3).

1

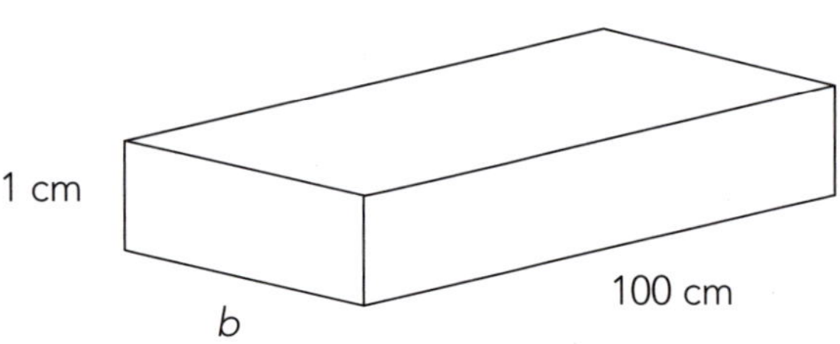

2

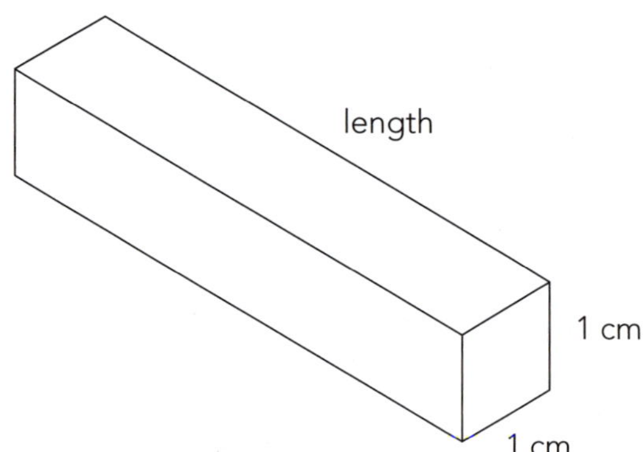

 ISBN: 9780170447218

3

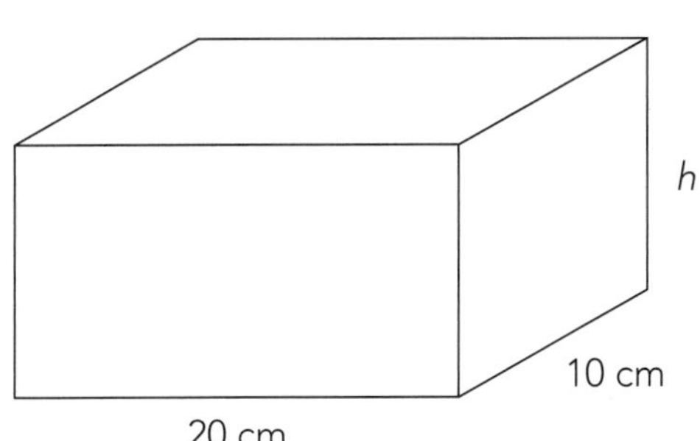

4

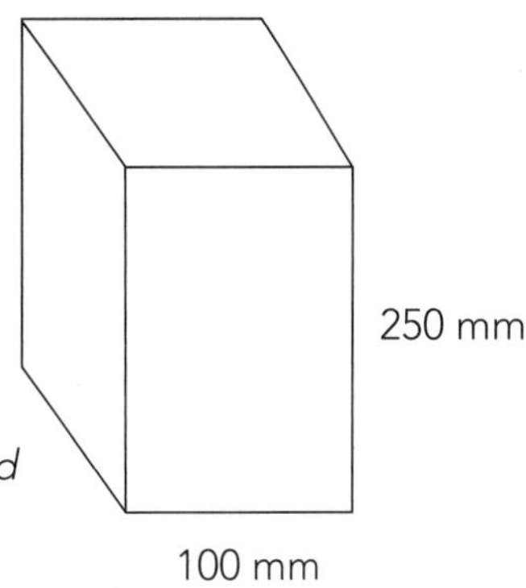

5 Write your answer in centimetres (cm).

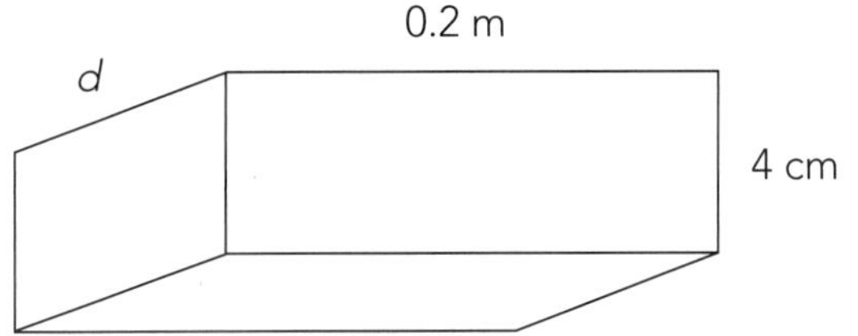

6 Write your answer in centimetres (cm).

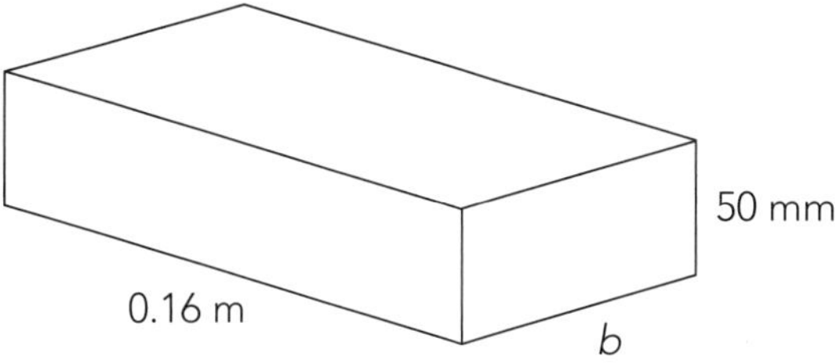

7 Write your answer in centimetres (cm).

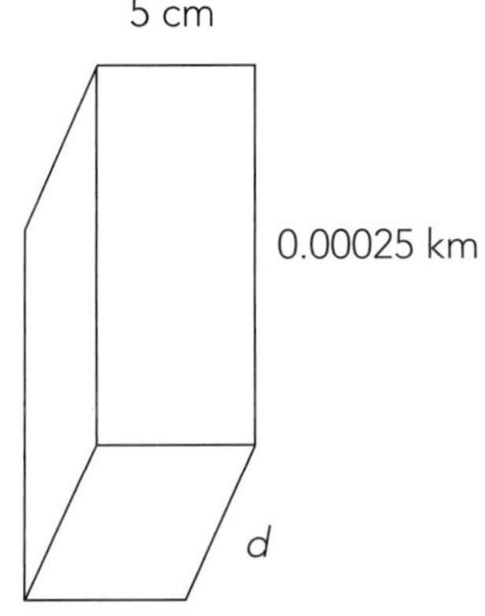

8

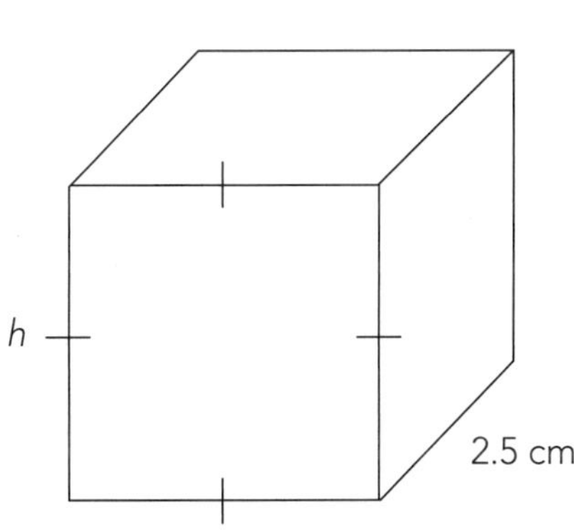

ISBN: 9780170447218

Revision 1

1 Write the abbreviations for these units.

a metre ______________ **b** milligram ______________

c litre ______________ **d** minute ______________

2 Write the meaning of these abbreviations.

a tsp ______________ **b** kg ______________

c s ______________ **d** c ______________

3 Convert these to 24-hour time.

a 5.34 p.m. = ______________ **b** 1.14 a.m. = ______________

c 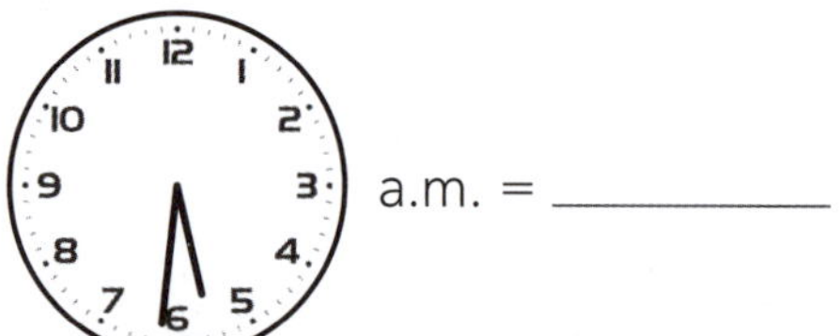

d 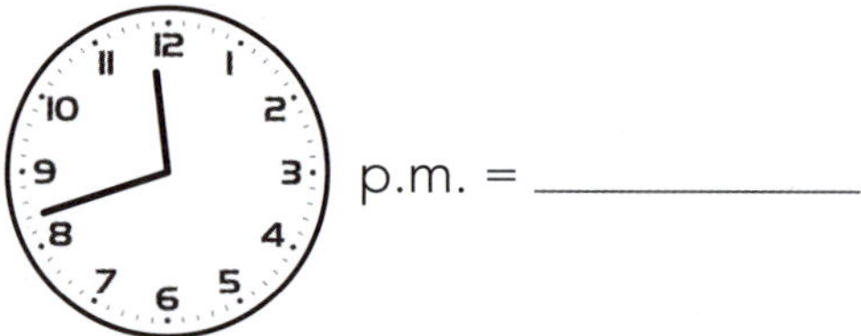

4 Convert these measurements.

a 84 min = ______________ s **b** 580 mm = ______________ cm

c 3500 g = ______________ kg **d** 3 L = ______________ mL

e 670 cm = ______________ m **f** 120 h = ______________ d

g 400 m = ______________ km **h** 95 g = ______________ mg

i 750 mL = ______________ L **j** 2.4 km = ______________ m

ISBN: 9780170447218

5 Circle or highlight the most likely unit of measurement for these items.

a The amount of time it takes to brush your teeth.

h mL cm min

b The length of your fingernail.

km L t mm

c The mass of a basketball.

ha kg m g

d The amount of milk in a cup of tea.

L km mL kg

6 Write down the measurements shown on these scales.

A = ____________ B = ____________ C = ____________

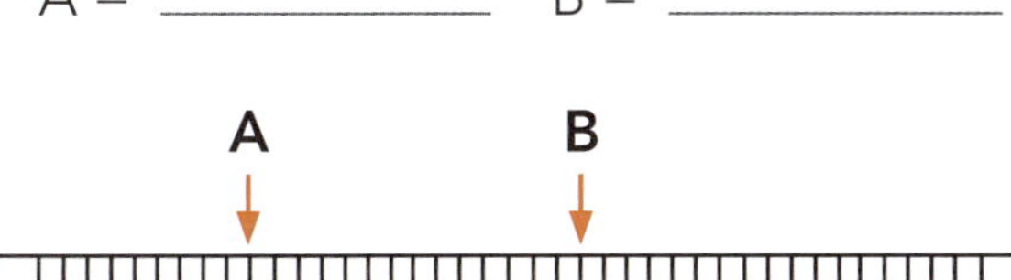

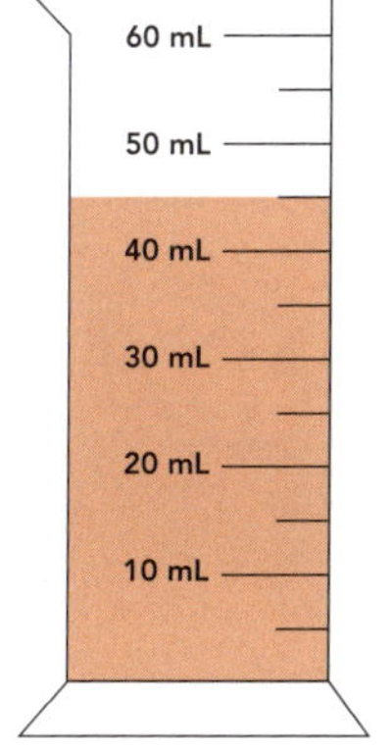

7 Colour these amounts on the scales.

a 70 mL

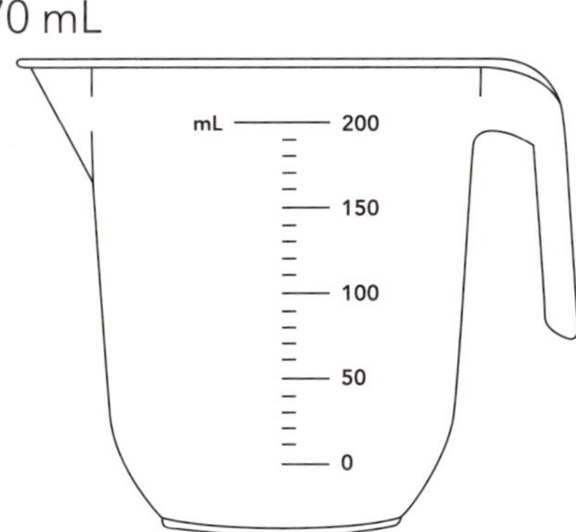

b 84°

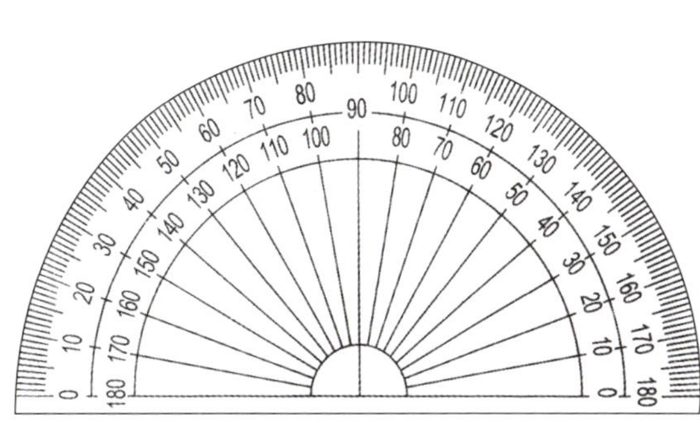

8 Calculate the perimeters of these shapes.

a

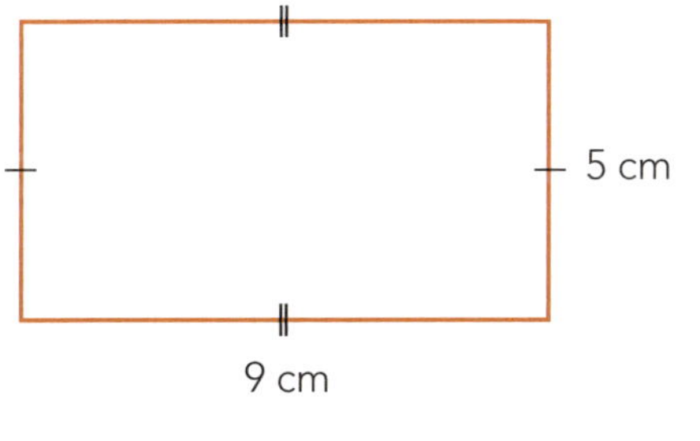

____

____

b

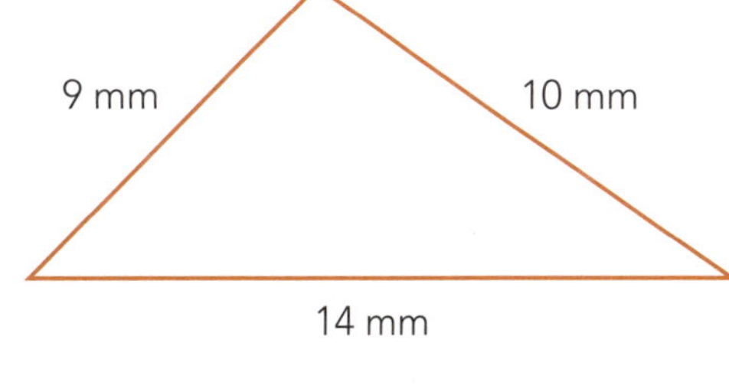

____

____

c

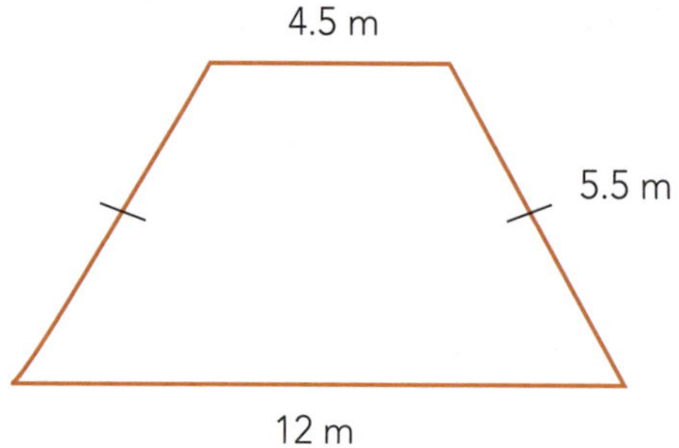

d

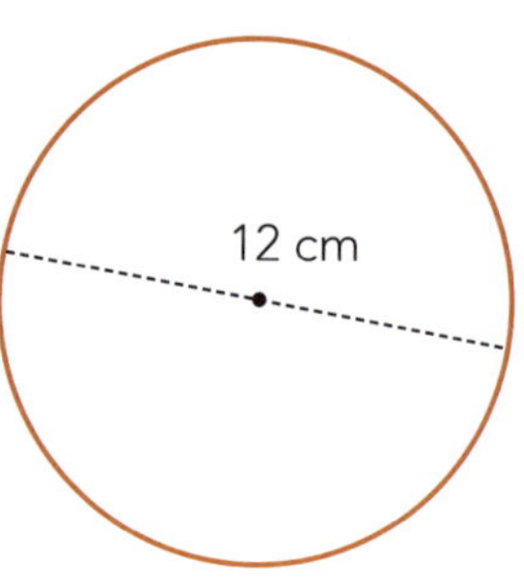

9 Calculate the areas of these shapes.

a

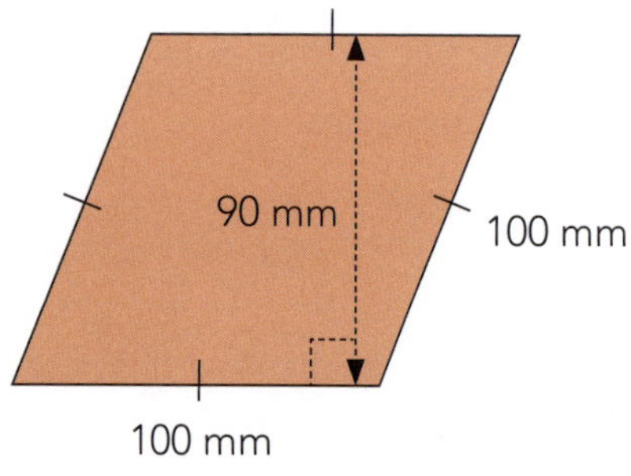

b

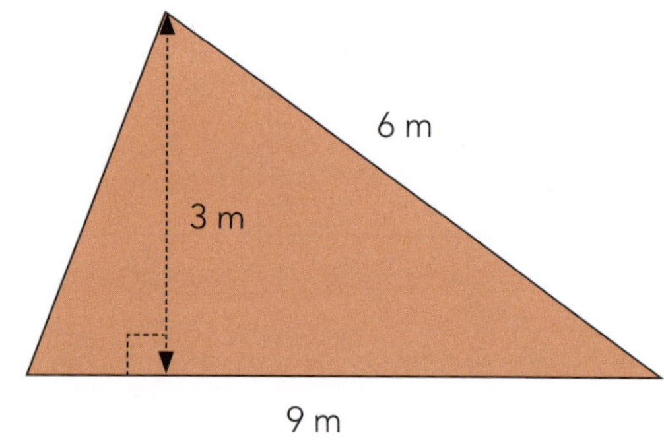

c

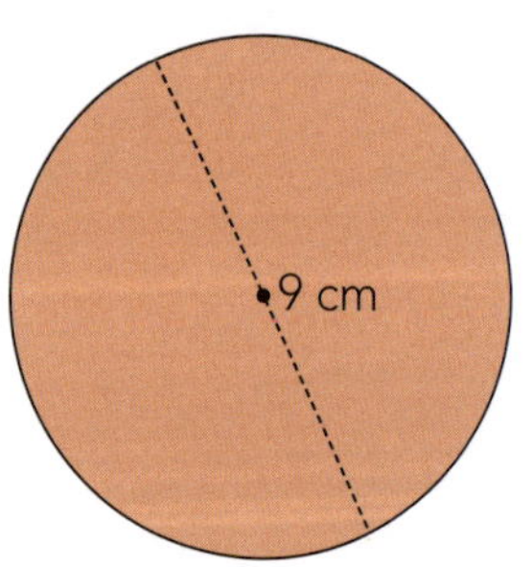

10 Calculate the volume of this cuboid.

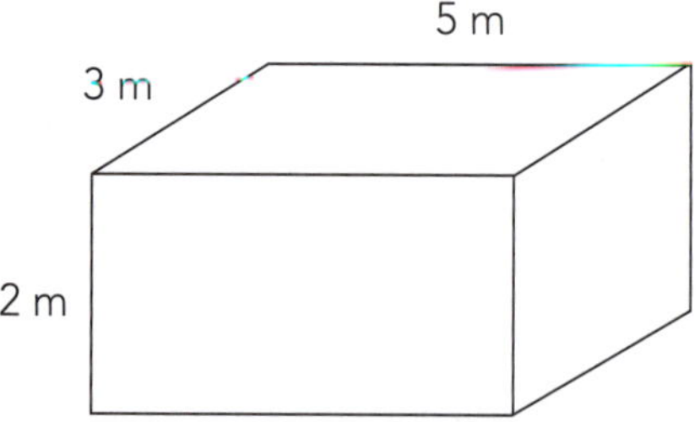

 ISBN: 9780170447218

Revision 2

1 Write the abbreviations for these units.

a kilometre ____________ **b** gram ____________

c millilitre ____________ **d** hectare ____________

2 Write the meaning of these abbreviations.

a kg ____________ **b** mm ____________

c t ____________ **d** °C ____________

3 Convert these to 24-hour time.

a 9.23 p.m. = ____________ **b** 6.52 a.m. = ____________

c 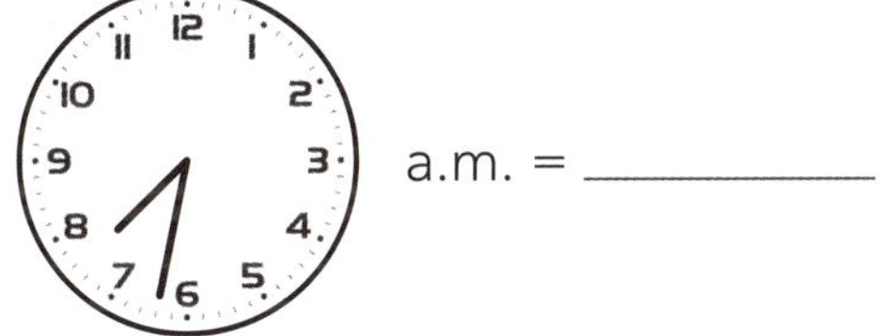 a.m. = ____________

d 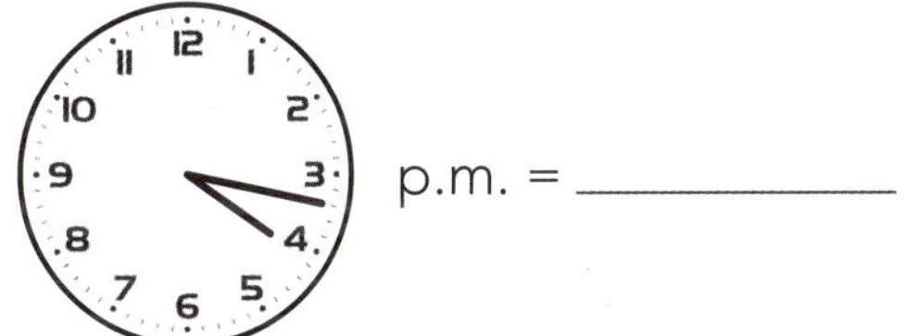 p.m. = ____________

4 Convert these measurements.

a 480 s = ____________ min **b** 5 L = ____________ mL

c 6 kg = ____________ g **d** 3.5 cm = ____________ mm

e 0.9 m = ____________ cm **f** 4.5 days = ____________ hours

g 1200 m = ____________ km **h** 250 mg = ____________ g

i 9500 mL = ____________ L **j** 5.1 km = ____________ cm

ISBN: 9780170447218

5 Circle or highlight the most likely unit of measurement for these items.

a The length of your big toe.

min mL cm mm

b The mass of your shoe.

km g cm kg

c The amount of food on your plate.

s kg g L

d The mass of your chair.

m kg L mg

6 Write down the measurements shown on these scales.

a ______________

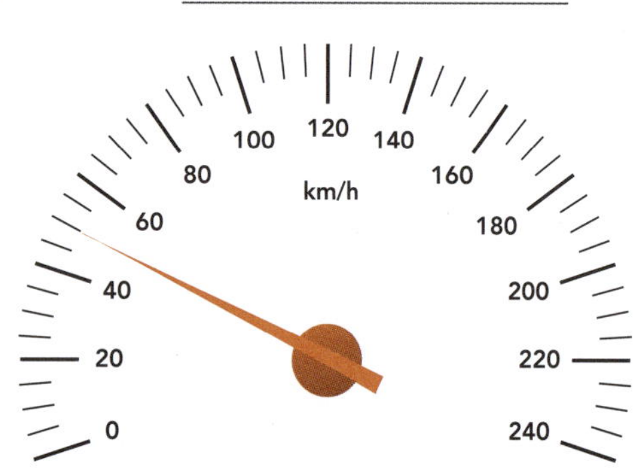

b A = ______________

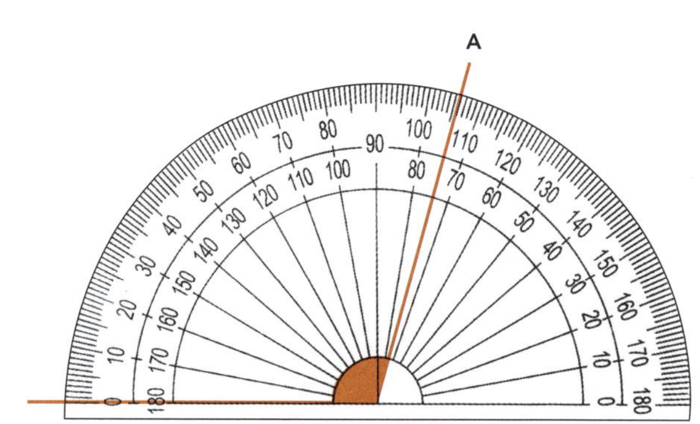

7 Add pointers to show these values.

a 64°C

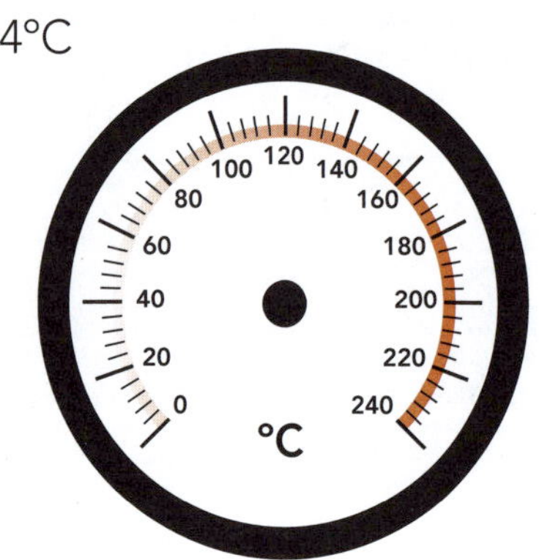

b A = 13.1 cm
B = 15.6 cm

11 12 13 14 15 16
cm

8 Calculate the perimeters of these shapes.

a

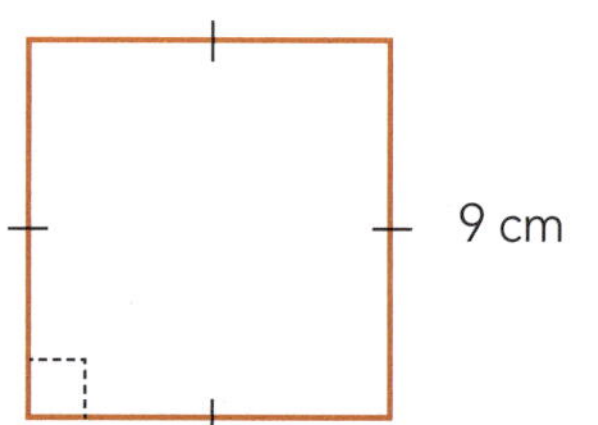

____

____

b

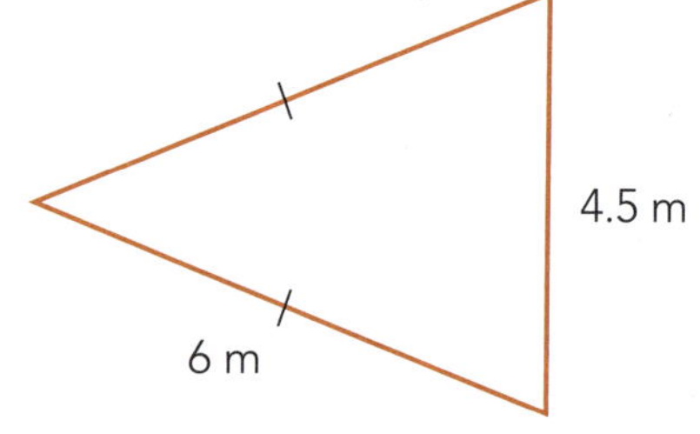

____

____

ISBN: 9780170447218

c

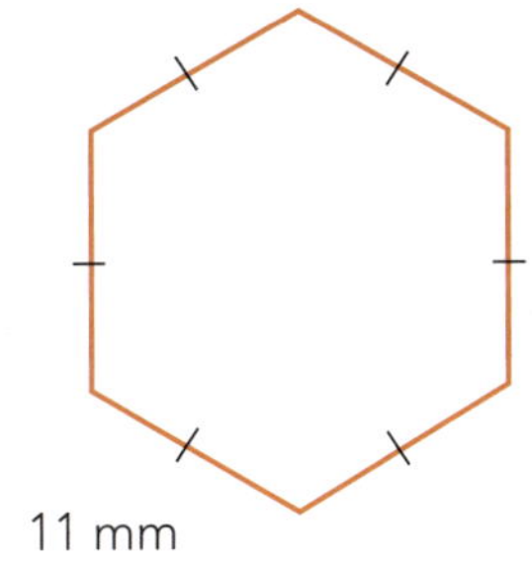

d

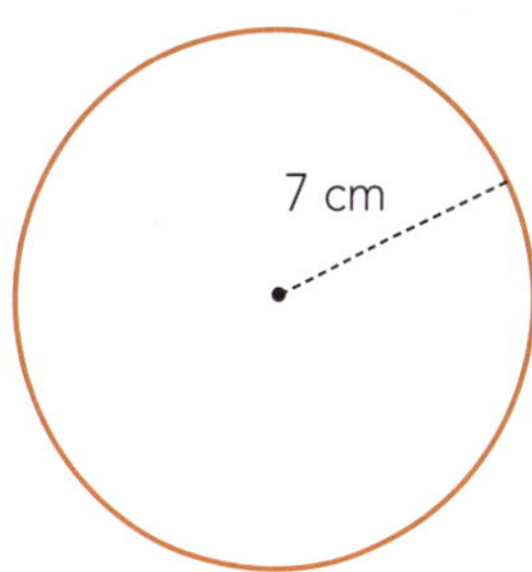

9 Calculate the areas of these shapes.

a

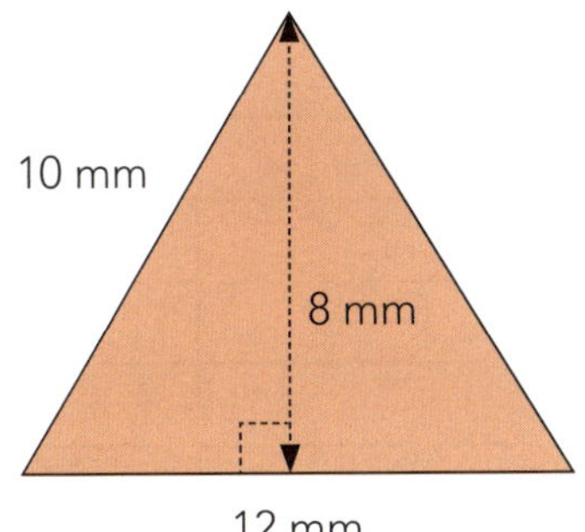

b

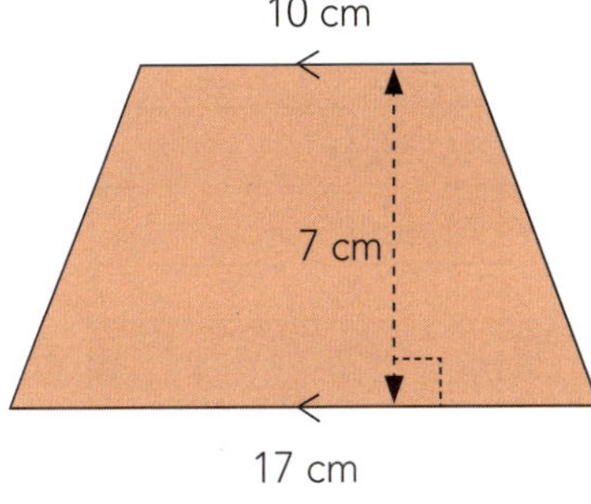

c

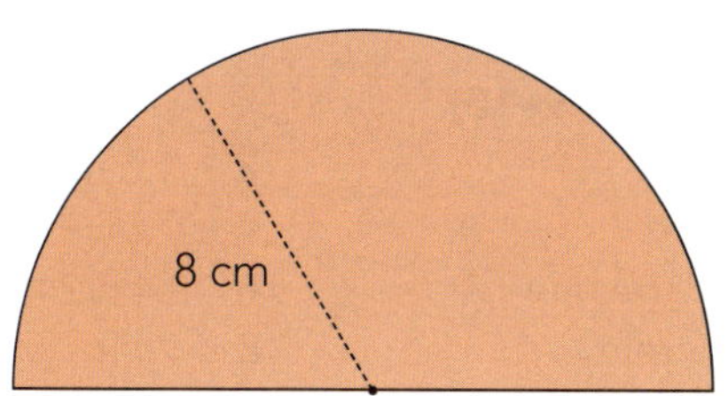

10 Calculate the volume of this cuboid.

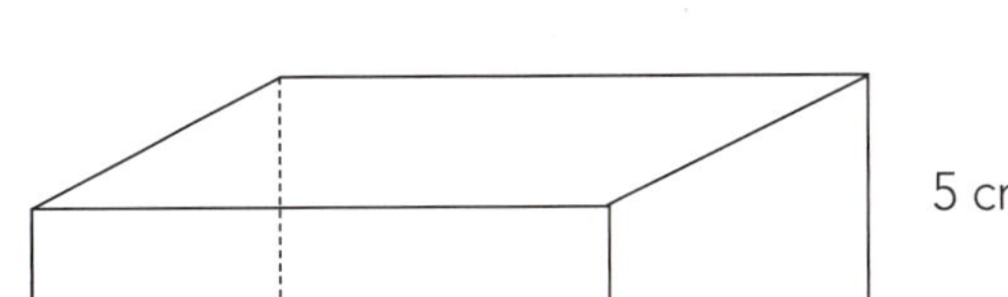

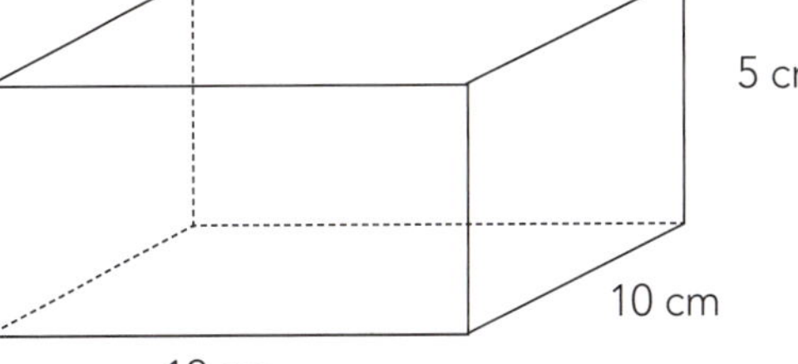

ISBN: 9780170447218

Answers

The language of measurement (pp. 6–7)

Length: distance, far, long, wide, reach
Time: long, period, age, fortnight, century, decade, generation
Volume/Capacity: room, bulk, space
Angle: incline, slant, steep, gradient, pitch, slope, flat
Temperature: warm, cold, heat, hot, icy
Mass: heavy, load, light

Term	Period of time
Fortnight	Two weeks
Month	About four weeks
Leap year	366 days
Generation	About 25 years

Term	Period of time
Century	100 years
Millennium	1000 years
Decade	10 years
Year	365 days

Measuring devices (p. 7)

Length: tape measure, ruler, pedometer, odometer
Mass: scales
Time: stopwatch, timer, clock
Temperature: thermometer
Capacity: cup, syringe, teaspoon, tablespoon, measuring cylinder
Angle: protractor, clinometer

Units (pp. 8–19)

Abbreviations (shortened versions) for units (p. 8)

Unit of measurement	Shortened version
Kilogram	kg
Centimetre	cm
Metre	m
Minute	min
Litre	L
Hectare	ha
Milligram	mg
Teaspoon	tsp
Dessertspoon	dsp
Day	d

Unit of measurement	Shortened version
Kilometre	km
Millimetre	mm
Degree Celsius	°C
Second	s
Tablespoon	tbsp
Tonne	t
Millilitre	mL
Cup	c
Gram	g
Hour	h

Length km, m, cm, mm	**Area** ha
Capacity tbsp, dsp, tsp, L, mL, c	**Mass** kg, g, mg, t
Temperature °C	**Time** min, s, d, h

Time (pp. 9–10)

1 2 h
2 1.5 min
3 3 d
4 7 min
5 2160 min
6 14 h 24 min
7 8 min
8 24 h
9 3 h
10 210 min
11 3600 s
12 5 d
13 3.5 h
14 2.5 d
15 2 min
16 3 d
17 301 min
18 8.5 min
19 3.5 d
20 1.5 d
21 3960 s, 0.05 d, 1.3 h, 84 min
22 180 000 s, 3003 min, 2.1 d, 50.5 h
23 minutes
24 seconds
25 days
26 hours
27 minutes
28 hours

ISBN: 9780170447218

Length (pp. 11–12)

1 0.2 m
2 0.5 m
3 2600 m
4 80 cm
5 90 mm
6 2000 cm
7 3 km
8 2500 m
9 17 m
10 95 mm
11 12 cm
12 35 m
13 5.4 km
14 650 mm
15 0.3 m
16 9000 mm
17 cm
18 mm
19 cm
20 km
21 cm
22 mm
23 m
24 mm
25 8848 m
26 9.6 mm
27 10.97 m
28 29.7cm
29 21 km
30 961 mm
31 81 mm

Mass (pp. 13–14)

1 1.5 kg
2 1800 g
3 2000 kg
4 2.6 g
5 16 000 g
6 900 kg
7 0.63 g
8 0.785 kg
9 94 000 mg
10 0.236 t
11 80 001 mg
12 5400 g
13 10 g
14 3000 kg
15 52 kg
16 1 kg
17 kg
18 kg
19 g
20 mg
21 t
22 mg
23 kg
24 g
25 284 g
26 22 g
27 28.4 kg
28 136 g
29 52310 t
30 10 mg
31 500 mg

Capacity (pp. 15–16)

1 0.6 L
2 1200 mL
3 1 mL
4 15 L
5 70 000 mL
6 0.45 L
7 9.8 L
8 4000 mL
9 15 000 mL
10 84 L
11 0.01 L
12 900 mL
13 1001 mL, 1100 mL, 1.2 L, 2.0 L, 2100 mL
14 0.91 L, 1.9 L, 9001 mL, 9010 mL, 9.1L
15 12 L
16 55 L
17 1.5 L
18 1.5 mL
19 1000 L
20 100 mL
21 350 mL
22 15 mL

Appropriate units (p. 17)

1 cm
2 mL
3 g
4 cm
5 min
6 mL
7 mL
8 cm
9 g
10 min
11 L
12 kg
13 mm
14 g
15 s
16 t

Estimating quantities (p. 18)

1 1.5 t
2 93 m
3 1300 g
4 150 g
5 8.4 cm
6 12 mL
7 2.1 m
8 28 m
9 76 cm
10 5 L
11 0.5 kg
12 28 mL
13 17 cm
14 5 g
15 80 L
16 400 mL
17 5 mm
18 50 cm
19 2.3 kg

Word questions (p. 19)

1 560 mL
2 8 kg
3 750 g
4 5.1 m
5 23.75 m
6 36.5 hours
7 **a** 0.4 m
b 12.5 days
c 2.695 kg
d 5.714 so 6 eggs
10 g left over

Time (pp. 20–22)

1 16:12
2 02:14
3 9.20 p.m.
4 19:17
5 3.51 p.m.
6 00:12
7 4.01 p.m.
8 14:17
9 8.42 p.m.
10 00:00
11 00:05
12 22:15
13 18:45
14 16:37
15 3.20 a.m.
16 14:00
17 4.16 p.m.
18 7.45 p.m.
19 10:01 a.m.
20 12:00 p.m.
21 13:05, 15:03, 3.15 p.m., 5.13 p.m., 10.53 p.m.
22 12.12 p.m., 12.21 p.m., 21:12, 22:11, 11.22 p.m.

		12-hour time	24-hour time
23	Nine minutes past midday.	12:09 p.m.	12:09
24	Twelve minutes before midnight.	11:48 p.m.	23:48
25	Just before lunch at five minutes to twelve.	11:55 a.m.	11:55
26	Quarter to one in the morning.	12:45 a.m.	00:45
27	One forty five in the afternoon.	1:45 p.m.	13:45
28	Ten to nine in the evening.	8.50 p.m.	20:50
29	Quarter to six in the morning.	5.45 a.m.	05:45
30	Quarter past midnight.	12.15 a.m.	00:15

ISBN: 9780170447218

Reading tables (p. 23)

1 17:29 **2** 11:01

3 19 minutes

4 **a** 13:52 **b** 13:17 or 1.17 p.m.

5 **a** 07:54 **b** 07:49 or 7.49 a.m.

Scales (pp. 24–27)

Reading scales (pp. 24–25)

1 A = 2.5 cm
B = 5.0 cm
C = 6.6 cm

2 D = 56°
E = 81°

3 150 km/h

4 F = 141°

5 G = 78 mm
H = 102 mm
I = 126 mm

6 25 mL

7 27.5°C

8 34 kg

Showing values on scales (pp. 26–27)

1

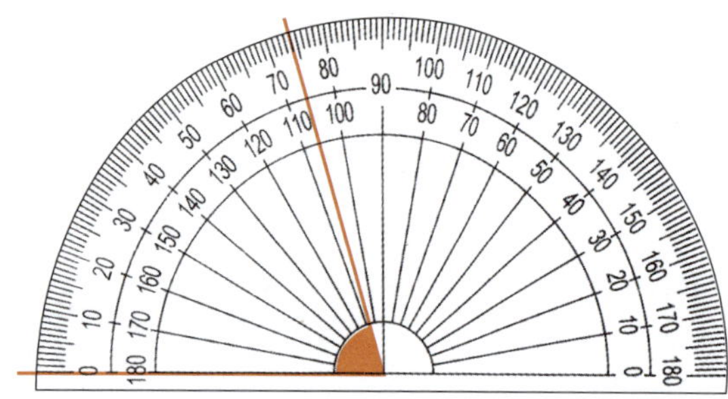

2

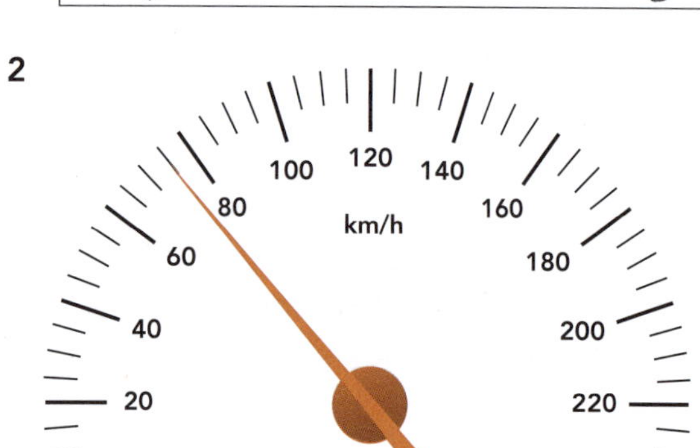

3

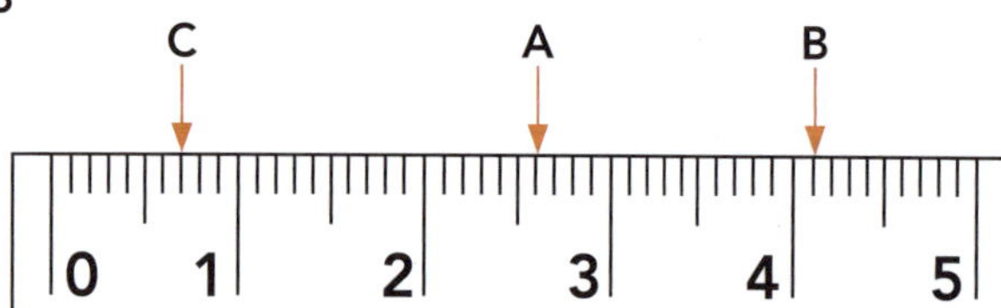

4

5

6

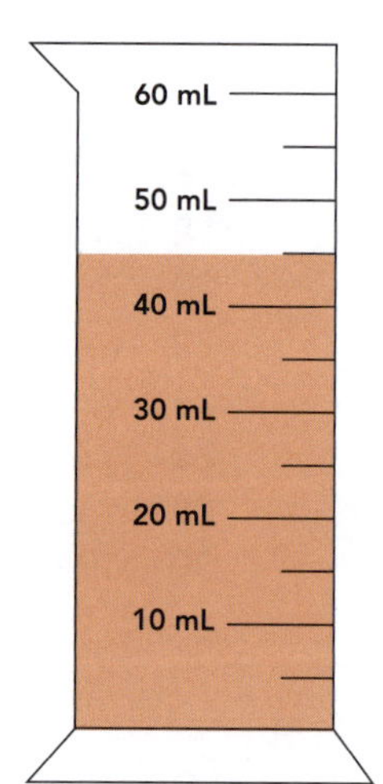

7

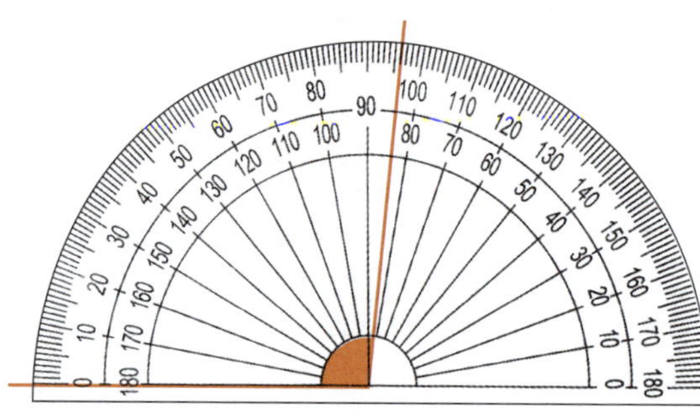

 ISBN: 9780170447218

8

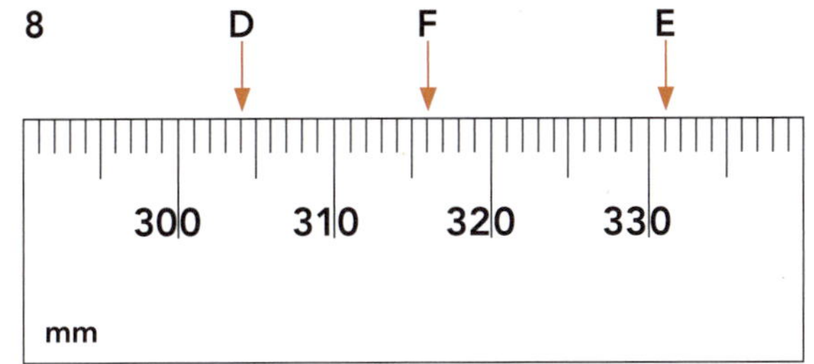

9

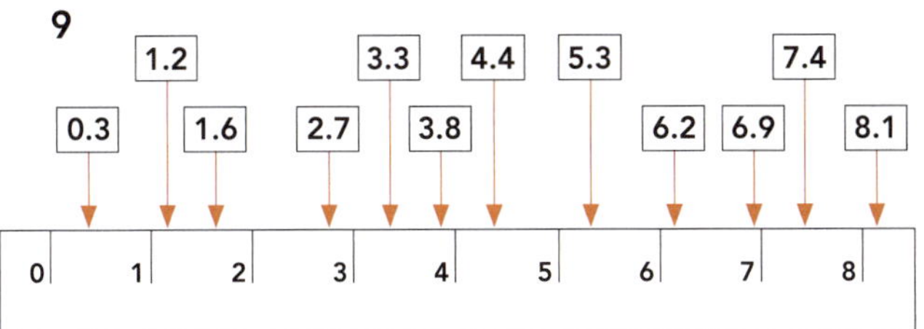

Perimeter (pp. 28–44)

Shapes on a grid (pp. 28–29)

1 A = 16 cm B = 20 cm
C = 16 cm D = 18 cm
2 E = 32 cm I = 36 cm
F = 28 cm J = 30 cm
G = 30 cm K = 40 cm
H = 28 cm L = 44 cm

Shapes with linear sides (pp. 30–31)

1 20 cm **2** 86 mm
3 26 m **4** 28 m
5 12 m **6** 26 cm
7 6 km **8** 21 cm
9 167 mm **10** 13 km
11 19.92 cm **12** 67.4 m

Things to look out for (pp. 32–34)

1 30 cm **2** 12 km
3 48 cm **4** 110 mm
5 8.4 m **6** 6.4 m
7 21 km **8** 344 mm
9 4 km **10** 28 cm
11 46 mm **12** 12 m
13 42 cm **14** 2800 m
15 16.3 m **16** 32 m

Challenge 1 (p. 35)

1 7 cm **2** 3.2 km
3 6 m **4** 80 cm
5 4 cm or 40 mm **6** 2.8 km or 2800 m

Circles (pp. 36–39)

1 21.99 cm **2** 9.42 km
3 56.55 m **4** 100.53 mm
5 37.70 cm **6** 15.71 km
7 39.58 m **8** 32.04 cm
9 75.40 cm **10** 18.85 km

Parts of circles (pp. 38–39)

1 64.27 mm **2** 15.42 km
3 21.42 m **4** 437.04 mm
5 14.28 cm **6** 3.21 km
7 6.71 m **8** 234.93 mm
9 15.42 m **10** 17.85 cm

Compound shapes (pp. 40–41)

1 240 mm **2** 24 cm
3 30 km **4** 130 mm
5 64 cm **6** 49 m
7 101.70 cm **8** 0.91 km

Word questions (pp. 42–43)

1 110.6 cm **2** 13 cm
3 **a** 110.4 m **b** 36.8 m
4 **a** 13.60 m
b 14.86 – 13.60 = 1.26 m
5 **a** 34 cm **b** It doesn't change.
c 34 cm **d** 34 cm
e Because the lines in all the perimeters could be arranged to form a 10 x 7 rectangle.
6 **a** 13.93 m **b** 1.07 m

Challenge 2 (p. 44)

1 121.55 cm **2** 5171.24 cm

Area (pp. 45–73)

Shapes on a grid (pp. 45–46)

1 A = 12 cm^2 B = 18 cm^2
C = 12 cm^2 D = 16 cm^2
2 E = 39 cm^2 L = 30 cm^2
F = 24 cm^2 M = 8 cm^2
G = 33 cm^2 N = 18 cm^2
H = 33 cm^2 O = 24 cm^2
I = 35 cm^2 P = 10 cm^2
J = 18 cm^2 Q = 11 cm^2
K = 30 cm^2 R = 24 cm^2

ISBN: 9780170447218

Challenge 3 (p. 47)

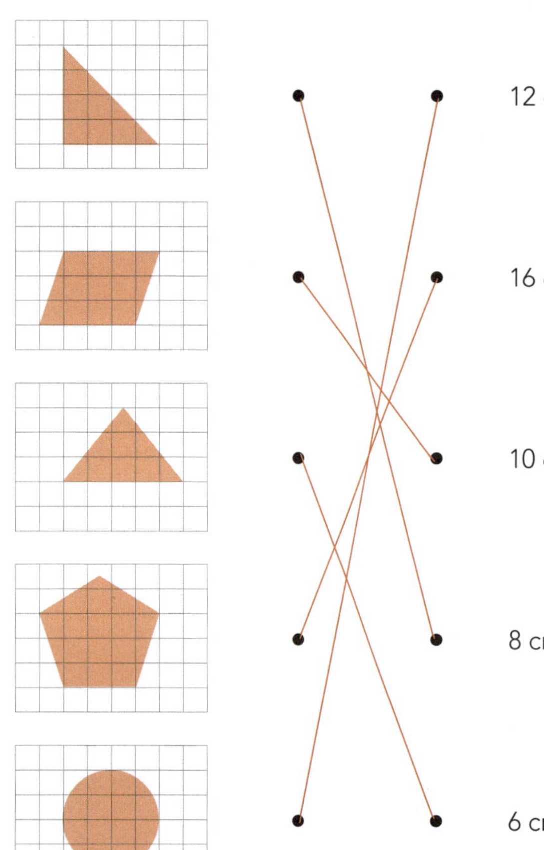

Quadrilaterals (pp. 48–53)

Square and rectangle (pp. 48–49)

1 40 m^2
2 49 cm^2
3 4 km^2
4 24 mm^2
5 60 cm^2
6 25 km^2
7 64 m^2
8 140 mm^2
9 35.75 cm^2
10 5.29 m^2
11 2493.18 mm^2
12 0.0009 km^2

Parallelogram and rhombus (pp. 50–51)

1 30 m^2
2 50 mm^2
3 18 km^2
4 24 cm^2
5 56 m^2
6 5400 mm^2
7 7.5 m^2
8 135 cm^2
9 0.4 km^2
10 90 m^2

Trapezium (pp. 52–53)

1 28 km^2
2 2625 mm^2
3 88 cm^2
4 135 m^2
5 1250 mm^2
6 0.585 km^2
7 265.625 cm^2
8 0.825 m^2

Triangles (pp. 54–55)

1 9 km^2
2 5000 mm^2
3 5 km^2
4 525 mm^2
5 12.5 cm^2
6 20 m^2
7 5.625 m^2
8 0.1125 km^2

Mixing it up (pp. 56–57)

1 40 cm^2
2 6 m^2
3 1425 mm^2
4 12 km^2
5 225 cm^2
6 45 m^2
7 0.2 m^2
8 210 m^2
9 150 km^2
10 440 mm^2
11 19.25 m^2
12 288 cm^2

Things to look out for (pp. 58–59)

1 0.4 km^2
2 6 km^2
3 2800 mm^2
4 270 cm^2
5 0.3 km^2
6 24 m^2
7 0.14 m^2
8 1000 m^2

Challenge 4 (pp. 60–61)

1 8 cm
2 6 m
3 4 km
4 70 mm
5 7 m
6 12 cm
7 9 cm
8 6 km
9 7 m
10 20 000 mm

Circles (pp. 62–65)

1 153.94 m^2
2 254.47 km^2
3 380.13 m^2
4 452.39 mm^2
5 283.53 cm^2
6 22698.01 mm^2
7 19.63 m^2
8 44.18 km^2

Parts of circles (pp. 64–65)

1 353.43 mm^2
2 12.57 km^2
3 190.85 m^2
4 353.43 mm^2
5 132.73 cm^2
6 3.39 km^2
7 126.71 m^2
8 236.27 km^2

Compound shapes (pp. 66–67)

1 1000 mm^2
2 45.5 cm^2
3 81 m^2
4 27 km^2
5 117 cm^2
6 410.07 mm^2
7 34.13 m^2
8 128 cm^2

Shapes with holes (pp. 68–69)

1 37 m^2
2 11 km^2
3 1825 mm^2
4 551.75 cm^2
5 46 m^2
6 12.43 km^2
7 3875 mm^2
8 2063.27 mm^2
9 27 cm^2
10 0.039 m^2

ISBN: 9780170447218

Summary (p. 70)
Complete the table:

Shape	Picture	Formula
Square and rectangle	height; base	$A = b \times h$
Trapezium	a; height; b	$A = \frac{a + b}{2} \times h$
Triangle	height; base	$A = \frac{b \times h}{2}$
Circle	radius	$A = \pi r^2$

Word questions (pp. 71–72)

1 13.12 m^2
2 8 m
3 a 7.5 m
b 9 m
4 a 14.73 m^2
b 17.57 – 14.73 = 2.85 m^2
5 a 30 cm^2
b Area 42 cm^2. Increases by 12 cm^2.
6 a 11.16 m^2
b 12.5 – 11.16 = 1.34 m^2
7 a 72 m^2
b 68.86 m^2

Challenge 5 (p. 73)

1 a

Black	10 cm^2
Orange	18 cm^2
White	53 cm^2

b

Black	18 cm^2
Orange	10 cm^2
White	53 cm^2

2

	Area	Percentage
Black	168 cm^2	17.3%
Orange	168 cm^2	17.3%
White	636 cm^2	65.4%

Volume (pp. 74–83)

Cuboids with cube blocks (pp. 74–75)

1 8 cm^3
2 8 cm^3
3 12 cm^3
4 27 cm^3
5 12 cm^3
6 10 cm^3
7 16 cm^3
8 72 cm^3

Cuboids (pp. 76–77)

1 84 m^3
2 7500 mm^3
3 216 m^3
4 4095 cm^3
5 216 000 mm^3
6 240 m^3
7 0.189 m^3
8 342.575 cm^3

Compound shapes with cube blocks (pp. 78–79)

1 6
2 10
3 16
4 24
5 36
6 29
7 24
8 51

Compound cuboids (pp. 80–81)

1 56 m^3
2 18 000 mm^3
3 120 m^3
4 4000 cm^3
5 283 500 mm^3
6 6669 cm^3
7 0.007 m^3
8 600 000 mm^3

One-litre challenge (pp. 82–83)

1 10 cm
2 1000 cm
3 5 cm
4 40 mm
5 12.5 cm
6 12.5 cm
7 8 cm
8 20 cm

Revision 1 (pp. 84–86)

1 a m
b mg
c L
d min
2 a teaspoon
b kilogram
c second
d cup
3 a 17:34
b 01:14
c 05:31
d 23:42
4 a 5040 s
b 58 cm
c 3.5 kg
d 3000 mL
e 6.7 m
f 5 d
g 0.4 km
h 95 000 mg
i 0.75 L
j 2400 m
5 a min
b mm
c kg
d mL
6 A = 0.9 cm
B = 2.3 cm
C = 45 mL

ISBN: 9780170447218

7 a 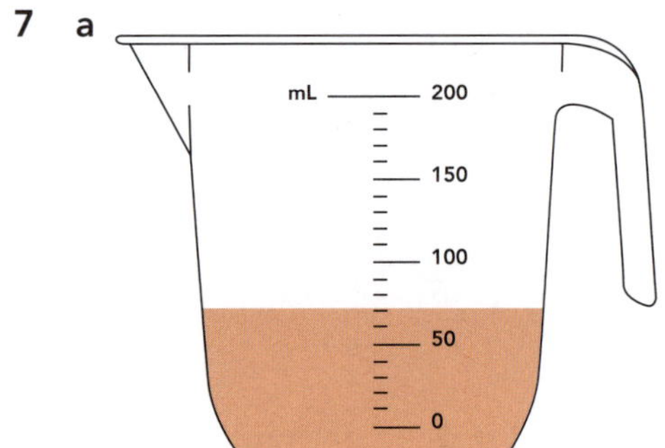

b 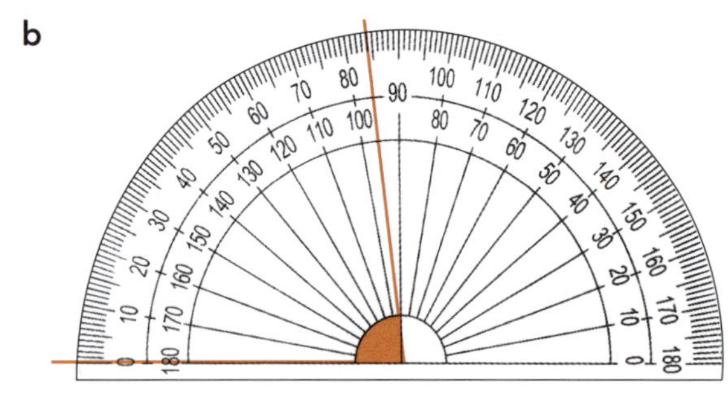

8 a 28 cm b 33 mm
c 27.5 m d 37.7cm
9 a 9000 mm^2 b 13.5 m^2
c 63.62 cm^2
10 30 m^3

Revision 2 (pp. 87–89)

1 a km b g
c mL d ha
2 a kilogram b millimetre
c tonne d degree Celsius
3 a 21:23 b 06:52
c 07:32 d 16:17
4 a 8 min b 5000 mL
c 6000 g d 35 mm
e 90 cm f 108 hours
g 1.2 km h 0.25 g
i 9.5 L j 510 000 cm
5 a cm b g
c g d kg
6 a 50 km/h b A = 106°
7 a 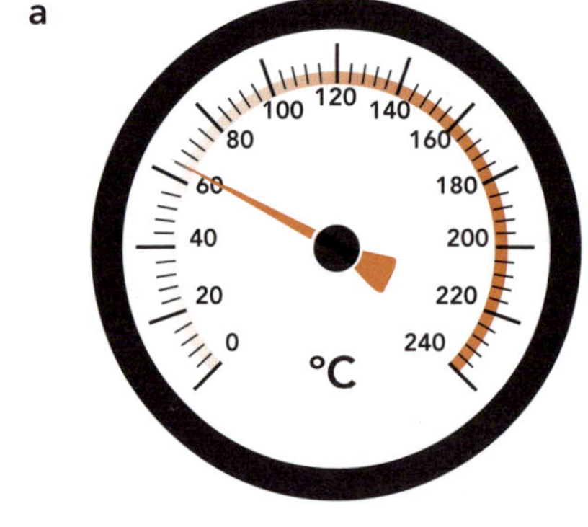

b 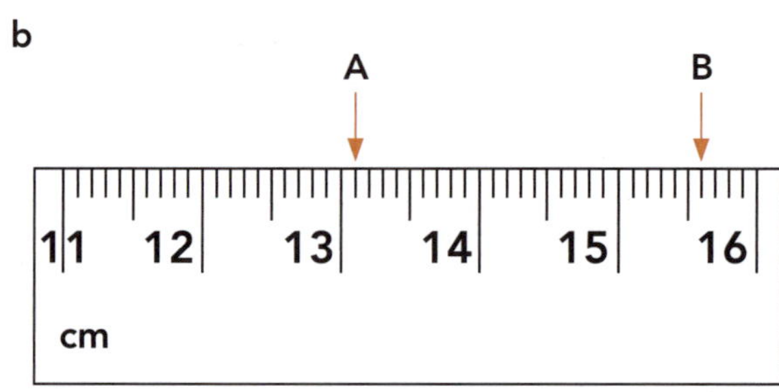

8 a 36 cm b 16.5 m
c 66 mm d 43.98 cm
9 a 48 mm^2 b 94.5 cm^2
c 100.53 m^2
10 600 cm^3

 ISBN: 9780170447218